D1571327

HISTORICAL FOUNDATIONS OF INFORMAL LOGIC

Historical Foundations of Informal Logic

Edited by
DOUGLAS WALTON
ALAN BRINTON

Ashgate

Aldershot • Brookfield USA • Singapore • Sydney

Published by
Ashgate Publishing Ltd
Gower House
Croft Road
Aldershot
Hants GU11 3HR
England

Ashgate Publishing Company
Old Post Road
Brookfield
Vermont 05036
USA

British Library Cataloguing in Publication Data

Historical foundations of informal logic
    1. Logic - History
    I. Walton, Douglas N. II. Brinton, Alan
    160.9

Library of Congress Catalog Card Number: 97-72075

ISBN 1 85972 588 0

Printed in Great Britain by Antony Rowe Ltd, Chippenham, Wiltshire

Contents

Contributors

James Benjamin is a Professor of Communication at The University of Toledo. He received his bachelor's degree in English and in Speech and Drama from Dakota State University and his M.A. and Ph.D. in Speech Communication from The Pennsylvania State University. He has authored articles that have appeared in journals including *Philosophy and Rhetoric*, *Presidential Studies Quarterly*, and *Communication Quarterly*. Professor Benjamin is the author of several textbooks including his recent *Principles, Elements, and Types of Persuasion* published by Harcourt Brace College Publishers.

J. Anthony Blair is Professor and Chair of the Department of Philosophy at the University of Windsor. He was educated at McGill University and the University of Michigan. Blair is coauthor with Ralph H. Johnson of *Logical Self-Defence* and with R. C. Pinto of *Reasoning: A Practical Guide* and has published widely on topics in argumentation theory and informal logic. He serves as coeditor of the journal *Informal Logic*.

Alan Brinton is Professor of Philosophy and Associate Vice President for Academic Affairs at Boise State University. He received his Ph.D. from the University of Minnesota in 1974. He has published articles on topics in informal logic and in rhetorical theory and its history in a variety of journals. He currently serves as a member of the editorial board of *Philosophy and Rhetoric*.

Rob Grootendorst is Associate Professor of Discourse and Argumentation Studies in the Department of Speech Communication at the University of Amsterdam, the Netherlands. His research is in the area of descriptive and normative pragmatics and has concentrated on argumentation. He is co-editor of the international journal *Argumentation*, and co-founder of the International Society for the Study of Argumentation (ISSA). His main books in English are *Speech Acts in Argumentative Discussions* (with Frans H. van Eemeren), *Argumentation, Communication, and Fallacies* (also with van Eemeren), *Reconstructing Argumentative Discourse* (with van Eemeren, Sally Jackson and Scott Jacobs), and *Fundamentals of Argumentation Theory* (with van Eemeren and Francisca Snoeck Henkemans).

Hans V. Hansen was born in Denmark. He took his first degree in philosophy from Lakehead University, the second from the University of Manitoba, and received his Ph.D. from Wayne State University. Hansen is consulting editor to *Informal Logic* and a member of the editorial board of *Philosophy and Rhetoric*, co-editor (with R. C. Pinto) of *Fallacies: Classical and Contemporary Readings*, and co-organizer (with C. Tindale) of the conference of the Ontario Society for the Study of Argumentation. Hansen's essays on logic have appeared in *Philosophy and Rhetoric* and *Logique et Analyse*. He teaches in the Liberal Studies Program at Brock University in St. Catharines, Canada.

Pamela Huby was educated at Oxford University and held the position of Lecturer, and then of Reader at Liverpool University. She is now retired. Ms. Huby is joint editor of *Theophrastus of Eresus: Sources for his Life, Writings, Thought and Influence* and author of many works on Theophrastus and other aspects of ancient philosophy, including neoplatonism, and of works on logic, parapsychology, and general philosophy.

Hud Hudson is Associate Professor of Philosophy at Western Washington University in Bellingham, Washington. He is the author of *Kant's Compatibilism*, co-editor of *Kant's Aesthetics*, and author of articles in the history of philosophy, ethics, and metaphysics which have appeared in *Kant-Studien*, *The Southern Journal of Philosophy*, *The Journal of Social Philosophy*, *The Journal of Applied Ethics*, and *The Australasian Journal of Philosophy*.

Ralph H. Johnson is Professor of Philosophy and also holds the position of University Professor at the University of Windsor. He received his Ph.D. from the University of Notre Dame. He is coauthor with J. Anthony Blair of *Logical Self-Defence*. Johnson has published widely in the areas of informal logic and argumentation theory. He currently serves as coeditor of the journal *Informal Logic*.

Raymie E. McKerrow (Ph.D., University of Iowa, 1974) is a Professor in the School of Interpersonal Communication at Ohio University, where he teaches undergraduate courses in argument and persuasion, and graduate courses in rhetoric and social theory. His research interests are in modern and contemporary rhetorical history and theory and in argument theory. He has published essays on argument theory in various Alta Summer Argument Conference Proceedings and in the Proceedings of the first and second conferences of the International Society for the Study of Argumentation. His work on Whately has been published in several journals, including *Church History*, *The Journal of the History of Ideas*, *Philosophy and Rhetoric*, and *Rhetorica*.

Alan R. Perreiah is Professor of Philosophy at the University of Kentucky, Lexington. Completing his Ph.D. at Indiana University, he has been a Fullbright Scholar in Poland, a member of the Institute for Advanced Study at Princeton, and a fellow of Villa i Tatti, the Harvard University Center for Italian Renaissance Studies in Florence, Italy.

John Poulakos is Associate Professor of Rhetoric in the Department of Communication at the University of Pittsburgh. He is the author of *Sophistical Rhetoric in Classical Greece*, which in 1995 won the Speech Communication Association Wichelns-Winans Award for Distinguished Scholarship in Rhetoric. Professor Poulakos is interested in rhetorical theory, the history of rhetoric, and the relationship of philosophy and rhetoric.

Russell Wahl is Professor of Philosophy at Idaho State University. He received his Ph.D. in Philosophy from Indiana University in 1982. His areas of research interest include Bertrand Russell's logic and philosophy of mathematics, and seventeenth century philosophy of science, epistemology and metaphysics. He has published in several journals, including *Synthese*, *The Journal of the History of Philosophy*, *History of Philosophy Quarterly*, *Philosophical Quarterly*, *The Australasian Journal of Philosophy*, *The Monist*, and *Russell*.

Douglas Walton is Professor of Philosophy at the University of Winnipeg and has been a Fellow-in-Residence in Argumentation Studies at the University of Amsterdam. He received his Ph.D. from the University of Toronto. Walton has published numerous books and articles on a wide variety of topics in informal logic. Recent books include *The Place of Emotion in Argument, Slippery Slope Arguments, Plausible Argument in Everyday Conversation, A Pragmatic Theory of Fallacy, Argument Structure: A Pragmatic Theory of Fallacy, Argumentation Schemes for Presumptive Reasoning,* and *Arguments from Ignorance.*

Acknowledgements

We wish to thank Tylee Kite, Stephanie Brinton, Damie Lasater, Diane Applegate, Elisa Hughes, Debi Reininger, and Ashgate's Rachel Hedges for their assistance in our preparation of the final manuscript.

1 Introduction

Douglas Walton and Alan Brinton

Does informal logic have a history?

Is there such a thing as the history of informal logic? No books or articles explicitly on its history or historiography appear to exist, and many would even question whether informal logic is a well enough established, or even a well enough conceived, discipline to have a 'history'. Yet, even so, self-proclaimed exponents of informal logic and argumentation studies (such as ourselves) often refer to what they take to be historical predecessors, sometimes disagreeing with them, sometimes making use of their ideas and methods. And these historical references and studies do seem to be an important aspect of the study of informal logic and to help to define it as a subject.

Informal logic does indeed have a *recent* history as a self-conscious field of specialization. The First International Symposium on Informal Logic in 1980 is an important landmark in that recent history, and a variety of similarly oriented symposia and conferences have come in its wake. Some aspects of this recent history are also traceable in the development of textbooks, in the publication of monographs and articles, and even in the emergence of the aptly named scholarly journal *Informal Logic*[1]. The recent history of informal logic is the subject of our last chapter, written by the editors of that journal, Ralph Johnson and J. Anthony Blair.

What, though, about earlier historical origins? In what sense can informal logic be said to have an earlier history? Well, the answer to this question depends in part on what we conceive informal logic to be. But, then again, the search for its history might influence our conception of what it is. In fact, part of the motivation for the current volume is a conviction that more careful and more systematic attention to the historical antecedents of the recent *informal logic* movement is likely not only to inform and enrich further discussion of particular aspects of its subject matter, but also to provide the basis for a clearer conception of what that subject matter is. It is time for deeper reflection by proponents of the study of informal logic - deeper reflection about what it is that we are up to; and an important aspect of that deeper reflection is the study of historical antecedents.

1

What would its history include, if it did have one?

So, for the moment we postpone the question of what exactly is meant by 'informal logic' – or, rather, we approach it by way of considering where we ought to look for its historical antecedents. Even if it does not make good sense to say that informal logic has an ancient history of its own, *formal* logic certainly has an ancient history, a history which the authors of a variety of books and scholarly articles have attempted to write. It may be best to begin our inquiry by thinking about our subject matter in relation to the history of formal logic.

Formal logic

Insofar as it involves the study of arguments, *formal logic* may be roughly characterized – with more confidence, it would appear, than that with which one might characterize informal logic – as concerned with the analysis and evaluation of arguments solely in terms of their form or structure. Generally, books on the history of logic, such as the Kneales' *The Development of Logic* (1962), have treated the development of formal logic systematically, but have tended to append treatment of matters most directly relevant to the study of informal logic to the treatment of more formal matters, presenting what is said about these matters as supplementary to the 'real' history of logic, namely the history of formal logic. Long articles in *The Encyclopedia of Philosophy* (1967) on the 'History of Logic', 'Modern Logic', and 'Traditional Logic' pretty much identify the history of logic with the history of formal logic. 'In formulating its theory of inference', writes the author of the entry on 'Modern Logic':

> logic considers arguments solely with respect to their *form*, not with respect to their content. It regards the validity of arguments as being independent not only of the truth or falsity of their premises and conclusions but likewise of their infinitely varied subject matter . . . Logic confines itself to those arguments whose validity rests exclusively on the *logical form* of the statements composing them . . .

'Thus modern logic', the author continues, 'like its ancestors, is a *formal* logic . . .' (5: 13). The authors of *The Encyclopedia of Philosophy's* long entry on the history of logic make occasional reference to matters likely to interest modern students of informal logic, but then tend either to focus attention on aspects of those matters which are of purely formal interest or else present them as deviations from the genuine study of logic. Plato's *Euthydemus*, for example, and Aristotle's *Sophistical Refutations* are mentioned for their attention to logical puzzles which play a role 'comparable to that played in modern times by the antinomies discovered in the early systems of the foundations of mathematics' (4: 513). It is said of the *Port Royal Logic*, in the same article, that the 'epistemological interests' of its authors 'certainly contributed much to the psychologism that was soon to infect logic', and that the *Port Royal Logic's* treatment of *method* 'opened the way to the discursive excesses that would soon masquerade as logic . . .' (536).

2

The approach taken in *The Encyclopedia of Philosophy* is representative of modern attempts to deal comprehensively with the history of logic[2]. William and Martha Kneales' monumental *The Development of Logic* begins with the statement that 'Logic is concerned with the principles of valid inference . . .', thus identifying the subject matter with *formal* deductive logic. The long and very informative entry 'The History and Kinds of Logic' in *The New Encyclopaedia Britannica* (15th edition, Macropaedia) refers to the contributions of the early Sophists to the understanding of argument, and even to the development of Zeno's paradoxes, as the 'prehistory of logic', though it acknowledges a 'wider sense' in which 'logic' may be said to include theories of language (23: 235).

But, despite the fact that there appears to be more consensus about the nature of formal logic, the boundaries of the formal in logic are not so clear, as is evident from the consideration of the works of Aristotle as also from even a casual perusal of written histories of formal logic. No formal logician, and certainly no historian of formal logic, has ever actually conceived of formal logic as concerned exclusively with the validity of arguments. The history of formal logic is a tale told about many things, and a good deal of that tale is about language, of which logic was conceived by some medieval logicians to be a science, a science which they conceived to be concerned not only with implication, but also with syntactical and semantical problems. And formal logicians still concern themselves with a variety of problems which are on the edges (if not outside the edges) of the formal.

The fact is that formal logicians are and always have been puzzled and perplexed by the extent to which significant aspects of what they find to be logically interesting are resistant to the appropriate kinds of formalization. In his *History of Formal Logic*, I. M. Bochenski (1961) acknowledges the difficulty of sharply defining, and the inadvisability of too narrowly delimiting, his subject matter. 'A complete history of the problems of logic', he writes, 'must then have formal logic at its centre, but treat also of the development of problems of semiotics and methodology' (Bochenski, 3). The Kneales acknowledge that '[t]he character of Greek logic cannot be explained wholly in terms of demonstration (*apodeixis*)' and regard the history of the early development of the concept of dialectic as germane to their study. But, interwoven with the more formal idea of dialectic as refutation of hypotheses by drawing consequences in that early history is the Socratic *elenchus*, which is more conspicuously dialectical in the sense of involving interaction between participants in inquiry and in argumentation. As the Kneales observe, the word 'dialectic' comes from the verb *dialegesthai*, which means to converse or discuss.

The 'pre-history' of formal logic

Also significant in the Kneales' account is their recognition (shared with that of the authors of the aforementioned article in *The New Encyclopaedia Britannica*) of the fact that the emergence of logic as a field of study has its origins in the conscious development of techniques of argument, tricks, puzzles, and sophisms in practical contexts, especially in Greek courts of law. Plato's *Euthydemus* and Aristotle's *De*

Sophisticis Elenchis, they observe, 'present clear evidence that the practice of public dispute according to set rules was well established' (Kneale and Kneale, 13). 'It seems likely', they add a few pages later, '. . . that some logical discussion suggested by the puzzles arising in everyday discourse was already taking place before Aristotle wrote' (15).

It is not only informal logic, then, which has problems of identity. Informal logicians can perhaps say that if we knew exactly what formal logic was, we could say that informal logic is the 'other part' or 'the rest' of logic.

In the light of the indistinctness of the borders between the formal and the informal in logic, it seems to us that informal logicians ought to read standard histories of logic. Despite their preoccupation with the formal, these histories are typically informative about a variety of matters which are relevant to the modern study of informal logic, especially in their efforts to provide full coverage to the logical works of Aristotle and of the most significant medieval logicians. They are informative (if a little too cryptic) about the so-called 'prehistory' of formal logic, which, with its emphasis on practical argumentation, on persuasive strategies and the like, would have to be regarded as falling more squarely within any early history of informal logic. In any case, an antipathy toward formal logic or even a benign neglect of its study seems to us to be clearly inadvisable for any student of argumentation. Among the conceptual skills and habits of exactness which are needed for the study of informal logic, some are best acquired through the study of formal logic.

The relevance of the so-called 'prehistoric' period is nowhere more obvious than in the case of the older sophists, who are the subject of our second chapter by John Poulakos. Of particular interest is the attention which he gives to features of rhetorical situations and aspects of argumentation – such as *opportunity, propriety, timeliness,* and even *playfulness* – which are not at all in the logical repertoire of formal logicians, but which are likely to strike informal logicians as relevant to their study (for example in relation to their struggles with the concept of *relevance*).

The relevance of the period is also apparent in the dialogues of Plato, not so much (from our point of view) in such contributions to the philosophy of formal logic as are found in later dialogues such as the *Sophist* and the *Theaetetus*, but rather in the self-conscious dialectical and argumentative methodology and conceptions of the earlier Socratic dialogues. Our third chapter, by James Benjamin, accordingly deals with Plato, emphasizing his character as a theorist and practitioner of argumentation, especially with reference to the Socratic dialogues. Poulakos and Benjamin both write as scholars whose background is primarily in rhetoric and only secondarily in philosophy, which provides for the former a kind of insight into the logic of sophistry which is likely to elude informal logicians whose background is in philosophy, and which gives the latter a familiarity with the kinds of misconceptions which rhetoricians tend to have about Plato.

If there is one historical figure who more than any other looms in the background of the work of informal logicians as well as in the beginnings and early history of formal logic, that figure is Aristotle. We have already taken note of the fact that two of his works which are especially significant for informal logicians, the *Topics* and the *Sophistical Refutations*, are given some treatment by historians of formal logic, and their accounts are worthy of the attention of informal logicians. Other of Aristotle's logical works are

4

also worthy of their attention, especially in what they have to say about language; and so is his *Rhetoric*. Our chapter on Aristotle, by Pamela Huby, accordingly emphasizes Aristotle's treatment of language and takes account of some relevant aspects of the *Rhetoric*. Huby draws attention to the fact that even the study of *grammar* is regarded by Aristotle as inseparable from his more narrowly logical inquiries, and she emphasizes the extent to which Aristotle's logical (and, or including, grammatical) studies are intertwined with his metaphysics. It is the role of Aristotle's wider conception of logical inquiry in its application to philosophical, rather than practical questions which is emphasized by Huby. Though the point is not explicitly made by Huby, it is our observation that there is a certain irony in the fact that many of the issues which have recently been addressed by informal logicians are issues which arise in a careful consideration of the reasoning and argumentation of philosophers themselves, despite their own preoccupation with formal logic.

Dialectic

Dialectic is clearly a subject which has a history of its own, one which, as has already been noted, plays a role in the development of formal logic, in medieval times as well as among the ancient Greeks. The relevance of dialectic (in various of its pre-Kantian senses) to their subject matter has been taken note of by late twentieth century informal logicians. One of the most significant contributions to the recent development of informal logic, C. L. Hamblin's *Fallacies* (1970), makes a strong case for the relevance of dialectic to the study of informal fallacies (and by implication, perhaps, to the whole of informal logic). The dialectical tradition has also been explicitly drawn upon by proponents of the 'pragma-dialectical' approach to the study of argumentation, for example in the work of Grootendorst and Van Eemeren, and by Douglas Walton in his examination of various issues in informal logic in terms of kinds of dialogue. The emphasis on *disputations* in medieval education makes medieval conceptions of dialectic especially relevant to the work of modern argumentation theorists and of informal logicians interested in dialogic contexts of argument. In our fifth chapter, Alan Perreiah examines forms of argumentation in medieval dialectic, with attention to its applications to both philosophical and practical reasoning and disputation. For readers who have an interest in dialogical or dialectical approaches to the study of argumentation, but who are intimidated by the prospect of inquiring into the works of medieval logicians, Perreiah provides an agreeable introduction and identification of sources.

Deviant old logics

We have already made mention of the supposed degradation of logical studies which is said to have its origins in the *Port Royal Logic*. Under the influence of the *Port Royal Logic*, and also partly under the influence of philosophers such as Descartes and Francis Bacon, a number of influential logics sprung up during the eighteenth century which tended to be more practical in orientation, to be critical of scholastic formalities, to de-emphasize the logic of categorical propositions, and to regard logic as a study of operations of the mind. These logics appeared mainly in English. The *Logick* (1725) of Isaac Watts is perhaps the most influential general logic of this type published in English. Also indicative of the dreaded 'psychologization' of logic is the appearance of a variety of works on what we should now call 'critical thinking', such as Watts's *Improvement of the Mind* and John Locke's *Of the Conduct of the Understanding*. The influence of these older psychologistic logics continued well into the nineteenth century.

The slaying of the dragon of logical psychologism is in fact generally supposed by philosophers to be a hallmark of the emergence of the truly modern formal logic. The period from the publication of the *Port Royal Logic* in 1662 until, say, the publication of Frege's late nineteenth century attack on psychologism constitutes, from the twentieth century formal logician's point of view, a sort of 'Dark Ages' of the history of logic. Bochenski, in his *History of Formal Logic*, takes a dim view of historians of logic as well as of logicians of the period.

> Most historians of logic in the 17th, 18th and 19th centuries treat of ontological, epistemological and psychological problems rather than of logical ones. Furthermore, everything in this period, with few exceptions, is so conditioned by the then prevailing prejudices that we may count the whole period as part of the pre-history of our period. (Bochenski, 4)

In chapter 6, Russell Wahl examines the *Port Royal Logic*, with particular attention to its approach and to what seems to us now to be its strange emphasis on *ideas*. In addition to Wahl's examination of the *Port Royal Logic*, which may be regarded as the fountainhead of logics of its type, chapters by Alan Brinton and Raymie McKerrow deal with what are perhaps the two most influential logics which follow its approach to the subject matter in terms of 'operations of the mind', Watts' *Logick* and Richard Whately's *Elements of Logic* (1831). The contents of these chapters leave little doubt that psychologized logic has, as a matter of historical record, had a great deal to say about matters which have more recently been discussed under the rubric of 'informal logic'. They also suggest that, however definitive the philosophical arguments may appear to be against the theoretical viability of a psychologistic conception of formal logic, more psychological conceptions of the nature of logic are conducive to some significant kinds of insightfulness about problems which occupy the attention of modern informal logicians and theorists of critical thinking.

In any case, the teaching of psychologistic logic has a history, which is traceable in terms of the publication of a number of influential textbooks. And those textbooks do address a large number of issues which are currently regarded as at the heart of the study of informal logic. It is during these Dark Ages of the history of logic, for example, that the theory of 'informal fallacies', as we find it expressed in mid-twentieth century standard textbooks, really begins to take shape, for example in the extended treatment in Whately's *Elements of Logic*.

Bentham, Mill, and Kant

Another important early nineteenth century general treatment of fallacies, though one which is relativised to politics and which is more oriented toward practice than Whately's, is Jeremy Bentham's *Handbook of Fallacies* (1971), which is the subject of a chapter by Rob Grootendorst. According to Grootendorst, the approach of the *Handbook of Fallacies* and its emphasis on political contexts bring into sharp relief the problem of whether these fallacies are best thought of as logical phenomena or as rhetorical phenomena, a problem which he believes is solved by a 'pragma-dialectical' approach.

There are a number of major figures in the history of western philosophy, in addition to Plato and Aristotle, whose works or significant aspects of whose work could be said to merit chapter-length treatment in a volume such as this – too many for a volume such as this. Some of them are given attention with regard to their influence on works to which chapters are devoted: The influence of Descartes, for example, is noted in the treatment of the *Port Royal Logic*, and that of Francis Bacon and of John Locke in the treatment of the *Logick* of Isaac Watts. John Stuart Mill, on the other hand, is a figure whose relevance to twentieth century informal logic is widely acknowledged and is even explicitly drawn upon in undergraduate logic textbooks. It is Mill's treatment of causal inferences which is typically covered in some detail in standard texts. But his treatment of informal fallacies, which is the subject of chapter 10 by Hans Hansen, has generally been neglected. Hansen examines the discussion and classification of fallacies in *A System of Logic* (1843) in relation to Mill's more general theory of inference and also in relation to more recent work on the informal fallacies.

Kant is one historical figure who has had a profound influence on nineteenth and twentieth century conceptions of dialectic, fallacy, analysis, and synthesis. His contributions to argumentation theory not only include his distinctive employment of the distinction between analytic and synthetic method and introduction of what he called the method of transcendental argument, but also include a strategy for exhibiting a surprising connection between argumentation theory and normative ethical theory. Moreover, in addition to reconceiving the theory of dialectic, Kant proposed a general theory regarding a kind of inevitable fallacy into which, he argued, human beings naturally fall. Finally, on the strength of his revolutionary views in epistemology, ethics, and political philosophy, Kant offered a new philosophical foundation for an old critique of rhetoric and the art of persuasion. These contributions, together with the inaccessibility of the corpus of relevant Kantian texts to many who work in informal logic, made it appropriate to include a chapter on him, which has been contributed by Hud Hudson. Because of the more direct influence and awareness of the importance of Kant in twentieth century thought, we have placed this chapter after those on British logicians who are chronologically subsequent to Kant.

Our final chapter by Johnson and Blair, mentioned earlier, provides a fairly comprehensive overview and assessment of more recent developments, to which Johnson and Blair have themselves made important contributions.

Scope of this volume

We observed at the outset that there is not an existing literature which sets out to investigate the historical background of informal logic as a subject in its own right. Some informal logicians make reference to, and others make extensive use of, what they take to be relevant historical materials. But there has been no general attempt to conceive of a history or to give any kind of systematic account of the historical antecedents to the current study of informal logic. Nor is the present volume a serious attempt to do either one of those things. What we have attempted to do is to produce a volume whose chapters inquire into historical materials which we feel ought to have an important place in any comprehensive inquiry into our subject. We are well aware that there are other figures, particular works, and developments for whose inclusion an equally good case could be made as for those which are represented in this volume. We have already mentioned a few of these, and other conspicuous examples come to mind. We considered including chapters on Peter Ramus, for example, on Schopenhauer's *Art of Controversy*, and on Alfred Sidgwick's *Fallacies, A View of Logic from the Practical Side* (1884). One could also make a case for including a chapter on Sextus Empiricus, or a chapter on the Pragmatists, perhaps on John Dewey's logic in particular.

We also want to make mention of the relevance of the history of classical rhetoric, in its various stages, to a great deal of the work currently going on under the rubric of 'informal logic'. Rhetoric, in contrast with dialectic, has generally been regarded by formal logicians and philosophers as having as little to do with logic as Athens was once said to have to do with Jerusalem; so, one finds at best only passing references to it in standard histories of logic.

Fortunately, a rather extensive and growing literature on the history of rhetoric exists, and this literature includes many works which are readable even by advanced undergraduate students of informal logic and argumentation. A good general introduction to the history of rhetoric is George Kennedy's *Classical Rhetoric and Its Christian and Secular Heritage from Ancient to Modern Times* (1980). Two periods stand out as of special importance: ancient rhetoric and early modern British rhetoric, especially the work of late eighteenth century Scottish rhetoricians.

Works about the ancient period which students of informal logic will find especially helpful include Kennedy's *The Art of Persuasion in Greece* (1963) and D. L. Clark's *Rhetoric in Greco-Roman Education* (1957). Among primary texts, in addition to Aristotle's *Rhetoric*, the rhetorical works of Cicero and Quintilian are especially useful and readable and are available in volumes of the Loeb Classical Library (Harvard University Press: Cambridge, MA). The pseudo-Aristotelian *Rhetorica ad Alexandrum*, the oldest surviving representative of the ancient rhetoric handbook tradition (and also available in the Loeb Library), is also well worth the attention of informal logicians.

The most important secondary works on early modern British rhetoric are also works on neglected periods of the history of logic, Wilbur Samuel Howell's *Logic and Rhetoric in England, 1500-1700* (1961) and his *Eighteenth Century British Logic and Rhetoric*. These two works are the closest thing we have to an earlier 'history of informal logic' and ought to be studied by informal logicians. Primary sources from the modern period in the history of rhetoric to which students of informal logic might first turn their attention are Hugh Blair's *Lectures on Rhetoric and Belles Lettres* (1783) and Richard Whately's *Elements of Rhetoric* (1828), the latter of which might of course be fruitfully examined in comparison with Whately's *Elements of Logic*.

A major recent contribution to argumentation theory which draws heavily on rhetorical traditions is *The New Rhetoric: A Treatise on Argumentation* by Ch. Perelman and L. Olbrechts-Tyteca (1969).

Further comments on the character of informal logic

As a matter of historical fact, formal logic has always maintained a place of prominence (if one that has wavered during different periods) both as a subject of research and as an important subject in the university curriculum.

Informal logic has yet to come together as a clearly defined discipline, one organized around some well-defined and agreed upon systematic techniques that have a definite structure and that can be decisively applied by users. Nothing analogous to the great flowering of formal logic of the past hundred years has occurred, or appears quite ready to occur in informal logic. There is, though, some agreement among self-proclaimed theorists and practitioners of informal logic about what sorts of issues and problems fall under its study – although there is a great deal of diversity in this regard as well.

There are inherent difficulties for informal logic's achieving the kind of disciplinary status that formal logic currently enjoys and has to a remarkable extent enjoyed for over two millennia. Most of these difficulties appear to arise out of the fact that it is an essentially practical subject that requires the interpretation of natural language argumentative discourse. It also seems to essentially require attention to the roles of participants in argument. If its aim were to understand the nature of persuasion and develop techniques of persuasion, these would not be obstacles. But its aim with respect to argument, like that of formal logic, is to provide the basis for judgments about correctness or incorrectness of inferences. Unlike the formal logician, however, the informal logician has to cast his or her eye in a number of very cloudy directions in an effort to grapple with much more than the form of these inferences.

We hope that the present volume will help to stimulate a more widespread and more thoroughgoing interest in and investigation of the historical antecedents of present day informal logic. We are confident that such investigations will significantly inform and improve the quality of discussion of issues which informal logicians currently discuss, and we are hopeful that they will play a significant role in reaching more of a consensus about the character of informal logic as a field of study.

Audience

Let us finally comment as to our intended audience. This volume is intended for students and scholars of informal logic, critical thinking, and argumentation theory, from the level of advanced undergraduate students and up; and we expect it to be of interest and value for persons from philosophy, communication, English, education, and various other disciplines.

Notes

1. Two other scholarly journals which have been especially important organs for the publication of recent work in the area are *Argumentation,* the journal of the International Society for the study of Argumentation, and *Philosophy and Rhetoric.* Also worthy of special mention as indicative of recent developments in logic and argumentation theory are the multi-volume proceedings of the First (1986), Second (1990), and Third (1994) International Conferences on Argumentation (Eemeren, et al. 1987, 1991, and 1995).

2. An exception is Dumitrou's *Istoria Logicii*, which appears to be the most truly comprehensive existing history of logic, and which considers in a more even handed way the development of contending conceptions of the subject matter. Its treatment of particular figures is uneven and often sketchy, but Dimitriu's work is well worth the attention of informal logicians in search of a history.

References

Blair, Hugh (1783), *Lectures on Rhetoric and Belles Lettres*, London.

Bochenski, I. M. (1961), *A History of Formal Logic*, translated by I. Thomas, Chelsea: New York.

Clark, D. L. (1957), *Rhetoric in Greco-Roman Education*, Columbia University Press: New York.

Dumitriu, Anton (1977), *History of Logic*, translated by D. Zamfirescu, D. Giurcaneanu, D. Doneaud, Abacus: Bucharest, Rumania.

Edwards, Paul (ed.) (1967), *Encyclopedia of Philosophy*, Macmillan: New York.

Eemeren, Frans H. van, and Rob Grootendorst (1984), *Speech Acts in Argumentative Discourse*, Foris: Dordrecht and Cinnaminson.

Eemeren, Frans H. van, and Rob Grootendorst (1992), *Argumentation, Communication and Fallacies*, Lawrence Erlbaum Associates: Hillsdale, NJ.

Eemeren, Frans H. van, Rob Grootendorst, J. Anthony Blair, and Charles Willard (eds.) (1987), *Argumentation: Across the Lines of Discipline: Proceedings of the Conference on Argumentation, 1986*, Foris: Dordrecht.

Eemeren, Frans H. van, Rob Grootendorst, J. Anthony Blair, and Charles Willard (eds.) (1991) *Proceedings of the Second International Conference on Argumentation, 1990*, ISSA: Amsterdam.

Eemeren, Frans H. van, Rob Grootendorst, J. Anthony Blair, and Charles Willard (eds.) (1995) *Proceedings of the Third ISSA Conference on Argumentation, 1994*, Sic Sat: Amsterdam.

Hamblin, C. L. (1970), *Fallacies*, Methuen: London.

Howell, Wilbur Samuel (1961), *Logic and Rhetoric in England, 1500-1700*, Russell and Russell: New York.

Howell, Wilbur Samuel (1971) *Eighteenth Century British Logic and Rhetoric*, Princeton University Press: Princeton.

Kennedy, George (1963), *The Art of Persuasion in Greece*, Princeton University Press: Princeton.

Kennedy, George (1980), *Classical Rhetoric and its Christian and Secular Heritage from Ancient to Modern Times*, University of North Carolina Press: Chapel Hill.

Kneale, William, and Martha Kneale (1962), *The Development of Logic*, Clarendon Press: Oxford.

The New Encyclopaedia Britannica, 15th edition, Macropaedia.

Perelman, Ch., and L. Olbrechts-Tyteca (1969), *The New Rhetoric: A Treatise on Argumentation*, translated by J. Wilkinson and P. Weaver, University of Notre Dame Press: Notre Dame IN.

Schopenhauer, Artur (1951), in his *Essays from the Parerga and Paralipomena*, translated by T. B. Saunders, Allen and Unwin: London.

Sidgwick, Alfred (1884), *Fallacies, a View of Logic from the Practical Side*, Appleton: New York.

Walton, Douglas N. (1992a), *The Place of Emotion in Argument*, Pennsylvania State University Press: University Park, PA.

Walton, Douglas N. (1992b), *Plausible Argument in Everyday Conversation*, State University of New York Press: Albany.

Watts, Isaac (1725), *Logick; Or, the Right Use of Reason in the Enquiry After Truth*, London.

Whately, Richard (1828), *The Elements of Rhetoric*, London.

Whately, Richard (1831), *The Elements of Logic*, London.

2 The logic of Greek sophistry

John Poulakos

Any attempt to discuss the Greek sophists as precursors of current developments in informal logic is problematic. Strictly speaking, there is little, if any, direct connection between sophistical and contemporary thought on valid inference in the domain of practical affairs. Even so, we still hold onto the belief that current notions are neither entirely random nor completely unique. In other words, we still believe that our notions are somehow tied to the notions of our predecessors, who include the sophists. Therefore, so the thinking goes, if the proper understanding of our present views on informal logic demands that we come to terms with our distant past, it behooves us to inquire into earlier thinking about this important area of study.

The belief, however, in our connection to our past is beset with difficulties, some theoretical, some historical. One of the theoretical difficulties concerns the tension between past significance and present meaning. If in our attempts to make sense of sophistical logic we assert the priority of our present categories and preoccupations, we run the risk of advancing anachronistic explanations. As Jaeger has noted in his discussion of the age of the sophists, 'it is historically incorrect, and it keeps us from understanding this important epoch in the history of culture, to saddle it with problems which arose only at a later stage of philosophical thought' (1: 291). If, on the other hand, we privilege an ancient mentality, a mentality to be recovered as it 'really' was, we are faced with an impossible task: discounting the perspective afforded us by our present intellectual predicament. If any object of inquiry must be seen from a particular perspective, and if our contemporary angle of vision is shaped by the discourses of our modernity, the object we wish to investigate can only be seen from the perspective of our present. As E. R. Dodds has pointed out, historical judgment is 'for ever in the making because the present is for ever in the making and we cannot see the past except by the light of the present' (92).

Beyond this theoretical dilemma, a second and perhaps more difficult problem stems from the fact that the sophists' doctrines are available to us mostly as fragmentary, inadequate, refuted, or ill-conceived notions, not as fully developed, self-sufficient, or internally valid units of thought. From the fourth century B.C. to the first part of the nineteenth century, the sophists have been discussed in negative terms (i.e., irrationalists, immoralists, etc.). Moreover, they have not had the good fortune of having their works survive them. Unlike philosophers like Plato or Aristotle, whose plentiful, lengthy, and systematic writings offer us more or less direct access to their doctrines on several subjects, the sophists can only offer us some hints and suggestions, and this from the pen of non-sophist others. While, then, we can read the Greek philosophers, we can only read *about* the sophists from their chroniclers (Philostratus, Diogenes Laertius), their critics (Isocrates, Plato, Xenophon, Aristotle) and, more recently, their sympathizers (Hegel, Grote, Nietzsche, Untersteiner, Havelock, Guthrie, Kerferd). However, the chroniclers are largely unreliable or irrelevant; the critics are generally less interested in explaining sophistical doctrines and more in advancing arguments against them; and the sympathizers are mostly telling us that there is more to the sophists than their critics thought.

With these difficulties in mind, what the sophists can be said to have contributed to the thinking about informal reasoning must necessarily be the result of a particular reconstruction from the materials attributed to them as well as the commentaries about them. But even in its reconstructed form, their 'logic' is useful in at least two senses. First, it offers us a glimpse into the kind of thinking the sophists' immediate successors found perplexing, troublesome, and ultimately unacceptable. Second, it provides a certain historical background against which the more familiar logics of Plato, Aristotle, and later thinkers make better sense. This twofold justification aside, the shape and direction of our investigation and conclusions will largely be determined by our starting point. If we start with the philosophers' rejection of sophistry, we would have to ask: How could the sophists have reasoned in ways that later thinkers of considerable stature found so faulty, so erroneous, so wrong? If the philosophers are right, how on earth did the sophists' contemporaries believe them? Couldn't they see through their deceptions, inconsistencies, and contradictions? To be sure, these are legitimate questions but their very legitimacy issues from our post-sophistical, that is, Platonic and Aristotelian ways of thinking. If, however, we were to suspend this kind of thinking, the line of our questioning would take a different turn: How did the sophists reason? Why? On what grounds did the philosophers of the fourth century B.C. reject the logic of sophistical thought?

In an effort to get to the logic of Greek sophistry, I attempt to answer only the second set of questions. This is so because the first presumes that the philosophers were right and the sophists wrong, a presumption I am not willing to make. Operating from some commonly known charges against the sophists, I try to show that sophistical reasoning was grounded on cultural conditions and needs. In carrying out this task, I assume throughout this essay that informal logic is not a singular mode of thinking on a trajectory of infinite development. Unlike Kneale and Kneale, who hold that logic is a science that grows over time (1978, v), I maintain that it is a time- and place-specific enterprise. This means that a given logic emerges alongside and in reaction to a set of cultural conditions, and declines as new conditions appear. But if this is so, the history of informal logic is not so much the story of a process of mental reflection undergoing continuous refinement as the story of an ongoing series of intellectual battles in which one logic prevails over another on account of particular circumstances. According to this way of thinking, the logic of Greek sophistry was as necessary as that of Greek philosophy. Further, both logics are equally justifiable but on different grounds. But if this is so, sophistical logic is not inferior to but different from its philosophical counterpart.

I. Practices and notions of the sophists

The Greek sophists are generally known to us in terms of a set of charges leveled against them by their immediate successors (Plato, Isocrates, and Aristotle). These charges are well known: the sophists were foreigners traveling from town to town teaching rhetoric and argumentation for a fee; they made exaggerated promises about worldly wisdom and success to their students instead of helping them inquire into purely intellectual subjects or ethically grounded matters; they traded in fickle opinions rather than firm knowledge; they favored probabilities over the truth; they deceived their audiences through the use of ambiguous words and confusing arguments; they advanced paradoxical and untenable rather than reasonable or commonsensical theses; they concerned themselves with appearances rather than reality; their reasoning was mostly fallacious; much of their thinking revolved around the accidental rather than the necessary or the usual; they were more interested in winning arguments at any cost rather than discovering correct answers to complex questions; they sought to make the weaker argument stronger rather than affirm the superiority of the stronger and the inferiority of the weaker; they often tried to refute their opponents with 'unreal' refutations; instead of acknowledging the import of expertise and the limits of knowledge, they professed to be polymaths who knew something about everything; they employed charming language in order to win over their audiences; and they were unsystematic in their teaching.

The fairness or unfairness of these charges aside, what concerns us here is the practices the sophists are reported to have engaged in and the notions they are said to have maintained, not what their critics thought about them. Accordingly, we will focus on some of these practices and notions, and attempt to derive a logic that can be said to inform them. Taking, in other words, the informational aspect of the critics' comments, we will try to elaborate on it and explain it. On our way to this project, we will also consider briefly the sociopolitical and intellectual context within which the sophists operated.

The sophists burst on the scene of the Hellenic culture in the midst of several monumental changes. These included the Periclean democratic reforms, which replaced rule by one or the few with government by the many, as well as Athens' transformation from a small city-state to a naval empire. The latter part of the fifth century B.C. also witnessed an increasingly secularized world, the development of a civic consciousness against the backdrop of the mythopoetic tradition, the displacement of poetry by prose, the growth of writing in a predominately oral culture, the rise of the middle class against a declining aristocracy, and the change from a sense of communalism to one of individualism.

The sophists were instrumental in solidifying some of these changes. Their presence in Athens as visiting intellectuals and teachers was part of what made this city-state the

14

cultural center of the known world. Their instruction in rhetoric and argument functioned so as to bolster participation in the affairs of the state while their professional success and popularity served as examples of the new possibilities opened up for the middle class. Finally, their exportation and importation of ideas from one city to another contributed to the realization that customs, laws, and institutions were not, as previously thought, the result of divine will or natural laws but of human agreements based on need and desire. From this realization to the next, that man-made arrangements differ significantly from one society to another, was only a short distance away.

The sophists, however, were not only agents of change; they were also subjects to a well-defined cultural tradition. Intellectually, they were the heirs of the pre-Socratics, who had portrayed the structure of the cosmos in terms of a set of binary oppositions (permanence and change, being and becoming, the one and the many, motion and rest, strife and love). The sophists, who turned away from the pre-Socratics' concern with natural phenomena and toward social and political matters, adapted the lessons of the cosmologists to the life in the polis. In so doing, they noted that human societies are characterized more by change than permanence, becoming than being, the manifold than the one, motion than rest, and strife than love. This, however, is not to say that the logic of binary oppositions was abandoned by the sophists altogether. On the contrary it can be said to have been perpetuated in Protagoras' notion of *dissoi logoi* (there are at least two opposing sides to every issue), and illustrated in Prodicus' tale of *Heracles at the Crossroads* (What is one to do when presented with two equipotent and contrary arguments?). Produced at a time when the issues surrounding 'proper' citizenly conduct were hotly contested, Protagoras' notion and Prodicus' story place the individual citizen in a sociopolitical environment characterized by competing and conflicting discourses, and make him responsible for his choices and their consequences.

The sophists were also the heirs of the poets. The poeticisms of their prose reveal their cultural indebtedness to a past generation of word-smiths working within the confines of metrical utterances. But while poetry had presumed an identity between word and thing, the rhetorical prose of the sophists pointed to their radical difference. Moreover, while poetry had sought to illuminate the way of the world by announcing the relationship between gods and mortals or praising the ideals of an age of heroes, rhetoric directed its attention to the relationship among people as social and political beings by addressing such civic concerns as public deliberation on communal issues and the adjudication of cases involving competing interests. But despite these differences, the prose of the sophists preserved some of the features of the poets' language; so much so, in fact, that Aristotle complained that the style of Gorgias' rhetoric was too affected by poetical devices to serve the purposes of prose.[1]

Finally, the sophists participated in two prevalent cultural dynamics: the ethic of competition and the aesthetic of exhibition. Contests between warriors (Achilles and Hector in Homer's *Iliad*), political opponents (Cleon and Diodotus in Thucydides' *History of the Peloponnesian War*), opposed discourses (the Just and the Unjust arguments in Aristophanes' *Clouds*), or intellectual adversaries (Socrates and Callicles in Plato's *Gorgias*) were commonplace in the Hellenic culture. Institutionalized in and through the Olympic games, the ethic of competition functioned so as to drive the contestants to excellence, be it physical or intellectual. Whether in combat or debate, the idea of contest was to challenge the already powerful, and in the process assure renewed thinking and rejuvenation in all forms of organized life. The sophists transferred the ethic of competition to the political and legal arenas. In so doing, they in effect posited that, like athletics, rhetoric is a mode of exertion now in the form of attacking now in that of defending arguments. Plato affirmed this view when he likened a sophist to an athlete of words (*Sophist* 231d-e) who uses words as weapons and pursues victory at any cost (*Euthydemus* 272a).

The aesthetic of exhibition was the second cultural dynamic within which the sophists operated. Like contests, spectacles in the Hellenic culture were also commonplace. Whether in the form of public festivals or dramatic performances in the theater, spectacles functioned as a means of diversion and entertainment for a culture that did not miss many opportunities to celebrate itself. As in the case of the ethic of competition, the sophists expanded the boundaries of the aesthetic of exhibition beyond the stage and into the discursive forums of the court and the Assembly. In this vein, it is hardly surprising that Plato should have portrayed the sophists as imitators and producers of images who are preoccupied with appearances, linguistic exhibitions (*Gorgias* 447c), and the pleasure of their audience *(Gorgias* 502a-d). Likewise, it is perfectly understandable that he should have described sophistical rhetoric as an art of deception (*Sophist* 240d) whose real business is entertainment (*Gorgias* 235a).

II. *Kairos, paignion*, and *to dynaton*

Thus far I have argued that the logic of the sophists is tied to their cultural circumstances, that is, the specific exigencies of their times as well as the broader cultural dynamics of competition and exhibition. By virtue of this link, it can be said to concern itself with situational forces, specific points of contention, and new visions of linguistic expression. In short, it must be a circumstantial, agonistic, and exhibitive logic. In what follows, I explain this logic by focusing on three interdependent sophistical notions: opportunity (*kairos*), playfulness (*paignion*), and possibility (*to dynaton*).

Before explaining each notion, a brief discussion of the idea of *dissoi logoi* (two arguments, two views, two positions) is in order because all three notions are informed by it. Each notion, that is, is not an in-itself but constitutes an answer to a particular binary opposition. Specifically, opportunity answers to the opposition between the proper and the improper, playfulness to the opposition between the stronger and the weaker, and possibility to the opposition between the actual and the ideal.

The Protagorean idea of *dissoi logoi* points to a symbolic world consisting of contrary discourses. At any given point in time, language manifests itself in at least two opposite ways. In a Protagorean world, universal agreement on any one matter is not possible. Everything that gets said can make sense or be understood only in terms of something other, different, opposite. Even the idea of *dissoi logoi* itself is intelligible as opposing and opposed by the idea of *heis logos* (one argument, one view, one position). In a univocal world, every utterance would have its place unquestionably, and there would be no need for debate. But in the polyvocal world we inhabit, the status of all things is questionable. That is why people often find themselves at odds with one another,

16

disagreeing, differing, and seeking to resolve their differences. But because every issue admits of at least two contrary *logoi*, and because the imperative to action generally permits only one to prevail in a given instance, people are always faced with perplexing dualities or multiplicities, which they must resolve.

Stressing perceptual as well as intellectual differences rather than identities, the idea of *dissoi logoi* demands of the human subject a multiple awareness, an awareness at once cognizant of its own position *and* of those positions opposing it. In fact, it goes as far as to posit that one's own position cannot even be expressed except against another's op-position. This means that any one discourse is oppositional and, as such, always directed against other discourse(s). Moreover, it means that in order to understand an issue, one must be aware of at least two opposing sides. Last, it means that in order to decide how to act, one must espouse one of the two opposing sides or come up with a third, which will also be opposed by yet another side.

Let us turn now to the notions of opportunity, playfulness, and possibility. Opportunity for the sophists is a momentary discursive opening inviting an answer or a temporary resolution at the border separating the proper and the improper. Springing from one's sense of placing a particular thing in a particular place and one's will to repeat, the proper alludes to the realization that speech exists in space and is uttered as a habitual response to a situation reminiscent of the past. According to this realization, occasions for speaking (e.g., funerals, festivals, trials) are finite in number, and have a way of reappearing from time to time. Thus any one encounter in and with the world constitutes a variation of a previously experienced situation, and calls for a more or less predictable restatement of what has already been said. In this sense, the proper represents a conventional principle according to which the production of meaning in language is historically determined. At the same time, it posits that in most respects the present resembles, and, therefore, must be understood in terms provided by the past.

The proper is the result of tacit or explicit agreements on what should be appropriate responses to recurring topics and occasions. As one grows within a set of parameters of rhetorical practice, one learns that in certain occasions and before certain audiences only certain utterances are appropriate. In the same vein, one also learns that speaking in public is highly regulated by established norms of appropriateness, norms one is expected to observe. Over time, these norms tend to harden to the point of becoming highly specific types of speech (e.g., the apology, the eulogy, the encomium). When employing these types of speech, one can be said to be addressing typical or atypical situations in typical ways.

The proper is opposed by the improper. Like the proper, the improper is largely the outcome of tacit or explicit agreements regarding inappropriate responses to particular topics and occasions. In other words, the improper, too, is learned historically and sustained by the force of accepted prohibitions against specific utterances. What is improper is so by virtue of its deviation from or disregard of normative rhetorical practices within a community of speakers and listeners. Insofar as the proper-improper opposition concerns itself with already settled discursive territories, it disregards the unique aspects of a given situation, and in so doing leaves out of account uncharted linguistic regions. These regions can begin to be settled when one creates or capitalizes on opportune rhetorical moments (*kairoi*).

Springing from one's sense of timing and the will to invent, *kairos* alludes to the realization that speech exists in time and is uttered both as a spontaneous formulation of and a barely constituted response to a new situation unfolding in the immediate present. According to this realization, time is understood as 'a succession of discontinuous occasions' rather than as duration or historical continuity. In the same vein, the present is conceived not 'as continuous with a causally related sequence of events' but as 'unprecedented, as a moment of decision, a moment of crisis'. In this regard, *kairos* represents 'a radical principle of occasionality' that sees 'the production of meaning in language as a process of continuous adjustment to and creation of the present occasion (White, 14).

The speaker who operates mainly with the awareness of *kairos* responds spontaneously to the fleeting situation at hand, speaks on the spur of the moment, and addresses each occasion in its particularity, its singularity, its uniqueness. In this sense, he is both a hunter and a maker of opportunities, always ready to address a topic improvisationally and confer meaning on newly emerging situations.

Because what gets said kairotically is unprecedented, it has no ready-made audience. As such it can surprise its listeners; and once the moment of its utterance has passed, it can well be forgotten, or remembered as an exception to the rule. But if it happens to fall on receptive ears and make unexpected sense, it will eventually find its place in the audience's linguistic repertoire and become available for future use. In this way, the unique can turn into the proper.

The reverse does not obtain. Because what gets said from the vantage of propriety is decided historically, it seeks to perpetuate or strengthen the formulaic character it has acquired over time. In this way, a proper utterance recommends itself as a criterion of the conventionally acceptable, and resists innovation except insofar as innovation constitutes a 'natural' extension of the tradition. Because it reinforces what listeners already know and because it reassures them of the continuing value of their discursive sensibilities, a proper expression can usually count on an already well-disposed audience.

By contrast, what gets said on the spur of the moment strives to expand the frontiers of language and invite its audience to settle them. In so doing, it ignores the proper-improper opposition and underscores the crucial role occasionality and temporality play in the practice of rhetoric. In effect, the notion of *kairos* demands the awareness that the proper-improper opposition is not especially useful at the precise moment of utterance. Further, it insists on the view that something is not proper or improper at all times and in all situations. What is said at any one time and in any one situation can be construed as appropriate or inappropriate regardless of precedents; but how it will be construed depends both on one's reading of the occasion of its utterance and on its persuasiveness.

That *kairos* may overturn the conventional categories of the proper and the improper and reverse their status does not mean that 'anything goes' – before anything can go, a great deal must be in place. Rather, it means that what is generally regarded as appropriate or the reverse has no necessary bearing on a discourse uttered in a specific temporal, occasional, and situational context. What is believed to be proper or improper is based only on prior norms marking the accepted boundaries of discourse in a society.

18

However, by virtue of their non-necessity, these norms are vulnerable to new linguistic expressions produced at the point where a particular utterance disturbs silence or precedent. Thus whether certain versions of propriety or impropriety will be acknowledged and invoked at any given time is indeterminate; and whether they will remain unchanged in the future is an open question. In the domain of rhetoric, every agreement is subject to review and dissolution whenever spontaneity manages to outweigh memory and habit. Second, the capacity of *kairos* to challenge a particular form of propriety means that what is considered appropriate today has not always been so; there was a time when that form, too, was introduced for the first time either in addition to or at the expense of other notions of propriety. The normative authority of the proper, then, attests to three things: a) it continues to be useful, b) it is accepted unquestionably, c) no opportunity has arisen that would challenge or displace it.

Viewed historically, the above discussion points to sophistry as an opportune response to the need for a new political education, an education with rhetoric at its center. In pre-sophistical times, education had concerned itself with the proper upbringing of the youth in the hands of the community's elders and the pursuit of higher knowledge in quasi-secretive societies like the Pythagoreans. But the advent of the city-state created the need for citizens who could attend to the affairs of the polis. And this need brought traditional education to a point of crisis, a crisis addressed by the new educational practices of the sophists. Soon thereafter, the intellectuals of the fourth century, most notably Isocrates, Plato, and Aristotle, argued that the logic of sophistry was so flawed that those who espoused it were of no help to the city-state. According to the philosophers, sophistry had focused narrowly on the individual but had failed to see the connection between citizen and polis, or the priority of the whole (polis) over its parts (citizens). Further, it had favored the circumstantial treatment of circumstances without understanding the significance of grounding oneself in principles, definitions, and the lessons of history. Moreover, it had concentrated on the accidental rather than the necessary or the usual. Because of these flaws, the philosophers posited, sophistry was one of the main causes for the political decline of Athens. In effect, they generally agreed that sophistry may have captured an opportune moment but had done so inappropriately.

The second notion of sophistical logic is playfulness. Sophistry's affinity for playfulness issues from the reputation of sophistical orators for playing with words, turning phrases in new ways, punning, and refuting opponents in jest. More importantly, it issues from their reputed practice of making the weaker argument (*to hetton*) appear the stronger (*to kreitton*). In rhetoric an argument is weaker in relation to another, stronger argument. What makes an argument weaker is the fact that the majority shuns it or is not persuaded by it. By contrast, a stronger argument is stronger because the majority has found it more persuasive than other alternatives. When advocating a weaker argument, the orator seeks to strengthen it and weaken its opposite(s) in the minds of his listeners. This he does by exploiting the resources of language to turn on itself and on people's ability to change their minds. To be successful in this endeavor means to reverse in some measure the established hierarchy of things within a specific linguistic community. Conversely, the orator who advances a stronger argument counts on the audience's familiarity with discourse that has already won their approval, and seeks to have them reinforce that of which they are persuaded. At the same time, he attempts to

19

point out, if only implicitly, that the weaker argument belongs precisely where it is: under the rule of the stronger argument. Success in this case means reaffirming the existing relations between stronger and weaker arguments and perpetuating in some measure some aspect(s) of the established state of symbolic affairs.

An argument or position is not weaker or stronger in itself but in relation to another argument and as a result of one or more rhetorical contests. To introduce two arguments by reference to their relative strength and weakness is to allude to a past verdict that pronounced a winner and a loser at the end of at least one competitive event. According to this agonistic view of rhetoric, an argument acquires or loses strength in action. No argument is victorious or vanquished once and for all. Because the circumstances calling for arguments change, any one argument can lose its power or overcome its weakness at some future contest. This is another way of saying that the status of an argument is always time and situation bound. Therefore, today's loser may be tomorrow's winner and vice versa.

A discursive contest requires at least two contestants. Often many contestants enter a round of discursive competition; but in the end, there are generally many losers and only one winner. Of the many discourses competing for victory in a given contest, it is usually only one that emerges victorious. Once a particular contest is over, the stronger argument concerns itself with how to avoid losing future challenges while the weaker becomes preoccupied with how to win next time. An argument that has lost a contest may never reappear to fight another round of symbolic competition; or it may reappear reworded and reformulated, ready to challenge the winner(s) of the past. By contrast, an argument that has won a contest may in time have to defend itself in future contests. In sophistical rhetoric, competition between arguments never ceases. As such, the social agreements and political arrangements of a people are always in the process of redefinition.

To enter arenas of symbolic competition means to be willing to play, win or lose. Whether one enters as a challenger or challenged, one, by virtue of his entry, helps perpetuate competition as a practice. In doing so, he not only agrees to play a particular game but also endorses the tacit understandings that have made 'the game' possible. By extension, one plays not only for victory but also for the pleasure inherent in playing. In rhetoric, one plays both specific games, as in the case of a legal battle or a political race, as well as the broader game of language. In the former instance, one generally seeks to win, which means to bring the game to a particular end. In the latter, one seeks pleasure, which requires that one prolong the game indefinitely. Within a specific rhetorical game, one wins not by having the stronger argument but by playing the game more skillfully than his opponent(s). Conversely, one loses by playing the game less skillfully than his opponent(s). In other words, it is skill in language that determines rhetorical strength or weakness in a specific game. But within the broader game of language, there are no winners or losers – only players; therefore, what matters is not so much winning or losing as bringing as many players into the game as possible.

Viewed historically, the above discussion points to sophistry as a playful practice, a practice exploiting the resources of language to coin new words and arguments out of a seemingly exhausted language. Through this practice, the sophists expanded the established linguistic and argumentative repertoire to satisfy the needs that the new sociopolitical realities had created. This expansion enlarged the discursive space within which their students could listen and speak. At the same time, it challenged the authority of preexisting phraseology by making its semantic field less stable and more complex. In effect, the sophists' lessons in rhetoric and argumentation brought into the game of language more players and showed them how to play it more effectively. Soon after the age of sophistry, the philosophers objected to the notion and practice of linguistic playfulness on the grounds that the sophists and their disciples were playing not only *by* but also *with* the rules of the game. Recognizing a tight connection between language and action, the philosophers thought that too many players and too much innovation in language were creating too much instability in the domain of sociopolitical action. In the sophists' love of paradox, deliberate use of ambiguity, or extravagant display of style, the philosophers saw a flirtation with absurdity and the consequence of that flirtation, a breakdown of the social and political orders. Accordingly, they took on the task of defining, this time seriously, the rules of the proper operation of language. Part of this task entailed the articulation of a logic according to which arguments were to be judged not in terms of their persuasive strength or weakness but their truthfulness and logical validity.

The third notion of sophistical logic is possibility. The background of this notion is the opposition between the actual and the ideal. Actuality refers to the way things are in the world. In rhetoric, actual is that which people believe to be so. Actual things are so by virtue of their presence and most people's conviction that they 'know' what is the case about the world around them, how it works, and why. When speaking from the frame of actuality, the orator emphasizes the 'here', the 'now', and the 'is'. More specifically, he highlights those aspects of the world that exhibit a certain fixity by virtue of which they can be had or mastered cognitively. In doing so, he not only draws for his listeners the boundaries of reality; he also confines them within those boundaries. The ends of this kind of rhetoric are within reach because they are construed as 'natural' extensions or necessary implications of the way things are.

That which opposes the actual is the ideal. In rhetoric the ideal is that which should be, or that which is envisioned about a world that can never be made actual. Ideal things are so by virtue of their absence and a few visionaries' conception of things in their perfect form. When speaking from the frame of ideality, the orator emphasizes the 'nowhere', the 'never', and the 'should be'. More specifically, he concentrates on a world that, no matter how untenable, one should strive to approach. In so doing, he not only disparages the world as it is commonly known but also prompts his audience to imagine a world that can never be actualized. The ends of this rhetoric are beyond reach, yet are construed as worthy of endless pursuit.

As a third alternative to the actual-ideal opposition, possibility refers to things that are not but can be. Possible things are possible by virtue of their absence and most people's proclivity to give primacy to what lies either near their immediate grasp or beyond their reach. When speaking from the awareness of possibility, the orator favors the 'there', the 'then' and the 'can be'. As such he underscores the fluidity, the elusiveness, and the malleability of human experience. In so doing, he acknowledges the known boundaries of the world but urges his listeners to go beyond them. The ends of this rhetoric can be reached because people are endowed with the capacity to see themselves and the world not only as they are but also as they can become.

21

In its various forms the possible avoids the actual-ideal opposition by negating the efficacy of either side, that is, by exposing the unactualizability of the ideal and the imperfections of the actual – it makes no sense to count on what can never come to be; and there is little or no incentive to stay where one is, perfectly content with the way things are. Recasting the ideal as a version of the impossible and the actual as a version of the unacceptable, the possible urges the kind of movement that oversteps the boundaries of the actual and undercuts the appeal of the ideal. Put another way, the possible refuses the actual ideal antagonism and offers itself as a third alternative. In so doing, it declares that actuality can only furnish the ground for endorsements of the facticity of the world while ideality provides a wide-open field of dreams. At the same time, it posits that the world need not be inhabited only by pedants and dreamers – there is always room for those between the extremities of immanence and transcendence. In effect, the possible cultivates the awareness that knowledge of and attachment to the actual hinders one from aspiring to transcend it while utopian ideals amount to unimpeded fantasy, the kind that refuses to come to terms with the materials of actuality. Finally, the possible advances the view that what is actual now has not always been so but has resulted from a sequence of possibles; by contrast, what is ideal now can always be expected to remain so.

As proposed, the possible often meets with the resistance or rejection of audiences unable to see the world under a different light. This is so because the possible is a version of the novel; and the novel is often dismissed on several grounds: it is 'really' a variation of the old, it demands too many or too radical changes, it offers no guarantees of success, and it has yet to be tested for its workability. But if the orator's display succeeds in firing the imagination of his listeners, and if their hopes triumph over their experiences, the possibilities before them are well on their way to actualization. When such a transformation does occur, new possibilities are in order.

Viewed historically, the above observations point to sophistry as an intellectual and practical possibility, a new way of speaking, thinking, and arguing. If the sophists' reported success and popularity are any guide, the promises sophistry made had a great deal of appeal. The fact that it subsequently was dismissed by the philosophers matters less than the fact that soon after its appearance it became part and parcel of the intellectual horizon of Greek antiquity. Had it remained a possibility, there is no telling what shape or direction the history of Western thought would have taken. In its actualized form, sophistry provided the provocation that made the emergence of formal philosophy possible. For its part, philosophy did acknowledge that possibilities in thought and language are infinite; but it went on to argue that because the infinite cannot be contained, what is needed is a world with limits. For Aristotle, the world has a knowable nature, a nature that constitutes the *arche* (first principle, origin, grounding) of all human activity. For Plato, the world has a knowable *terminus* (end, border) a *terminus* marked by the Forms. As for Isocrates, a curious figure at the intersection of rhetoric and philosophy, the limits of the world are provided by the lessons of history.

III. Conclusion

If the above analysis is correct, the logic of sophistry situated man in the midst of changing circumstances, competing arguments, and open-ended limits. Further, it posited that the only means of coping in this situation was language. Through this instrumentality, man could capture and create opportune moments, challenge the authority of traditionally strong arguments, and suggest new possibilities for thought and action. Created in a period of cultural confidence and experimentation, this logic served a set of social and political needs in the latter half of the fifth century B.C. A new set of needs in the aftermath of the Peloponnesian war gave rise to self-consciousness and inward reflection. Carried by and reflecting the spirit of this change, the philosophers of the fourth century worked on a new logic, a logic whose first task was to refute the logic of sophistry.

Note

1.   See Aristotle's *Rhetoric* 1404a20-35.

References

Aristotle (1978), *On Sophistical Refutations*, translated by E. S. Forster, Harvard University Press: Cambridge.

Backman, Mark (1991), *Sophistication: Rhetoric and the Rise of Self Consciousness*, Ox Bow Press: New York.

Cope, E. M. (1854), 'The Sophists', *Journal of Classical and Sacred Philology*, Vol. 1, pp. 145-88.

Cope, E. M. (1855), 'On Sophistical Rhetoric I', *Journal of Classical and Sacred Philology*, Vol. 2, pp. 126-69.

Cope, E. M. (1856), 'On Sophistical Rhetoric II', *Journal of Classical and Sacred Philology*, Vol. 3, pp. 34-80.

Cope, E. M. (1856), 'On Sophistical Rhetoric III', *Journal of Classical and Sacred Philology*, Vol. 3, pp. 253-288.

Crowley, Sharon (1989), 'A Plea for the Revival of Sophistry', *Rhetoric Review*, Vol. 7, pp. 318-337.

Dodds, E. R. (1973), 'The Sophistic Movement and the Failure of Greek Liberalism', *The Ancient Concept of Progress and Other Essays on Greek Literature and Belief*, Clarendon Press: Oxford.

Grote, George (1888), *A History of Greece from the Earliest Period to the Close of the Generation Contemporary with Alexander the Great*, John Murray: London.

Guthrie, W. K. C. (1971), *The Sophists*, Cambridge University Press: Cambridge.

Havelock, Eric (1957), *The Liberal Temper in Greek Politics*, Jonathan Cape: London.

Hegel, G. F. (1963), *Lectures in the History of Philosophy*, translated by E. S. Haldane, Humanities Press: New York.

Jaeger, Werner (1970), *Paideia: The Ideals of Greek Culture*, translated by Gilbert Highet, Oxford University Press: New York.

Jarratt, Susan C. (1991), *Rereading the Sophists: Classical Rhetoric Refigured*, Southern Illinois University Press: Carbondale.

Kerferd, G. B. (1981a), *The Sophistic Movement*, Cambridge University Press: Cambridge.

Kerferd, G. B. (1981b), *The Sophists and their Legacy*, Franz Steiner Verlag GMBH: Wiesbaden.

Kneale, William, and Martha Kneale (1978), *The Development of Logic*, Clarendon Press: Oxford.

Moss, Roger (1982), 'The Case for Sophistry', in Vickers, Brian (ed.), *Rhetoric Revalued*, Center for Medieval and Early Renaissance Studies: Binghamton, NY, pp. 207-224.

Oscanyan, Frederick S. (1973), 'On Six Definitions of the Sophist: *Sophist* 221c-231e', *Philosophical Forum*, Vol. 4, pp. 241-259.

Plato (1961), *The Sophist*, translated by H. N. Fowler, Harvard University Press: Cambridge.

Poulakos, John (1984), 'Rhetoric, the Sophists, and the Possible', *Communication Monographs,* Vol. 51, pp. 215-226.

Romilly, Jacqueline de (1992), *The Great Sophists in Periclean Athens*, translated by Janet Lloyd, Oxford University Press: New York.

Sprague, Rosamont K. (1972), *The Older Sophists*, University of South Carolina Press: Columbia.

Untersteiner, Mario (1954), *The Sophists*, translated by Kathleen Freeman, Philosophical Library: New York.

White, Eric (1987), *Kaironomia: On the Will-to-Invent*, Cornell University Press: Ithaca.

24

3 The roots of informal logic in Plato

James Benjamin

No major figure in the history of rhetoric is more misunderstood than Plato. The Sophists against whom he argued have developed their defenders; his most famous student is often treated as if ideas sprang full-grown from the brow of his pupil, Aristotle. Consequently there are at least three myths that should be dispelled before we explore the roots of informal logic in Plato.

The first misconception to be resolved concerns Plato's idealism. Plato was not the impractical idealist a rapid reading may lead one to assume. While Plato did advocate that we pursue ideals and truth, Platonism is not a Quixotic quest. Plato rejected taking the easy way out; he argued against following the mandates of the crowd or the too easily adopted prejudices of the past. Plato's mandates that issues be subjected to close scrutiny and refined argumentation, that the mind must seek further than the shifting surface appearances, and that Truth is knowable were all challenges to both popular sentiment and accepted wisdom. In fact, Plato was a skilled administrator and a profound humanist, aspects of his character that are overshadowed by a quick and popular reading of his works. Only by delving deeply into Plato's work do we see his substantive contributions to the history of argumentation. It is the goal of this chapter to reveal his pragmatic role in the development of informal logic.

A second misconception is that Plato was dogmatic. In fact, it was his open mindedness that led him to challenge the often contradictory and dangerously enticing views of the Sophists. To accept unchallenged positions like Gorgias' assertion that 'nothing exists' would be to surrender to a solipsistic existence, confined to a realm of mere perceptions of a void that doesn't exist. To accept Gorgias' argument that 'if anything exists, it cannot be known' would be to accept the shifting uncertainty of a relativistic epistemology, offering no fruitful way to come to know anything. To uncritically believe Gorgias' claim that 'if anything can be known, it cannot be communicated' would be to embrace an irrationalism so extreme as to be incoherent in its own expression.

Plato's counterarguments that Truth exists, that it can be known, and that it can be communicated were far from dogmatic; they were liberating for the soul.

Aeschylus, Sophocles, and Euripides depicted the dramatic qualities of man's emotions, the play and conflict of his passions. They held them up for contemplation, as a spectacle for *theoria*. Plato, it can be said, depicts the dramatic qualities of man's thinking, the play and conflict of his ideas, the spectacle of his mind. Plato raised the Greek passion for seeing life as it is to the level of philosophy, to the vision of the realm of ideas – which has its abode, not in some impossible Heaven, but in the discourse of men – in man talking – in the drama of the Life of Reason. (Randall, 3)

A third misconception common among students of rhetoric is that Plato rejected rhetoric in favor of dialectic. Given only the interpretation of rhetoric offered in the *Gorgias*, it is easy to understand why this myth is perpetrated. A full reading of Plato with special attention to his *Phaedrus*, reveals a more balanced interpretation of the role of rhetoric. Plato was realistic; he recognized that not all citizens would have the patience and the clarity of mind to engage in a dialectical inquiry into every issue. Furthermore, he recognized that people are easily swayed by glib interlocutors and unscrupulous arguers.

Plato's problem with rhetoric was not that it was inherently evil but rather that its monologue form did not permit inquiry or sharp focus on countervailing views that were inherent in and encouraged by dialectic's dialogue format. This point is clear in Plato's depiction of the frustration Socrates feels when interlocutors give long speeches in lieu of answers in dialectical encounters. In his dialogue with Gorgias, for example, Socrates says,

> Would you be willing, Gorgias, to continue our present method of conversing by question and answer, postponing to some other occasion the lengthy discourses of the type begun by Polus? You must not, however, disappoint us in your promise but show yourself ready to answer the question briefly. (*Gorgias* 449b)[1]

Plato was, in fact, a master of the art of rhetoric. When the occasion allows, as it does in the *Phaedrus*, Plato's Socrates is not only comfortable with monologues; he demonstrates his mastery of the rhetorical art form in a series of speeches. Writing about Plato's rhetorical speech in the *Phaedrus*, Thomas Cole claims,

> It is as accomplished and effective a piece of continuous rhetoric as survives from antiquity, rivaled only by certain speeches of Demosthenes and Cicero, sections of Plato's own *Gorgias* and *Phaedo*, and, of course, the whole of his *Apology*. The last can be counted a rhetorical failure only on the mistaken assumption that its passionate, unyielding defense of Socrates' philosophical mission is directed at an actual Athenian jury, rather than at the audience of literate intellectuals, unsuited by taste or talent for an active political life and the compromises it requires, for whom Plato was in fact writing. (Cole, 9)

Plato did not reject rhetoric; he rejected the misuse of rhetoric just as he rejected the misuse of dialectic, which he called eristic, when it was used for base purposes.

Plato was a skilled and practical teacher. He offered open minded inquiry into important issues, but he demanded from others that same open mindedness. He was able to use the twin argumentative arts of rhetoric and dialectic to assure the continuation of truth and to eliminate false conceit.

Plato and informal logic

Since this is a chapter on the origins of informal logic in Plato, it is entirely appropriate, one might even say Platonically mandatory, that we define informal logic. Douglas Walton represents informal logic as concerned with 'arguments as they occur in natural language in the real marketplace of persuasion on controversial issues in politics, law, science and all aspects of daily life' (Walton, ix). Walton's characterization provides the organizing principle for the following pages. First, we will examine the Platonic concept of argument with particular attention to the relationship of argumentation to dialectic and rhetoric. Next, we will consider Plato's view of natural language as it relates to argumentation and informal logic. Finally, we will map the 'real marketplace of persuasion' in Plato's world.

Dialectical and rhetorical argumentation

For the Greeks, argumentation was both a national passion and a national pastime. An educated individual was expected to argue for his position in legislative assemblies, to defend himself or prosecute his action in the law courts, and to engage in intellectual discussion in social settings. Argumentation was ubiquitous in Greek society. One's effectiveness as a citizen was judged on the basis of one's ability to argue effectively in a variety of public settings. It is little wonder that the skill of arguing ably was both sought and taught.

The public setting of argumentation required skill in the complementary discursive arts of dialectic and rhetoric. A close examination of these argumentative arts provides insight into the origins of informal logic in Plato's thought. First, consider the Platonic art of dialectic.

While Aristotle gave little credit to Plato for developing dialectic as an argumentative art (Ryle, 117), Plato has long been associated with the origin of dialectic as a method for advancing understanding. Most commentators agree with Robinson that Plato does not offer a concise definition of dialectic (Robinson, 69), but his dialogues demonstrate that Plato posited dialectic as an epistemic procedure that combined the question and answer process with a constructive use of *elenchus* or interrogation.

Plato's dialectical method served four important functions in the context of Greek society. First, there was a pedagogical purpose. Students in the Academy would practice dialectic by defending their theses against attack and by learning to critique other people's theses. A second use of dialectic was periastic. By engaging in close argumentation with another, arguers were protected from complacency and from making reckless arguments. Third, the dialectical process served a sporting purpose; the Greeks enjoyed the sport of verbal wrestling as much as they enjoyed the sport of physical wrestling. Finally, there was the epistemic function of dialectic. Ryle described this fourth function as dialectic in which 'serious philosophers engage in duels with each other from an interest in philosophical issues themselves' (Ryle, 91-92).

Plato apparently combined the question and answer format with the critical force of *elenchus* to create a positive form of argumentation. Gilbert Ryle suggests that the question and answer format appears to have been originated by Euclides and the Megarians (Ryle, 94), but H. D. Rankin argues that Prodicus' *Horai* offers:

> the dialogue form, which, though stilted in comparison with Plato's powerful style, seems less artificial when compared with the texture of Xenophon's Socratic works. In a sense what we confront in the *Horai* is a primitive stage in the development of the philosophical dialogue, the evolutionary antecedent of Plato's dialogue; also those of Xenophon and the *Sokratikoi Logoi* of Aischenes and other writers. (Rankin, 49)

Whatever the origins of the dialogue form, Plato elaborated on the cross examination technique and imbued the question and answer method with a constructive force. According to Richard Robinson, the question and answer process 'was unconditionally necessary to the Socratic *elenchus*. As such it entered into the blood of Socrates' pupil Plato . . . The *elenchus*, which is a purely destructive instrument, went forward by its own inertia into Plato's new constructive instrument of dialectic' (Robinson, 94). More recently Hugh Benson traces the development of Socratic *elenchus* and concludes that Plato added to the negative force of Socratic *elenchus* by positing a further constructive step. Benson argues that by the time Plato wrote the *Meno* he was 'advancing beyond the Socratic/elenchic goal of eliminating false conceit to provide for the first time a substantive view about how knowledge might then be acquired' (Benson, 130).

A troublesome issue in Plato's dialogues is the difference between dialectic and eristic. While to some readers it seems that the condemned form of dialectic known as eristic consisted in the use of fallacious arguments, Socrates himself occasionally engaged in such sophistic reasoning. Richard Robinson indicates that by the term 'eristic' Plato meant 'the art of quarreling' whose objective 'is to win the argument, whereas the aim of dialectic is to discover the truth' (Robinson, 85).

Instead of viewing eristic as fallacious reasoning and dialectic as valid reasoning, the differentiation should be viewed in terms of a difference in the motivation of the participants. Platonic dialectic was pursued though the technique of serious questions and answers, whereas eristic used the question and answer technique for less lofty purposes.

Typically, the interlocutors in a dialectical encounter were expected to further the argument by posing and answering questions. To pose a question was the first move in the dialectical process. Questions were typically open ended, inviting the interlocutor to provide an answer which would be explored by additional, probing questions. This good faith give-and-take sought to explore and to test ideas in a dynamic development of irrefutable truths.

In contrast, eristical questions were motivated by a desire to show the superiority of the questioner rather than a desire to examine the issue. The interrogatory form would be employed and the challenge of *elenchus* would be used, but the intent was not serious questioning to explore issues. Instead the eristic arguers would maneuver to force the interlocutor into a paradox or into silence, thereby allowing the arguer to achieve victory in the argument. Argumentative chicanery, paradoxical propositions, ridiculous wrangling, and amusing wit were all eristical tactics intended to accomplish the goal of besting the interlocutor.

A term often used in connection with eristic is 'antilogic'. There is a close connection between these two terms. That relationship is clarified by Edward Schiappa.

> Plato criticizes *antilogike* on two grounds. First, he implies that it is easy to abuse: the practice of *antilogike* can be for the mere purpose of defeating an opponent through tricks in argument. It then becomes eristic – *eristike* – which Plato blames for misology . . . His second criticism is of the implicit ontology of the *antilogike*: opposites exist only in the phenomenal world, thus they participate only imperfectly in the Ideal Forms. Hence, as long as Sophists are tied to the fickle *doxa* of the public – claiming that an act is now just, now unjust, etc. – their art will always be inferior to the art of discovering the true nature of reality: dialectic. (Schiappa, 165-66)

In a sense, the roots of differentiating legitimate forms of argument from illegitimate forms of argument, an issue that remains relevant to contemporary studies of informal logic, began with Plato. Plato's concern in differentiating dialectic from eristic and antilogic provided the foundation for the more detailed account in Aristotle's *Topics* and *Sophistical Refutations* (Robinson, 22). Plato, then, provides the foundation for an examination of fallacy in informal logic.

Plato did not limit his consideration of the informal logic of argumentation to dialectic; he also treated informal logic in his exploration of rhetoric. In Plato's discussion of rhetoric we see more of the foundations of informal logic.

The two central dialogues on the subject of rhetoric are the *Gorgias* and the *Phaedrus*. While these two dialogues appear to offer contradictory views of rhetoric, many scholars have noted an essential unity of the two works. Edwin Black, for example, argued that 'the *Phaedrus* is the constructive complement of the *Gorgias* and the two dialogues taken together constitute a consistent view of rhetoric' (Black, 78). In other words, in the *Gorgias* rhetoric is base but in the *Phaedrus* rhetoric is noble if it is preceded by first establishing the truth of the rhetor's position. In Everett Lee Hunt's view, Plato's *Phaedrus* offered a view of the rhetorician as a philosopher, a logician, a psychologist, and a master of the language (Hunt, 135-36). Since we are primarily concerned with Plato's constructive concept of rhetoric and the use of informal logic in rhetorical situations, we will focus our attention on the *Phaedrus*.

Aristotle is usually credited with the origination of both inductive and deductive logic, but I. M. Bochenski argued that 'nearly everything in Aristotle's logic, if we except the analytic syllogism and some doctrines connected with it, is most probably a reflex elaboration and development of procedures used already, at least in a rudimentary way, by Plato' (Bochenski, 16). In short, it can be argued that Plato's notion of collection and division (*synagoge* and *diairesis*) provided the groundwork for Aristotle's later development of inductive and deductive reasoning which, in turn, took the rhetorical forms of example and enthymeme. The Platonic concepts of *diairesis* and *synagoge* are therefore strong candidates for further exploration.

It has been frequently noted that the method of *diairesis* or division is plainly described and clearly illustrated in the *Phaedrus*. Perhaps the most extensive commentary on this issue can be found in Seth Bernardete's *The Rhetoric of Morality and Philosophy: Plato's Gorgias and Phaedrus*. Bernardete claims that 'Socrates' speech exemplifies the analytic way' (Bernardete, 179). In Socrates's first speech in the *Phaedrus* the concept 'desire' is divided into natural and controlled types. Natural desire is then further subdivided into excessive forms like gluttony, alcoholism, and eros. In contrast with the first speech, Socrates' second speech in the *Phaedrus* serves as an antistrophe to the first speech. In the second speech Socrates divides the concept of 'madness' into human and divine types. Divine madness is then further subdivided into divination, initiation, poetry, and eros. The process of *diairesis*, so aptly illustrated in the two speeches, is a method of informal logic.

What is not so clearly recognized is the operation of *synagoge*. If we consider *diairesis* to be a rhetorical version of mathematical analysis or separation, then it is reasonable to consider *synagoge* to be a rhetorical version of synthesis. In that case, Ian Mueller's description of analysis and synthesis proves to be helpful. Mueller writes that:

> analysis can be thought of as the process of looking for the proof of an assertion *P* by searching for propositions that imply *P*, propositions that imply those, and so on until one reaches propositions already established; in synthesis one simply writes down the proof discovered by analysis, that is one goes through the steps of analysis in reverse order (Mueller, 175).

Since *diairesis* divides the key concept into its constituent parts, the carving process described in the *Phaedrus*, then *synagoge* would reverse that process by collecting seemingly disparate elements into a broader genus. Those instances which share common properties are accepted into the genus, and those instances which bear only a superficial resemblance to the collection are rejected. This process is clearly illustrated in the *Phaedrus* by the preamble of Socrates' first speech:

> All good counsel begins in the same way; a man should know what he is advising about, or his counsel will all come to nought. But people imagine that they know about the nature of things, when they don't know about them, and, not having come to an understanding at first because they think that they know, they end, as might be expected, in contradicting one another and themselves. Now you and I must not be guilty of this fundamental error which we condemn in others; but as our question is whether the lover or non-lover is to be preferred, let us first of all agree in defining the nature and power of love, and then, keeping our eyes upon the definition and to this appealing, let us further enquire whether love brings advantage or disadvantage. (*Phaedrus* 237b1-d5)[2]

Clearly, then, Plato's method of topic analysis for rhetorical endeavors consisted of both *diairesis* and *synagoge* to determine the starting points for rhetorical argumentation. These procedures were fundamental in developing the informal logic of rhetorical endeavors. It is interesting to note that they also laid the foundation for Aristotle's development of rhetorical reasoning through enthymeme and example, even though Aristotle did not explicitly acknowledge Plato as a source of these ideas.

Natural language

'Sophistication of theory cannot obscure the truth that there are but three ways for language to affect us', wrote Richard M. Weaver, a neo-Platonic rhetorician. 'It can move us toward what is good; it can move us toward what is evil; or it can, in hypothetical third place, fail to move us at all' (Weaver, 6). Clearly both Weaver and Plato believed in the moral dimension of argumentation through language.

Plato's concept of truth and knowledge is closely linked to his concept of words. Knowing, for Plato, was intimately and irrevocably linked to language (see Nettleship, 278). In Plato's view of language, key lexical items may be either positive terms, which have generally accepted definitions, or disputable terms, like 'justice' and 'goodness', which do not have undisputed definitions (*Phaedrus* 263a). Therefore, coming 'to know' was a matter of arguing to determine the appropriate definitions of disputable terms.

For Plato, natural language was both the means and an object of argumentation. It was the means because argumentation, whether rhetorical or dialectical, was carried out in natural language. It was intellectual conversation or well grounded speeches that advanced understanding and justice. Thus natural language was the means for argumentation.

Natural language was also an object of argumentation. Exploration of disputable terms was a critical aspect in defining a concept or in starting a logical sequence of questions and answers to gain knowledge. Many of Plato's dialogues take such definitional forms. Plato addresses the definition of justice in the *Republic*, the meaning of courage in the *Laches*, and the concept of virtue in the *Meno*. These are but a few examples of his definitional approach. In short, an understanding of natural language was a main point of argumentation as well as the means of argumentation.

Hence, the Platonic concept of natural language argumentation, or informal logic, provided people with ways to accomplish either positive or negative objectives. On the positive side, language and argumentation could lead people to understanding and truth. On the negative side, in the hands of a dissembler, language and argumentation could mislead people and draw them toward confusion and false impressions.

The real marketplace of persuasion

In Athens the Agora was a marketplace for both goods and ideas. The real marketplace of persuasion was in the Agora, in the courts, and in the political assemblies. To prepare its citizens to compete in these public arenas, the educational system of ancient Athens placed an emphasis on facility in argumentation.

The method of instruction in the Academy reflected Plato's emphasis on argumentative arts. According to H. I. Marrou, 'Besides lectures, a prominent place was given to the kind of friendly conversation that went on during the drinking parties . . . ; these, judiciously used, remained for Plato one of the essential elements of education' (Marrou, 68). It is not surprising, then, that Plato would give instruction in dialectic, what Ralph Waldo Emerson terms Plato's science of sciences: 'Dialectic . . . is the Intellect discriminating the false and the true. It rests on the observation of identity and diversity; for to judge is to unite to an object the notion which belongs to it' (Emerson, 432).

Contentious disputes were rife and the practitioners were even respected in Athens (see Taylor, 86n), but the motive of such sophists was self-aggrandizement, and the opponent in a sophistic dispute was to be defeated and bamboozled. Plato condemned such practices because they would lead people to distrust everyone and to doubt everything (*Republic* 539b). Argumentation, whether dialectical or rhetorical, needed to be practiced in accordance both with strict rules of fairness and with proper motives of enlightening rather than confusing or confounding (see, for example, *Sophist* 235b-e and *Phaedrus* 260-261). Thus, argumentation was neither good nor evil but depended upon the moral character and intellect of the practitioners to arrive at legitimate conclusions, to practice legitimate inquiry rather than contentious quibbling.

The marketplace for dialectical argumentation was cogently described by Mortimer Adler. In his book on dialectic, Adler writes the following.

> The method of criticism, which he [Plato] himself called dialectic, was one of taking an opinion as a premise and explicating it. Contrary opinions are suggested and the dialogue proceeds by the alternative examination of the grounds and implications of several hypotheses. In most cases the dialogue ends inconclusively. Plato makes no attempt at synthesizing the errors of his predecessors into any final truth of his own. He allows oppositions to stand unregenerated, and among them are the doctrines which tradition now calls Plato's own. The conversation is left, as it is begun, without anything more being known or believed in, but with the possible meanings of many things made clearer. The talkers meet by accident, find their themes in the statements of each other, and leave to keep appointment or return to bath or dinner. They are enriched philosophically by what they experience; but they are not in possession of greater knowledge or more truth, nor is it likely that they ever believe the last remarks which Socrates has made. They have been enriched by the philosophical exercise of their own minds. They have been philosophers in that they have argued, not in order to believe one thing rather than another, but merely for the experience of dialectic itself. (36)

The rhetorical arts were practiced in a wide variety of public settings. Aristotle was to establish labels for the three genres of rhetorical transactions common in his era but carried forward from the rhetorical practices in Plato's marketplace. These marketplaces were the political arenas for deliberative oratory, the law courts for forensic rhetorics and the social settings for epideictic discourse. The political arena included civic assemblies in which statesmen debated public policy. The courts offered another arena for rhetorical activity. Court cases were handled by the litigants, although logographers, or speech writers, were often hired to construct speeches for those less skilled in the rhetorical arts. Social settings that provided the forum for epideictic rhetoric included funerals, festivals and other public performances. This appears to be the type of forum Phaedrus is returning from when he encounters Socrates in Plato's dialogue on rhetoric which bears his name.

The marketplace for dialectical and rhetorical argumentation, and therefore for informal logic in discourse, extended from the law courts to political assemblies and from private discussions to public disputes. In short, the real marketplace of informal logic was anywhere minds were influenced by words (*Phaedrus* 261a-e).

Conclusions

While Aristotle is often credited with the discovery of logical forms and processes, Plato's role in the origins of informal logic is more complicated. It is clear that his thoughts were important precursors to Aristotelian logic. Plato's work provided the fertile soil that Aristotle so brilliantly tilled in developing his detailed depiction of the dialectical and rhetorical arts. In our investigation of the origins of informal logic in Plato, we have considered the following ideas.

First, Plato provided the roots for the development of both dialectical and rhetorical argumentation. Drawing upon his predecessors but adding his own innovations, Plato developed dialectic as a positive form of interrogation. Using his method of collection and division, Plato provided rhetoric with a method of analysis that provided the foundation for a positive form of extended argumentation.

Second, he linked a concept of natural language to the importance of dialectic and rhetoric in their epistemic functions. It was natural language that was both the object of and the method in argumentation. Informal logic, in the form of dialectical and rhetorical argumentation, used natural language to advance the epistemic goals of the speaker.

Third, the marketplace of ideas in Plato's era extended beyond the narrow confines of academic debate. The process of living in the real world was a process of arguing in law courts, in civic assemblies, and in the agora. Litigants in the law courts relied upon both rhetoric and dialectic to press their cases. The argumentative arts were used in political assemblies to resolve issues of public policy. In epideictic settings, informal logic was used to underscore civic virtues. In each of these arenas informal logic offered the means for success.

In summary, Plato's role as a founder of informal logic is complicated. While he did not explicitly identify the techniques and concepts that have come to be identified as the field of informal logic, his works stand as rich precursors to the topic. Plato remains a model for the full humanity of argumentation through natural language in social settings.

Notes

1.   Quotations from the *Gorgias* are from Plato, 1961, with translation by W. D. Woodhead.

2.   Quotations from the *Phaedrus* are from Plato, 1937.

References

Adler, Mortimer J. (1927), *Dialectic*, Harcourt Brace: New York.

Benson, Hugh H. (1990), 'Meno, the Slave Boy and the *Elenchos*', *Phronesis*, Vol. 35.

Bernardete, Seth (1991), *The Rhetoric of Morality and Philosophy: Plato's Gorgias and Phaedrus*, University of Chicago Press: Chicago.

Black, Edwin (1965), 'Plato's View of Rhetoric', in Crocker, Lionel and Paul A. Carmack (eds.), *Readings in Rhetoric*, Charles C. Thomas: Springfield, IL.

Bochenski, I. M. (1963), *Ancient Formal Logic*, North-Holland Publishing Company: Amsterdam.

Cole, Thomas (1991), *The Origins of Rhetoric in Ancient Greece*, Johns Hopkins University Press: Baltimore.

Emerson, Ralph Waldo (1992), 'Plato; or the Philosopher', in Atkinson, Brooks (ed.), *The Selected Writings of Ralph Waldo Emerson*, Modern Library: New York.

Gorgias (1972), 'On the Nonexistent or On Nature', translated by George Kennedy in Rosamond Kent Sprague, *The Older Sophists*, University of South Carolina Press: Columbia, pp. 42-46.

Hunt, Everett Lee (1965), 'Plato and Aristotle on Rhetoric and Rhetoricians', in Black, *Readings in Rhetoric*.

Marrou, H. I. (1982), *A History of Education in Antiquity*, translated by George Lamb, University of Wisconsin Press: Madison, WI.

Mueller, Ian (1992), 'Mathematical Method and Philosophical Truth', in Kraut, Richard (ed.), *The Cambridge Companion to Plato*, Cambridge University Press: Cambridge.

Nehamas, Alexander (1990), 'Eristic, Antilogic, Sophistic, Dialectic: Plato's Demarcation of Philosophy from Sophistry', *History of Philosophy Quarterly*, Vol. 7, pp. 3-16.

Nettleship, Richard L. (1961), *Lectures on the Republic of Plato*, Macmillan and Company: New York.

Plato (1937), *The Dialogues of Plato*, translated by Benjamin Jowett, Random House: New York.

Plato (1961), *The Collected Dialogues of Plato*, Hamilton, Edith and Huntington Cairns (eds.), Princeton University Press: Princeton.

Randall, John Herman (1970), *Plato: Dramatist of the Life of Reason*, Columbia University Press: New York.

Rankin, H. D. (1983), *Sophists, Socratics, and Cynics*, Croom Helm: London.

Robinson, Paul (1968), *Plato's Earlier Dialectic*, 2nd ed., Clarendon Press: Oxford.

Ryle, Gilbert (1971), 'The Academy and Dialectic', in *Collected Papers*, Barnes and Noble: New York.

Schiappa, Edward (1991), *Protagoras and Logos*, University of South Carolina Press: Columbia.

Taylor, A. E. (1966), *Plato: the Man and His Works*, Butler and Tanner, Ltd.: London.

Walton, Douglas N. (1989), *Informal Logic*, Cambridge University Press: Cambridge.

Weaver, Richard M. (1965), 'The Phaedrus and the Nature of Rhetoric', in *The Ethics of Rhetoric*, Henry Regnery: Chicago.

4   Aristotle and informal logic

Pamela Huby

Aristotle (384-322 B.C.) is known as the father of formal logic, which he set out in his *Prior Analytics*. But he was also a pioneer in the field of informal logic, and laid the foundations of much later work. He was for twenty years a close associate of Plato, first as pupil and then as colleague, taking part in the teaching and discussions of the Academy. After Plato's death in 348 B.C. Aristotle spent several years away from Athens, partly in Asia Minor, and partly in the Kingdom of Macedon where he was in some sense a tutor to the young Alexander the Great. In 335 he returned to Athens to set up his own school, the Peripatos, where he taught and researched until he had to withdraw again in 323 on the death of Alexander and a backlash in Athens against Macedonian influence. He died a year later.

Those works of his which have come down to us are nearly all connected with the teaching he gave during most of his adult life. That is, they were not composed, as some of his lost works were, for publication, but are more like lecture notes. Some have been seen as notes made by pupils, but most are more like the notes which Aristotle had before him when he lectured. It is even possible that over the years his notes accumulated marginal comments, which are now part of the text. In any case, what we have now, in the Aristotelian Corpus, is an organized group of writings put together by editors over many centuries. A few are not by Aristotle, and many titles, like *Politics* and *Metaphysics*, cover a number of smaller sections which were originally separate; in addition, many probably include passages dating from various parts of Aristotle's career. As a result, there is little agreement about the dating of much that he wrote, and it is still possible to explain discrepancies in his views in a variety of ways, depending on how systematic a thinker he is thought to be. My own view is that when teaching he was concentrating on putting his ideas across to his students in the most appropriate way for them, and not thinking all the time of the wider whole. But he did introduce many new ideas and ways of expressing them, and they are to be found scattered throughout his works, showing that the wider whole was always there in the background. The systematic arrangement we now have may well reflect Aristotle's own ordering of his works, as it perhaps was in the library of the Peripatos.

For us, the most important works come at the beginning of the Corpus, in what later became known as the Organon. 'Organon' means 'tool', and logic was seen as the tool of philosophy, placed therefore at the beginning of the whole system. It includes not only the great work in which Aristotle may be said to have founded formal logic, the *Prior Analytics*, but also the *Categories* and the *De Interpretatione* (of which the Latin title is usually kept because the English equivalent, *On Interpretation*, is misleading), the *Posterior Analytics* and the *Topics*. It is appropriate to begin with the last work, because much of it is very early and because it is concerned with what Aristotle called dialectic, a form of arguing different from the strict scientific form found in the *Analytics*. Plato had reserved the word 'dialectic' for the highest form of argument, which he hoped would lead to perfect knowledge; it is therefore at first sight surprising that Aristotle used it for a method that was indeed important but for him ranked below syllogistic argument. The most likely explanation is that it was only after some time spent in teaching dialectic, starting in Plato's Academy, that Aristotle conceived of the idea of syllogistic, and worked out the formal relationships now standard. Until then the way of arguing he was using, as reflected in the *Topics*, was the only one he knew, and its name was 'dialectic', which it kept. But he was also a keen scientist, and a pioneer in biology in particular, and his syllogistic was, for him, particularly appropriate for science. But dialectic remained as the foundation of other kinds of argument, and it is significant that, in a final section of his dialectical enterprise, at the end of the *Sophistical Refutations* (183b16-184b8), Aristotle claims to have invented the method set out in the *Topics* entirely himself: before him teaching in argumentation had been only by handing out examples. And he is clearly taking credit for what he has done, and not relegating it all to the scrap-heap.

Before the development of the syllogism argumentation was much less strictly organized. The *Topics* contains hundreds of topics, or starting-points and general patterns for argument, arranged loosely in groups, which can be used by people in their actual arguing. That way of putting it is appropriate because as a young lecturer Aristotle seems to have been given the task of training the students of the Academy to take part in competitive arguments, in which one contestant had to state and defend some position, and the other to attack it. Lively accounts of how this was done, with much background material, are to be found in Ryle (1965, 1968). By this means the students learned to argue. What they had learned might then be put to other purposes, particularly in public debate in politics and the lawcourts, and in the working out of philosophical problems; but here also the idea of individuals arguing was not far away. It is likely that the students were expected to memorize the topics: we are told by Averroes that Theophrastus, Aristotle's pupil and colleague, slightly changed Aristotle's ordering to make memorizing easier. It seems that in ancient times the memory was exercised successfully in a way difficult for us to comprehend; it is probably not a coincidence that the word *topos*, which primarily means 'place', was used in connection with the 'place-system' of memory, well described in Sorabji (1972, 22-34). In that, items to be memorized were assigned places in some system of images, and could be read off from it.

We must also take account of the fact that some of the methods suggested in the *Topics* strike us as less than honest. This is best explained by supposing that there was still no clear idea of formal argument as distinct from convincing argument: a good argument was one that would win a victory over one's opponent. Even in the *Prior Analytics* the same line is taken in book II, 19-20. But this point must not be overemphasized. There is much good material in the *Topics*, and after a long period of neglect its importance is now recognized. The formal syllogistic of the *Prior Analytics* was of strictly limited value, and in practice Aristotle made little use of it in his own works. Many of his key ideas are already to be found in the *Topics*, although here too he left work to be done. It was Theophrastus who produced a definition of 'topic' itself, and organized the theory involved with the use of other technical terms.

At this point I propose to follow a different line of approach. As I have said, Aristotle's works as they have come down to us have been organized in a way that may be based on his own arrangement. Roughly speaking, the *Categories* is on words, the *De Interpretatione* on sentences, the *Prior Analytics* on arguments formed by putting sentences together, and the *Posterior Analytics* on actually proving things by using arguments. In addition the *Topics* covers methods of argument outside the standard syllogism, including some that are not valid, and the *Rhetoric*, among other things, deals with aspects of the use of arguments in speeches. All these are concerned primarily with the use of language to persuade or prove something, but in other works Aristotle develops aspects of language to further philosophical and metaphysical speculation, as in the *Metaphysics* itself. In addition there is an odd section in the *Poetics* which deals with what we would now call grammar. Grammar, like everything else, took time to develop, and clarifying its foundations is as much a logical matter as a purely linguistic one. The fact that Aristotle (like medieval logicians) did not regard the study of language as falling outside the purview of logical studies is significant in relation to the amount of attention given by modern informal logicians to matters of language. I propose therefore to start with the treatment of grammar in the *Poetics*.

Chapter 20 of that work includes a difficult treatment of parts of speech. This is the first chapter of three that seem to be independent of the rest of the *Poetics*, and which some have, probably wrongly, thought not to be by Aristotle. It has been little studied, but for us there is a good account in Pinborg (1975, 72ff). It opens (1456b20) with a list of terms: letter, syllable, *sundesmos*, *arthron*, noun, verb, case, and *logos*, which here must mean 'sentence'. Each is then discussed separately. Clearly *sundesmos* and *arthron* are additions to the two parts of speech, *onoma* (roughly 'noun'), and *rhema* (roughly 'verb'), recognized by Plato and by Aristotle himself in the *De Interpretatione* (16a19 and 16b6). Later these terms acquired precise meanings, but here things are not so easy. Both are given two definitions, each beginning with 'non-signifying sound'. But Aristotle's words have been corrupted, and we can make little of them. Some examples are however given, and we can be sure that *sundesmoi* included *men* and *de*, a pair of Greek words normally rendered 'on the one hand' and 'on the other'. These are also given in the *Rhetoric* (1407a23). *Arthra* include the preposition 'about'. One might then suppose that Aristotle added the conjunction and the preposition to the list of the parts of speech, but we should rather conclude with Pinborg's observation (75) that 'we can here gain an insight' into Aristotle's difficulties in defining the segments of speech, and that his analysis was in terms of meaning and logic. Another problem with the list given above is the meaning of *ptosis*, here translated by 'case'. In fact this had a far wider meaning for Aristotle than our 'case', covering the declensions of verbs and other situations where the form of a word is modified. Already Theophrastus raised problems

38

about this list, and it was a long time before the traditional account, thereafter accepted until modern times, was worked out.

Although Aristotle was still at sea with grammar, he well understood that grammatical form may be misleading. Thus he developed a sophisticated account of different kinds of verbs, pointing out that if I see something I have also seen it, but if I am building something I have not yet built it. This point is used in a number of ways: at *Metaphysics* 1048b18-35 it helps to explain the difference between an activity (*energeia*) and a movement (*kinesis*); in the *Sophistic Refutations* (178a9) if someone has denied that it is possible to do and to have done the same thing at the same time, it is effective to reply that one can see and have seen the same thing at the same time; and in the *Nicomachean Ethics* (1174a14-3) it helps us to understand what pleasure is, something complete and not a process. So far so good, but modern scholars have disagreed about exactly what Aristotle is getting at here, as is shown by Ackrill (1965).

Aristotle also sees that grammatical forms can be misleading: at *Sophistical Refutations* 166b15-18 he points out that the verbal forms for *hygiainein* (thriving) and *temnein* (cutting) are the same, but the former relates to a quality or state, and the latter to an action. Again, not all nouns are names of things in a straightforward way, and, for example, a thing is called a threshold only because of its position: if the same piece of wood or stone had been placed elsewhere it would not have been a threshold but, perhaps, a lintel (*Metaph.* 1042b19, 1043b9-10). Again, he says that a dead hand is not a hand, nor indeed is a dead man a man, except homonymously, and the same is true of a metal hand (*Part. anim.* 640b34-641a7 and elsewhere). These cases illustrate Aristotle's methods: he needs to make certain distinctions for metaphysical purposes, and in the course of making them he lights upon important logical points.

A crucial development in his thinking came with the realization that some words are related to others by what has recently been called 'focal meaning', first explored by Owen (1960). An example is 'healthy': a man may be healthy, but so also may be a climate, a complexion, and so on. These are healthy in different ways, and we could not give a single definition that would cover them all. But a healthy climate is one that helps to keep people healthy, and a healthy complexion is one that looks as if its owner is healthy. All are related in one way or another to health. So we have here a class of words which involve neither complete identity of meaning nor complete difference, and for philosophical purposes they conceal many traps. Aristotle himself picked out 'good' and 'being' and its related terms like 'is' as being of this kind. He said that they were to be found in all categories, whereas most words belong to one category only. That is, Socrates can be good, but so can health and an opportunity.

Within the limits of this chapter I cannot follow this subject further, but some pioneering work on it which is worthy of the attention of informal logicians interested in problems of language has been done by R. G. Tanner (1970).

We can now turn to the *Categories*, for which Ackrill's translation and notes (1963) are of great value. It opens with a couple of important preliminary points about language. First, it observes (at 1a1-6) that language contains some words with more than one meaning, which Aristotle calls homonyms. Or rather, in the *Categories* it is the things referred to by such names that he calls homonyms, and this illustrates one of the difficulties in studying him, that he does not think about words and things in quite the way that we do. But the point we share with him is that in a case of homonymy or ambiguity the sounds, and for literate peoples the spellings, are the same, but the meanings are different, like 'tap' meaning faucet and 'tap' meaning rap. And elsewhere, for example in several places in *Topics* book I, chapter 15, it is natural to take him as saying, with many examples, that it is individual words, not what they refer to, that are homonymous. He puts this point to practical use in the fifth book of the *Metaphysics*, which has been described as a philosophical dictionary: he teases out the various meanings of many important words such as 'prior' and 'part' and 'nature'. The second preliminary point made about language in the *Categories* (at 1a16-20) is that words can be used either by themselves, we might say as in lists, or combined with others according to grammatical rules, as in sentences. This is further explored in the *De Interpretatione*.

In the *Categories* there follows his exposition of the actual categories. This groups the majority of words into ten (elsewhere eight) mutually exclusive groups. These have been seen as covering the types of questions that might be asked about an individual object like a man or a horse, like 'What is it?' and 'How big is it?'. The most important is the category of substance, which includes both the bearers of proper names like 'Socrates', and nouns like 'man' and 'tree'. There is a complication here to which we will return later. There follow the categories which have come to be known as those of quantity, relation, and quality. The rest, treated much less fully, are *where, when, being in a position, having, acting,* and *being acted upon.* Thus it can be said that Socrates (a substance) is in Athens (where or place) and is six feet tall (quantity or size). In every case the subject of the sentence will be a substance, and the predicate will contain something in another category, with the one exception that we can have sentences like 'Socrates is a man' where, as well as the subject, the predicate contains a substance word. A further development led to what has been called the distinction between first and second substances, not actually found in so many words in Aristotle. Socrates, and any individual object, is a first substance, while man, and anything that encompasses a group of objects is a second substance. Note that while it is clear that we should write 'Socrates' and not "Socrates" here, it is not so obvious how we should write *man*. We are still at the beginning of logical theory.

This is the place to point out that Aristotle lacked the linguistic conventions that enable us to distinguish clearly between words and the things to which they refer. We can easily tell whether we are concerned with the name 'Socrates' or the man Socrates, but Aristotle was using Greek written with little in the way of punctuation, and certainly no quotation marks; and although Greek is flexible and has certain ways of saying things which are not available in English, it is difficult for us sometimes to be sure whether he was aware that a distinction needed to be made, and it is likely that at least at times he was not.

One aspect of the theory of categories reflects Aristotle's rejection of the metaphysics of Plato. Against Plato's view that the most real things were forms or ideas, on the level of universals in our way of thinking, Aristotle held that the most real things were individual substances, and so for him these were primary.

As well as the categories themselves the *Categories* contains discussions of other aspects of language such as a treatment of opposites. These are used extensively in the accounts of the individual categories. One question raised is whether items in a particular category admit of opposites. Substances, whether individual, like Socrates, or universal, like man, do not have opposites, nor do quantities in the strict sense, like *six feet tall*. But relatives do, at least sometimes, though the examples he gives are puzzling, and qualities do, again at least sometimes; for while red does not have an opposite, white is opposite to black. He also uses the notion of *more and less* in the same way, asking whether it applies in each category. Thus something cannot be more or less a substance, nor can a quantity be more or less a quantity, but some relatives and qualities do admit the more and less, or as we might say, degrees. A thing can be more or less hot, for example. A feature of substances is that although not having contraries they do admit of contraries: a man can be hot at one time and cold at another, and it is substances, and substances only, that undergo changes, as from hot to cold or from dark to pale. We can see that Aristotle is sensitive to and attempts to address a number of logical problems in language use which may occur in argument and which require attention to more than what is covered in the more formal approach of the *Prior Analytics*.

As the account of the categories proceeds it becomes clear that there are many complications. Apparent quantities, for example, may turn out to be relatives. At 5b13-38 *great* and *small* are candidates for being quantities, but are rejected because 'nothing is said to be great or small in itself, but only by reference to something else'. Thus a mountain will be said to be small only in comparison with other mountains. So great and small must be relatives, not quantities. Further, great and small are not opposites (6a5-8), for the same thing can be both great and small (in relation to other things) at the same time, but one and the same thing cannot entertain opposites at the same time.

Again, quality is not a single notion, and Aristotle distinguishes four types of quality: (a) states, like being courageous; (b) capacities, like being (naturally) healthy or sickly - and, unexpectedly, 'hard' is introduced here because it means having a capacity not to be divided easily; (c) 'affective qualities' like sweetness and hotness which affect other things; and (d) shape and the like. There follows a rejection of the suggestion that *open-textured* and *dense* and *rough* and *smooth* are qualities, for they depend upon the arrangement of the parts of which they are composed; as Ackrill says, it is not clear into what category these terms would fit, and we are hampered by the fact that we lack a full discussion of the later categories.

Many of the themes of the *Categories* occur also in the *Metaphysics*. In particular, book X discusses a number of concepts connected with being and unity.

In the *De Interpretatione* Aristotle turns to words in combination, distinguishing, as we have seen, between names (or nouns) and verbs, the two together being the basic elements of sentences, and then discussing negation and affirmation, and finally sentence and statement. He says that written marks are symbols of spoken sounds, which vary according to the language of the user, and spoken sounds are symbols of thoughts, which are likenesses of actual things.

A sentence has meaning by itself, and sentences include not only statements but prayers (and commands, for example). The word here translated 'sentence' is *logos*; this translation is appropriate in this context, but it is a word with many meanings. Aristotle's particular concern here is with sentences which are statements, and which can be true or false. These must contain, explicitly or implicitly, a verb, and are either affirmations or negations, the latter containing a negative term like 'not'. A simple statement affirms or denies something of something, and has a time reference. At this point Aristotle touches on formal logic with a discussion of ways in which negatives and double negatives and universals and particulars may be used in logical arguments, and that is beyond our scope; but it is indicative (as is much of his treatment of language) of Aristotle's interest in the intersection of what we now tend to distinguish as 'formal logic' and 'informal logic'.

The terms 'universal' and 'particular' take up something we have already met, the distinction between first and second substance. Socrates (first substance) is a single individual and is a particular; *man* (second substance) can be applied to many individuals, and so is a universal. But first substances can be referred to not only by what we would call proper names, but also by expressions like 'a man' and 'this man'. These always refer to just one single item; but there are other words like 'some' which enable us to refer indefinitely to one or more items, and words like 'all' which can be used only to refer to the totality of items within some grouping. It is with the aid of these that Aristotle develops his formal logic, and we will not follow him there. But it should be noted that the treatment of 'some' and 'all' not only anticipates what we now call 'quantification theory', but also is relevant (as is quantification theory) to the treatment of the informal fallacies of *composition* and *division* and more generally to problems of ambiguity which have interested informal logicians.

Aristotle recognizes that there are linguistic problems that arise in the exercise of setting up formal logic. It is clear that many verbal groupings which have the form and appearance of being simple statements are not in fact like that. As we have seen, Aristotle's first treatment of such matters is to be found in his *Topics*, and much of that contains ways of attacking the proponent of a thesis. In the course of this many important distinctions are made, some of which are relevant to treatments of *definition* by modern informal logicians. His approach is to consider the ways in which the subject and predicate of a sentence may be related, for the thesis being defended or attacked will be a single proposition with, or apparently with, one subject and one predicate. The predicate may give a definition of the subject, by genus and differentia, or some property that is supposed to belong to it and it only, or an accident of the subject, i.e. something that belongs to the subject but also belongs to other things. The idea of a property in this sense seems to be Aristotle's own invention: it is introduced carefully in the introduction to the *Topics*, and is the subject of book V. It is different, of course, from the notion of *property* current in more modern logic.

Another Aristotelian innovation is what philosophers now usually refer to as 'accident', a notion that plays a great part in Aristotle's theories and was also of later importance. It will be seen that all of this depends on certain suppositions about the nature of the world and of language, that complex items, like substances, have a number of features which belong to them permanently, while there are many others which may belong to them at one time but not at others, and these are accidents. Further, among those features which belong permanently it is possible to pick out a nucleus which is the basis of a definition, while the rest are mere properties. Definitions are essential for science and knowledge of all kinds. Plato had already set out rules for arriving at definitions: he saw that items of all kinds can be organized in groups by means of relations of resemblance. Much of this we do naturally, seeing, for example, that many different trees, while

42

different, are still considerably alike, and using the word 'tree' to pick them out. But there are many other groupings which need more thought to discover, and Plato recommended a way of surveying the relevant field and dividing it up appropriately – Collection and Division – so that one might get an effective definition which would tell one something about both a thing's nature and its position in its field. Aristotle now refined this procedure, though with a difference. Ferejohn (23-24) distinguishes between Plato's and Aristotle's two methods. The final result was shortened, and the definition was to consist of but two words, giving the genus of what was to be defined and the differentia by which it could be picked out from other members of the same genus. A famous example is that of man as rational biped. 'Biped' picks out the genus, which includes birds as well as men; 'rational' picks out men within this genus because they are all rational, and only they are rational. A system of this kind involved the assumption that there were, or could be invented, a sufficient number of words to fit as many species as there might be of a genus, or rather twice as many, one for the species name, and one for the differentia. The art of formulating definitions involved finding words that were appropriate and immune to attack. As Solmsen says, it seems that in the *Topics* 'the desire to refute definitions is somewhat stronger than the desire to establish or defend them' (57), which is indicative of the relevance of the treatment to contexts of practical argumentation as well as to contexts of scientific or philosophical disputation. But, also, it can be explained by the fact that the best way to establish a definition could be thought to be to expose it to attack. Indeed Aristotle held that it was impossible to prove a definition deductively. The relation between demonstration and definition is treated in the *Posterior Analytics*, especially book II, chapters 3-8, for which see Ferejohn, 38-61.

While Aristotle's classification by way of *genus*, *species*, and *differentia* developed ultimately into the kind of rigid classification familiar to us from biology, his own use of these terms was much looser, and species and genera could be distinguished on what we would regard as many different levels. We can see him working away at problems of classification and definition in the opening chapters of his *On the Parts of Animals*, chapters which serve as an introduction to his whole work on zoology. He shows the difficulties in Plato's system, and in any systems that use bipartite division. There is a full study of biological classification in Pellegrin (1986), who shows the close connection between metaphysics, logic, and biology.

Whereas in the *Categories* Aristotle took as his model subject an individual thing – usually living, like Socrates, in the *Topics* many other items come up for definition. The *Topics* may be seen as covering the whole field of human discourse, while the *Categories*, under metaphysical pressures, has a more limited range. The *Topics* even considers geometrical and ethical definitions. It is concerned with arguments that have premises which are not certain, as scientific premises are supposed to be, but which, while not being self-evident and therefore certainly true, are held by all or most people, or by wise men, and therefore have a good claim to be true. An example of the latter is: 'Good and evil are the same' (as Heraclitus said) (159b30), and of a commonly held view: 'Happiness is preferable to justice and courage' (117a21). Faced with such a proposition, the protagonists are to use other widely accepted propositions to defend or refute it. The first group of topics is concerned with contraries, which are particularly helpful in deciding whether a term under discussion is ambiguous or not. Thus the pleasure of drinking is opposed to the pain of thirst, but there is no similar contrary to the pleasure of seeing that the diagonal of a square is incommensurate with the side. So 'pleasure' in these two cases must have different meanings (106a-b). Books II and III are concerned with accidents, book IV with genus, V, as we have seen, with property, and VI with definition.

There is also a short list of topics in the *Rhetoric* (1397a7-1400b25), but as a contribution to logic it is disappointing. There are only twenty-eight of them, in no obvious order, and only some overlap with the *Topics*. Most are illustrated with examples from history and poetry.

After the eight books of the *Topics* is a single book called the *Sophistical Refutations* or *Sophistici Elenchi*, generally described as being on fallacies. This and its progeny are fully treated by Hamblin (50-134), and Kirwan's treatment (1979) is ingenious. There is no Greek word that exactly corresponds to our 'fallacy'; but 'sophisma' is the nearest. And this work deals with various types of arguments used typically by the sophists to win arguments by foul means. Among the aims Aristotle gives is that of training would-be sophists in the use of fallacious arguments, but he also wants to make his audience proof against deception by these means. As in the *Topics* some devices he mentions are psychological and would come under the heading of gamesmanship. Thus to speak at length, and rapidly, can upset your opponent. But he also laid the foundations of the traditional theory of fallacies. His work falls into two parts: how fallacies arise, and how they may be solved or avoided. He gives six dependent on language, and seven not so dependent. It is inevitably an untidy subject, and Aristotle's methods have added to the untidiness. But as well as trivial cases he covers several that have become established; though, as Sir David Ross has said, 'in many cases his meaning has been misunderstood, and in others counsel has been darkened by the wilful application of his terms to entirely different types of fallacy' (1923, 61). We have already seen that in the *Categories* Aristotle dealt with ambiguity, and here he points out that ambiguity can be used to mislead. Other misuses of language are unlikely to mislead, he believes, though they are available to sophists, and perhaps to humorists. Unfortunately, the account of the first, that of *accident*, is very difficult to follow, not only because of the technical term 'accident'; we cannot deal with it here. The second is the fallacy known as *secundum quid*: it involves applying a term absolutely or without qualification when it should not so be used, because for example it would be wrong to say that an Ethiopian is white because he is white as regards his teeth. The third, which Hamblin calls 'misconception of refutation', but which still also goes by the name of *ignoratio elenchi*, involves not knowing what is required for a valid refutation, and the fourth is still called '*petitio principii*', or, in an expression now frequently misused by journalists, 'begging the question'. This means trying to prove something by assuming it is the case. This is also covered in *Topics* VIII, 162b34-163a13. (See Woods and Walton, 1982.) The fifth is 'treating a non-cause as cause' – using 'cause' in a very broad sense. We might say that it involves introducing an irrelevant premise into a deductive argument, drawing a conclusion that is obviously false, and claiming that it is the irrelevant premise that is at fault. A complication is that in the *Rhetoric* (1401b29-34) Aristotle gives a different account of what amounts to what is known as *post hoc propter hoc* with the example that Demosthenes' policy was the cause of evils because after it came the war.

44

In a sense, says Aristotle, all these fallacies can be seen as cases of *ignoratio elenchi*; but it is still useful to know in what way they are such. And for those wishing to use or avoid them this detailed treatment is valuable. This work is the origin of much of the later doctrine of fallacies, though, as Hamblin has shown, there was much confusion later. Many of Aristotle's classes depend on different kinds of ambiguity. For ambiguity is sometimes, as we have seen, a simple matter of a word having two meanings, but it is also possible for words which by themselves are not ambiguous to be joined with others to produce ambiguities. This is partly a matter of grammar, and, as with single words, will depend on the grammar of the language used; but the principles are universal, at least until someone produces a perfect language. An English example might be 'He asked for his father's pardon', which could mean either that he asked someone else to pardon his father, or that he asked his father to pardon him himself. And it is still very easy at least to bewilder, if not to deceive, by means of a play on words. It is probably not for nothing that there is a reference to the Sophists in the title, for some sophists at least had tried to teach their pupils to win arguments by such dubious means. But those who can analyze the moves and produce replies can themselves learn important philosophical lessons. Some of Aristotle's arguments were directed against Plato's Theory of Forms, starting a process, which continues to this day, of suggesting how that ingenious structure depended on misunderstandings about how words could and could not be used. Or, to be fair to Plato, we might say that Aristotle was carrying on a process that Plato himself had begun in his *Parmenides*.

As we have seen, the *Topics* is concerned with accepted beliefs, those held by the majority of people or by wise men, and the syllogisms of the *Prior Analytics* are supposed to have as their premises known scientific truths. The *Posterior Analytics* occupies a different position again: one early question is about the nature of these reliable premises. They must be true, and primitive in the sense that they are not derived from anything else, and immediate, and more familiar than and prior to and explanatory of the conclusion. Aristotle has seen, then, that to get scientific knowledge one must not only be able to argue in a correct formal way, but one must also be able to judge whether one's premises or starting-points are correct. That there must be some premises which are not derived from anything else is clear. Otherwise one would go back to infinity. It is not possible within the scope of this chapter to enter into the question of modal logic, which involves the use of the terms 'necessary' and 'possible', but Aristotle did hold that the propositions involved in scientific demonstration are all necessary ones. And the necessity of the premises would be passed on to the conclusions, and so on in a chain. For the problems of this procedure see the introduction to the Barnes translation of the *Posterior Analytics*.

Aristotle uses the word 'axiom' in this connection, though it is not entirely clear how far he would extend this usage. It certainly covers some logical and mathematical principles, and there are similarities between Aristotle's approach and that of Euclid, who was of a generation later than Aristotle but built on earlier work which Aristotle knew. It appears that the latter had a vision of fully established sciences, empirical as well as mathematical, all depending on firm axioms.

At the end of the *Posterior Analytics*, in book II, chapter 19, Aristotle gives what has been described as an empiricist account of the acquisition of knowledge. He says that we start with sense-perceptions, which can, in men, persist as memories, and we can organize these on the basis of similarity in such a way as to produce what we might call concepts or universals. From these come knowledge and skills. At this point Aristotle introduces the term *epagoge*, which has been seen as equivalent to our word 'induction', though there are problems here. Aristotle certainly does not treat it in exactly the same way as John Stuart Mill, for example, did, and it plays a comparatively small part in his thinking. It is connected with the idea of leading a man to a conclusion by means of examples, and is not treated in as abstract a way as we use 'induction'. But in places it comes very close. Thus he even says that there are only two sources of conviction about anything, syllogistic reasoning and *epagoge* (*Pr. An.*, 68b13-14). But he goes on in a confusing way to try to give a syllogism for the reasoning involved here, and this chapter has been seen as a *tour de force* rather than a complete study of the matter. He next introduces argument by example, where a conclusion about a single case is reached from a single example of the same kind. This is a procedure appropriate to rhetoric. And he distinguishes it from *epagoge* only by saying that in the latter all individual cases are covered.

The *Metaphysics* contains fourteen books, confusingly known by Greek letters which after the first do not correspond as expected to their numerical equivalents. Thus book 4 is also known as book Gamma. The work was not composed in this form by Aristotle, but is a collection of separate items put together by later editors. The title means 'After' or 'Beyond Physics', either because the work was placed after the *Physics* in the Aristotelian corpus, or because its subject matter was seen as more fundamental than physics. Aristotle's own name for the subject was 'First Philosophy', and it is a study of concepts that apply to all that exists.

Book Gamma is concerned with what later became known as the Laws of Thought, the law of non-contradiction, that a thing cannot be both X and not-X at the same time and in the same respect, and the law of excluded middle, that a thing must be either X or not-X, and no third possibility exists. There are two questions about these laws: what do they cover, and can they be proved? On the latter point Aristotle produced a variety of proofs of varying degrees of effectiveness. For a thorough study see Kirwan, 92-121. Aristotle admits that they cannot be proved by being deduced from other prior laws, but argues that without them rational thought and communication would be impossible. On the first point, what the laws cover, a moment's thought shows the limitations of the formulations. Plato had already argued that a man may be tall and short at the same time, that is, by comparison with other individuals, and this opens up a whole area of possibilities. And it is important to distinguish between, say, white and black on the one hand and white and not-white on the other. For any colored object that is not white must be not-white, but something may come between white and black and be grey.

An idea that has had a most curious history since Aristotle discussed it is that of the enthymeme. One must distinguish Aristotle's own account from later developments, for they pick out one thing that he said but ignore much else. Put shortly, in this later usage the central notion is that of arguments in which not every premise is stated, and some steps are expected to be supplied by the hearer or reader. In Aristotle, however, the enthymeme is introduced at the very end of the *Prior Analytics* (70a3-b38). And it is described as a syllogism from probable premises or signs, signs in this case being features which are always related to something else in the way that a sign A is a proof of the existence of something B. Aristotle gives the example of a proof that a woman is pregnant being the presence of milk in her breasts. The examples given are mainly from the fields of medicine and physiognomy, and all one can say is that there is here a kind of reasoning different from the strict kind of demonstration found in the theory of categorical syllogisms. (It has been suggested that there is a connection between the post-Aristotelian account of enthymemes and the fact that one later manuscript of Aristotle has the word 'incomplete' inserted before 'syllogism' in a quotation from Aristotle given by a later copyist. But what that connection was is obscure, and it is certain that it was not in Aristotle's original text.) (See Burnyeat, 1994.)

Aristotle's main treatment of enthymemes is in the *Rhetoric*, where the emphasis is on the use of arguments to persuade. It may be desirable here to get the audience's cooperation and sympathy by letting them join in an argument, and this can be done by letting them supply some missing steps. This is purely a psychological matter; the steps in the argument will be the same whether they are stated or not. So right at the beginning (1356b4-5) Aristotle defines enthymeme as a rhetorical syllogism, and in a full discussion in book II, chapters 21-24 he says that an enthymeme is a syllogism dealing with practical subjects. But the examples he gives are not in syllogistic form, and, as we have seen, one of the rhetorical aspects of the enthymeme is that it may be couched in a form which conceals its logical framework. And he does not limit himself to the figures of syllogistic argument of the *Prior Analytics*, but includes arguments like 'Temperance is beneficial, for licentiousness is hurtful', which resemble some discussed in the *Topics*. He does however distinguish between enthymemes, as used in rhetoric, and the arguments in the *Topics*, which need to be set out in a rigorous way because the purposes of dialectical argument differ from those of rhetoric. Finally Aristotle allows that there are spurious enthymemes just as there are spurious syllogisms.

Putting all this together, we may conclude that Aristotle used the word 'enthymeme' primarily for valid arguments that (a) are not in strict syllogistic form, (b) are particularly concerned with matters of practical interest, and (c) where the effect on an audience is important.

If Aristotle had been nothing but a logician, he would probably not have covered as much ground in logic itself as he did. For he had to tackle difficult questions in many fields, from physics to aesthetics, and these forced him to tease out matters of language and logic that he might not otherwise have encountered. He was then able to apply what he had learned in one field to difficulties in another, and so make advances on many fronts.

Note on the works of Aristotle

Greek texts of all mentioned works of Aristotle are to be found in volumes of the Loeb Classical Library (Harvard University Press: Cambridge, MA, and Wm. Heinemann: London), with facing English translation. The Clarendon Aristotle Series (Oxford University Press: Oxford) has: Aristotle's *Categories* and *De Interpretatione* translated with notes by J. L. Ackrill (1963); the *Posterior Analytics* translated with notes by

Jonathan Barnes (1975); *De Partibus Animalium* (On the Parts of Animals) I, etc. translated with notes by D. M. Balme (1972); and *Metaphysics*, Books Gamma, Delta and Epsilon translated with notes by Christopher Kirwan (1971). W. D. Ross's *Aristotle's Prior and Posterior Analytics* (1949) with introduction and commentary (Oxford University Press: Oxford) includes valuable notes. And *Aristotle on Fallacies or the Sophistici Elenchi* (1886), edited by E. Poste with a translation and notes (London) is still useful.

Translations of all of Aristotle's works are to be found in The Oxford Translation in 12 volumes, under the editorship of J. A. Smith and W. D. Ross (1908-52) Oxford University Press: Oxford).

[NOTE: For referring to passages in Aristotle the normal practice has been followed, using a system of marginal references as in '35b10', which gives the page, the column ('a' or 'b') and the line as in the 1837 Oxford edition of Becker's Greek text.]

References

Ackrill, J. L. (1965), 'Aristotle's Distinction between *energeia* and *kinesis*', in Bambrough (1965), pp. 121-41.

Ackrill, J. L. (1981), Aristotle's Theory of Definition: Some Questions on *Posterior Analytics* II, 8-10, in Berti (1981), pp. 359-84.

Balme, D. M. (1961), 'Aristotle's Use of Differentiae in Zoology', in Mansion, pp. 195-212 and (revised) in Barnes, *et al.* (1975), pp. 183-93.

Bambrough, R. (ed.) (1965), *New Essays on Plato and Aristotle*, Routledge: London.

Barnes, J., M. Schofield, R. Sorabji (eds.), *Articles on Aristotle*, Vol. 1: *Science* (1975); Vol. 2: *Ethics and Politics* (1977); and Vol. 3: *Metaphysics* (1979), Duckworth: London.

Berti, E. (ed.) (1981), *Aristotle on Science: The 'Posterior Analytics'*, Padua.

Burnyeat, M. (1994), 'Enthymeme: Aristotle on the Logic of Persuasion', in Furley, David J. and Alexander Nehamas (eds.), *Aristotle's Rhetoric: Philosophical Essays*, Princeton University Press: Princeton.

Evans, J. D. G. (1977), *Aristotle's Concept of Dialectic*, Cambridge University Press: Cambridge.

Ferejohn, Michael (1991), *The Origins of Aristotelian Science*, Yale University Press: New Haven, CT.

Frede, Michael (1981), 'Categories in Aristotle', in O'Meara, D.J. (ed.), *Studies in Aristotle*, Catholic University of America, Washington D.C. Reprinted in Frede's *Essays in Ancient Philosophy*, pp. 29-48. University of Minnesota Press: Minneapolis.

Halliwell, S. (1986), *Aristotle's Poetics*, Duckworth: London, Appendix 4, 'Aristotle on Language'. Discusses Chapter 20.

Hamblin, C. L. (1970), *Fallacies*, Methuen: London.

Kirwan, C. (1979), 'Aristotle and the So-Called Fallacy of Equivocation', *Philosophical Quarterly*, Vol. 29, pp. 35-46.

Kneale, William, and Martha Kneale (1962), *The Development of Logic*, Oxford University Press: Oxford.

Lear, J. (1980), *Aristotle and Logical Theory*, Cambridge University Press: Cambridge. Includes a chapter on proof by refutation.

LeBlond, J. M. (1979), 'Aristotle on Definition, in Barnes, *et al*. (eds.), Vol. 3, pp. 63-79. Originally published in French in 1939.

Mansion, S. (ed.) (1961), *Aristotle et les problèmes de méthode*, Louvain.

Moravcsik, J. M. E. (ed.) (1967a) 'Aristotle', Macmillan: New York.

Moravcsik, J. M. E. (1967b), 'Aristotle's Theory of Categories', in Moravcsik (1967a), pp. 125-45.

Owen, G. E. L. (1960), 'Logic and Metaphysics in Some Earlier Works of Aristotle', in During, I. and G. E. L. Owen, *Aristotle and Plato in the Mid-Fourth Century*, Göteborg, pp. 163-90. Reprinted in Barnes, *et al*. (1979), Vol. 3, pp. 13-32, and in Owen (1986), pp. 180-199.

Owen, G. E. L. (1965), 'Aristotle and the Snares of Ontology', in Bambrough (1965), pp. 69-75, and reprinted in Owen (1986), pp. 259-78.

Owen, G. E. L. (ed.) (1968a), *Aristotle on Dialectic: The Topics*, Oxford University Press: Oxford.

Owen, G. E. L. (1968b), 'Dialectic and Eristic in the Treatment of the Forms', in Owen (1968a), pp.103-25, and in Owen (1986), pp. 221-38.

Owen, G. E. L. (1971-2), 'Aristotelian Pleasures', *Proceedings of the Aristotelian Society*, Vol. 72, pp. 135-52. Reprinted in Barnes, *et al*. (1977), pp.92-103, and in Owen (1986), pp. 334-46.

Owen, G. E. L. (1986), *Logic, Science and Dialectic*, Cornell University Press: Ithaca, NY.

Pellegrin, Pierre (1986), *Aristotle's Classification of Animals*, translated by A. Preus, University of California Press: Berkeley. Originally published in French.

Pinborg, Jan (1975), 'Classical Antiquity: Greece', *Current Trends in Linguistics*, Vol. 13, pp. 72-75.

Ross, W. D. (1923), *Aristotle*, Methuen: London. (Many later editions).

Ryle, Gilbert (1965), 'The Academy and Dialectic', in Bambrough (1965), pp. 39-68 (as 'Dialectic in the Academy'), and in Ryle (1971), Vol. 1, pp. 89-115.

Ryle, Gilbert (1968), 'Dialectic in the Academy', in Owen (1968a), pp. 69-79, and in Ryle (1971), Vol. 1, pp. 116-25.

Ryle, Gilbert (1971), *Collected Papers*, Hutchinson: London.

Smith, R. (1986), 'Immediate Propositions and Aristotle's Proof Theory', *Ancient Philosophy*, Vol. 6, pp. 47-68.

Solmsen, F. (1968), 'Dialectic without the Forms', in Owen (1968a), pp. 49-68.

Sorabji, Richard (1972), *Aristotle on Memory*, Duckworth: London.

Sorabji, Richard (1981), 'Definitions: Why Necessary and in What Way?', in Berti (1981), pp. 205-244.

Tanner, R. G. (1969), 'Aristotle as a Structural Linguist', *Transactions of the Philological Society*, pp. 99-164.

Weil, E. (1975), 'The Place of Logic in Aristotle's Thought', in Barnes, *et al*. (1975), pp. 88-112. Originally published in French in 1951.

Woods, John, and Douglas N. Walton (1982), 'The Petitio: Aristotle's Five Ways', *Canadian Journal of Philosophy*, Vol. 12, pp. 77-100.

5 Forms of argumentation in medieval dialectic

Alan R. Perreiah

Dialectic is the art of arts and the science of sciences providing a way into the principles of all methods. For dialectic alone disputes probatively concerning the principles of all of the other arts and for that reason dialectic ought to come first in the acquisition of the sciences.

Peter of Spain, Summulae Logicales, I

Introduction

Medieval people with an interest in learning would have known that dialectic was the art of effective argumentation. An argumentation was successful if it moved someone from doubt to conviction about the truth or falsity of some proposition. Greater familiarity with dialectic would have shown its differences both from science and from rhetoric. The job of the scientist was to demonstrate necessary truths about the natures of things. The task of the orator was to persuade an audience to pursue or to avoid a particular course of action. The function of the dialectician was to investigate critically any significant opinion that was controversial and that fell beyond the scope of science or rhetoric. Thus, dialectic was useful in everyday reasoning about human affairs whether personal, political or religious. It was essential to the conduct of commercial, legal and medical proceedings. As a critical discipline dialectic guided discovery of the premises of science as well as those of oratory. Finally, dialectic influenced education by offering principles and methods for instruction, exercise and examination.

Modern scholars employ the term 'dialectic' broadly to designate almost any exercise of rational thought. In this sense 'dialectic' would include what we have called scientific as well as rhetorical argumentation. More precisely, in this essay the term denotes rational discourse that is 'probable' (*probabilis*) or sophistical (Hugh of St. Victor, 1961, bk. II, ch. 30; John of Salisbury, 1971, bk. II, ch. 3; Peter of Spain, 1947, ch. 7; William of Sherwood, 1966, ch. 4; Robert Kilwardby, 1988, 277-282; William Ockham, 1974, part 3, tract 1, ch. 1). 'Argumentation' refers to the full elaboration in speech or in writing of a chain of reasoning; it is distinguished from 'argument' which is the logical

51

structure or purely formal component of a chain of reasoning (Boethius, 1988, bk.I, 27ff.; 1978, bk. 2, 43; Peter Abelard, 1970, 462-463; Peter of Spain, 1947, ch. 5, sect. 5.02). This study proposes to examine four main forms of argumentation that were used in the Middle Ages. First acknowledged in Aristotle's *Topics*, these forms of argumentation were cultivated in the ancient Greek and Roman worlds (Aristotle, 1984, 162a 15-20; 165b 1-9). When the *Topics* became available to scholars in the twelfth century the forms were revived and became crucial to the way in which ordinary argumentation was conceived (John of Salisbury, 1971, p.196). Since dialectic involved inferences various sets of rules were invoked to justify them (e.g. categorical syllogistic, hypothetical syllogistic, topics or *consequentia*); however, very little will be said here about those rules. Almost nothing will be said about issues in purely formal logic that modern scholars have claimed to find in the medieval texts (see, for example, Moody, 1953; Bochenski, 1961; Kneale, 1962; Kretzmann, Kenny, Pinborg, 1982; Pinborg, 1984; Stump, 1989).

Dialectic versus science and rhetoric

Dialectic is a distinctive discipline that differs both from science and from rhetoric. As elaborated by Aristotle in the *Posterior Analytics* science is a body of knowledge about a definite and invariant subject matter (Aristotle, 1984). Thus, the subject-matter of physics is the nature of what moves, that of biology the nature of living things, that of psychology the nature of psychic life, that of political science the nature of social order, etc. In each case a definite kind of thing is the subject of universal and necessary propositions that explain why those things operate as they do. Because a science gives the reasons for certain facts it begins with first principles or law-like sentences (the axioms, definitions, postulates), in short, the basic formulas of the science. It proceeds by categorical syllogism to derived propositions; these are the theorems of the science. First principles are universal, necessary and true; they are self-evident, immediate and indemonstrable. They should be appropriate to, better known than, and causally explanatory of, the conclusions. Conclusions themselves must accord with the basic facts of the science. When the propositions of a science are ranked in order from the universal to the particular, where the latter are deducible from the former, they constitute an axiomatized science of the subject in question. Although this model of science from Aristotle's *Posterior Analytics* is rarely, if ever, exemplified in those scientific texts of Aristotle that have come down to us, it outlined a science like Euclidean geometry and later influenced medieval scientists no less than theologians.

Scientific demonstration is one kind of argumentation that is called in the ancient texts 'philosopheme' (*philosophema*) (Aristotle, 162a5-20). Its structuring principle is the categorical syllogism that Aristotle presented in the *Prior Analytics*. Here is an example of scientific demonstration:

1. Any body that from any position casts a curved shadow on another is spherical. (Major premise)

2. The earth during eclipse casts a curved shadow on the moon. (Minor Premise)

3. Therefore, the earth is spherical. (Conclusion)

Schematically,

$$[p_1, p_2] \Rightarrow q$$

'p' and 'q' stand for declarative sentences asserted by someone on some occasion; and 'q' is a different sentence from every 'p'. '⇒' stands for an inferential relationship between ps (premises or antecedents) and q (conclusion or consequent). This relationship is governed by rules of categorical syllogism that specify valid combinations of sentences. Validity is a property of the form of the argumentation; it does not depend in any way upon the meaning of the words or sentences that it contains.

Several examples of demonstrative argumentation survive in the scientific treatises of late antiquity. In the philosophical tradition, Plotinus' *Enneads* were organized by Porphyry in a quasi axiomatic format, and Plotinus attempts to prove particular propositions from general theses. His criticisms of dialectic are aimed at the practice of dialectic as a purely formal method of investigation detached from the content of questions that it treats (Plotinus, 1956, First Ennead, tr.3, ch. 4-6). Nonetheless, his own procedure often involves refutation of views that he opposes, and this is the central function of dialectical argumentation. The idea of theology as science in a stricter sense could be explored only after Aristotle's model of axiomatized science in *Posterior Analytics* became available to theologians in the thirteenth century.

Few medieval people would have laid claim to scientific knowledge as defined by Aristotle (see Clagett, 1961; Grant, 1974; Lindberg, 1978). Practically everyone, however, was exposed to public communication, and rhetoric was the art of such communication. The task of the rhetorician was to persuade through the use of enthymeme and example (see Erickson, 1974; Murphy, 1974). Enthymemes are argumentations by means of signs, for example 'If the enemy is amassing weapons on our border, they will probably attack. Therefore, we must prepare for an attack'. An argumentation by means of example: 'The Speaker and ten members of the house accepted $100 in exchange for their support of the bill. Is this the value of a vote in our legislature? Support legislative reform'. Aristotle called dialectic the complement (*antistrophe*) of rhetoric because it aided in the discovery of starting premises as well as lines of argument. Rhetoric fashions speech for the needs of specific audiences in particular circumstances; dialectic offers methods of reasoning that can be used with any respondent in any situation.

Dialectic: *epicheireme*

The basic argumentation form of dialectic is the dialectical syllogism or epicheireme (*epicheirema*). Because it deals with controversial matters, every epicheireme begins with a question posing two alternatives. Consider the following example.

Is exercise healthy or unhealthy?

Dialectical argumentation consists in examining one of these alternatives by means of question and answer. The above question might be posed to someone who doubts the benefits of exercise or who believes that it is unhealthy. The dialectician then asks a series of questions whose answers imply the opposite of that belief, viz. exercise is healthy. For example,

Dialectician: Does exercise promote circulation?

Respondent: yes.

Dialectician: Does exercise further digestion?

Respondent: yes.

Dialectician: Does exercise develop muscle tone?

Respondent: yes.

Dialectician: Is the improvement of circulation, digestion and muscle tone healthy?

Respondent: yes (Therefore, exercise is healthy.)

It is a principle of dialectic that a line of questioning could just as well have been performed on the alternative proposition, 'Exercise is healthy', and from different premises the opposite proposition, 'Exercise is unhealthy', could have been proved. In actual dialectical exchanges there is a contest between questioner and answerer. Like our example, the questioner would strive to overturn the opinion held by the answerer. Unlike our example, the answerer would try to uphold the original opinion.

The pattern of dialectical reasoning is the following:

? [q or not-q]

$q \mathbin{/\!/} [? \, p_1, ? \, p_3, \ldots ? \, p_n] \rightarrow$ not-q;

alternately,

54

? [q or not-q]

not-q // [? p_2, ? p_4,... ? p_{n+1}] → q.

'p' and 'q' stand for sentences asserted by someone on some occasion. q is distinct from every p. '→' stands for an inferential relationship between p and q governed by topical rules or rules of *consequentia*. Initial '?' indicates the dialectical question. Initial 'q' is called the thesis and must be a plausible opinion on the matter in question. Subsequent occurrences of '?' indicate that the argument proceeds by questions and simple 'yes' or 'no' replies. Each answered 'p' is approximately true or true for the most part. If the questioner succeeds, the opposite of the original thesis follows; if the answerer successfully resists the questioner's efforts at rebuttal, the original thesis stands.

Medieval logicians formulated a variety of rules to justify inferences from premises granted by respondents to conclusions that followed from them. Aristotle's *Topics* catalogued a large number rules and techniques used by ancient dialecticians to secure conclusions from propositions granted by willing respondents (Aristotle, 1984). Boethius' *De topicis differentiis* developed a system of topical rules for discovering how to prove a conclusion once its subject and predicate terms were identified (Boethius, 1978). He listed a number of general maxims that could be used as major premises with appropriate minor premises to prove desired conclusions. Although adopted widely in the Middle Ages, Boethius' system was replaced by others. Peter of Spain's *Summulae logicales* presented topical rules that could be used to confirm or disconfirm the validity of inferences in dialectical exchanges. In the later Middle Ages *consequentia* rules replaced topical rules as means of supporting inferences in dialectic (see Bird, 1960, 1962, 1969; Green-Pedersen, 1984). Whether *consequentia* rules were reducible to categorical syllogistic or vice versa was a theoretical issue in later medieval logic (as in Jean Buridan, 1985, 3.2.1). It is noteworthy that wherever any of these systems of rules made use of categorical syllogism, they borrowed its logical form and filled it with content appropriate to dialectical investigation. Instead of propositions that were universal, necessary, true, etc. as required by science, they included propositions that applied to contingent subject-matters and were plausible or 'true for the most part'. Unlike science that expresses truth; dialectic yields verisimilitude, what in the exchange between questioner and answerer appears to be true. Dialectic remains a discipline *toto caelo* different from science.

Medieval philosophical literature is replete with examples of dialectical argumentation. Often these appear under different guises. Augustine's early *Soliloquies, Concerning the Teacher*, and *On Free Will* are dialogues that exhibit dialectical form (Augustine, 1948). A large number of Augustine's theological writings, e.g. *City of God, On the Spirit and the Letter, The Enchiridion, On Grace and Free Will*, are treatises addressed to particular persons (Augustine, 1948). Because their principal purpose is the refutation of one or more theses, e.g. Pelagianism, they have a dialectical structure. Augustine's *Confessions* pose numerous dialectical questions on a wide variety of issues from ethics, epistemology and metaphysics. The Manichean question, 'Is evil material or immaterial?'; the Skeptical problem, 'Are the senses reliable or unreliable?', the theological issue, 'Is God bodily or nonbodily?', the metaphysical conundrum, 'Is time real or unreal?' – are but a few of the problems examined in the *Confessions*. They are dialectical because Augustine's espoused purpose is to resolve doubts in his own mind or in that of his reader. Of all his works, only Augustine's *On the Trinity* aspires to present something like scientific argumentation: combining central ideas of Scripture with observations from human experience, he attempts to deduce an account of the triune God (Augustine, 1948).

Boethius' *Consolation of Philosophy* similarly abounds with dialectical argumentation (Boethius, 1969). Dame Philosophy subjects Boethius' grievances – that he has been imprisoned unjustly, that fortune has been unkind to him, that the existence of God is incompatible with evil, that divine governance cancels human free will – to dialectical investigation. Each book of the *Consolation* is devoted to a series of interrogations whereby Boethius is compelled to admit the opposite of his earlier beliefs. The therapy that Dame Philosophy promises him is just the exercise of dialectical argumentation, and it is clear by the end of the work that Boethius has replaced his original confusion and doubt by a certainty that is essential for his emotional health.

Finally John Scotus Eriugena's *On the Division of Nature* from the ninth century shows the durability of dialectical argumentation. This major neoplatonic work is written in a dialogue form, and the principal structuring principle of dialogue is the epicheireme as we have seen (John Scotus Eriugena, 1853).

Dialectic: *aporeme*

As noted earlier, the skilled dialectician is able to argue from premises accepted by a respondent to *either* of the alternatives posed in the original question. When both alternatives are submitted to dialectical interrogation a new form of dialectical argumentation is born. Because it creates an impasse in thought it is called 'aporeme' (*aporema*). Perhaps owing to its complexity, the aporeme is the most neglected of medieval argumentation forms. This is regrettable since its presence is ubiquitous in medieval literature (see e.g. Curtius, 1953, Vance 1987).

A familiar example of aporetic argumentation is St. Augustine's famous perplexity about time in *Confessions* (Augustine, 1948). Here is a sketch of the dialectical reasoning Augustine pursues with himself and before his readers.

Is time real or unreal? (Dialectical Question)

Time is real. (First thesis)

Does the past exist? No.

Does the future exist? No.

Is not the present simply a transition between future and past? Yes.

Can there be a relation between two things that do not exist? No.

Therefore, time is not real. (Denial of First Thesis)

Time is not real. (Second Thesis)

Is time divided into past, present and future? Yes.

Are past, present and future parts of some whole? Yes.

Is not time the whole of which these are parts? Yes.

Therefore, time is real. (Denial of Second Thesis)

The results of these two sequences of argumentation are conjoined to support the dilemma: Time is both real and unreal.
The aporeme has the following form:

? (q or not-q)

$$q \mathbin{/\!/} [? \, p_1, ? \, p_3, ... ? \, p_n] \rightarrow \text{not-q},$$

and,

$$\text{not-q} \mathbin{/\!/} [? \, p_2, ? \, p_4, ? \, p_{n+1}] \rightarrow q.$$

Therefore, q and not-q.

with 'p', 'q' and '→' defined as previously, initial '?' indicates that the answerer selects one of two mutually contradictory theses. Then, the denial of that thesis is proved by a series of questions to which the answerer replies simply 'yes' or 'no'. Again, the opposite of the remaining thesis is proved by the same method.

What is the utility of this kind of argumentation? Ancient and medieval people recognized that no one could learn a subject that he already knew or believed that he knew. Learning requires docility and that implies an admission that one does not know the subject at hand. The aporeme was the standard way to bring about a disposition to learn in the mind of the student. Plato's dialogues, Aristotle's treatises, and a broad range of school texts throughout the Middle Ages attest to the importance of the aporeme in preparing students for the task of learning. We noted its importance for Augustine's *Confessions*. Boethius' *Commentary* on Porphyry's *Introduction* (*Isagoge*) to Aristotle's *Categories* that introduced the problem of universals to medieval thinkers is precisely a battery of aporetic arguments (Boethius, 1929, 70-99). The conclusion of these arguments is that the universal predicates of language are neither unitary nor multiple. Whatever exists, however, is either one or many. Therefore, universals that are indispensable to all thought and discourse seem not to exist. These aporemes challenged medieval students to explain how meaningful human discourse was possible. Beyond this specialized area of medieval philosophy, the aporetic form of argumentation is found in a wide variety of texts. Abelard's *Sic et Non* sets forth conflicting lines of testimony from the Church Fathers on 158 points of Christian belief (Abailard, 1977). From the viewpoint of argumentation-theory this pioneering effort in medieval theology exhibits the aporetic form of argumentation throughout.

Similarly, Moses Maimonides' *Guide for the Perplexed* utilizes the aporeme to deal with many questions such as creation versus the eternity of the world, chance versus providence, the nature of prophecy, etc. (See Maimonides, 1963; Hyman, 1989, 35-51). Moses weighs one side of an aporetic argument against the other in order to work out his own opinion on particular problems. At times one must choose between opposing alternatives; at other times one must develop a new opinion incorporating elements from both alternatives. For example, in the arguments concerning the eternity of the world Moses concludes that the creationist thesis is more plausible. Again, he reviews five opinions on the question whether providence rules the universe. Setting aside Epicurus' claim that the universe operates by chance, he considers a range of views from Aristotle that limit providence to the sublunar species to others that extend providential control to animals, plants and minerals. Comparing these rival claims and the arguments that support them, Moses concludes that providence extends to humans in proportion as they partake of intellectual reasoning. Thus, Moses uses the aporetic form of argumentation to weigh competing views and to arrive at a balanced interpretation of a subject.

Finally, Giles of Rome's *Errors of the Philosophers* (*Errores philosophorum*) pits arguments from Christian belief against the reasoned opinions of Greek and Arabic philosophers. When both lines of argumentation are taken into account they produce aporemes whose effect is to create doubt in the mind of the reader (Giles of Rome, 1944).

Dialectic: *sophisma*

Sophistry or the art of spurious reasoning has always had a productive connection with the serious study of argumentation. One way to show the strength of valid reasoning is to compare it with invalid or ineffective reasoning. Moreover, a capacity to spot weaknesses in an opponent's arguments has always held a peculiar attraction for western thinkers. In the twelfth century with the introduction of Aristotle's *Topica* and *Sophistical Refutations* medieval authors got a first-hand look at examples of sophistical reasoning from the ancient world. Perhaps the most famous sophism of the ancient world that was discussed extensively in the medieval school tradition was the liar paradox (Spade, 1975). Epimenides the Cretan declares, 'All Cretans are liars'. Is Epimenides telling the truth? If he is, then in saying that all Cretans are liars he is not telling the truth. If he is not telling the truth, then in saying that all Cretans are liars he is telling the truth. Thus, Epimenides tells the truth if and only if he does not tell the truth. How can this be? A simpler form of the same kind of paradox is that of the person who says 'I am lying'; if he is lying, he is speaking the truth, and vice versa.

Sophisms were also known as insolubles (*insolubilia*) because they gave rise to difficult linguistic puzzles and to problems that seemed impossible to solve. Paul of Venice's *Logica Parva* catalogues the major kinds of insolubles that a student could expect to encounter in academic pursuits. An insoluble is obvious (*apparens*) if it refers explicitly to its own truth or falsity; it is concealed (*non apparens*) if its truth or falsity is established by the context in which it is expressed. Obvious insolubles may occur in all of the major forms of statements:

1. Categorical statements

    a. Singular: 'I am saying something false'.

    b. Particular: 'Some particular proposition is false'.

    c. Universal: 'Every universal proposition is false'.

    d. Exclusive: 'Only Socrates says something true'.

    e. Exceptive: 'No one except Socrates says something true'.

2. Hypothetical statements

    a. Conjunctive: 'God exists and no conjunctive proposition is true'.

    b. Disjunctive: 'No God exists or no disjunctive proposition is true'.

Examples of concealed insolubles:

    1. 'Socrates will not have a dime'.

    2. 'Plato will not cross the bridge'.

The latter propositions could be problematic in a context where only persons who speak the truth will get a dime or cross a bridge. Then, Socrates says truly, 'I will not have a dime'. As a truth-teller Socrates will have a dime; but as a truth-teller of the negative proposition he will not have a dime. Similarly, Plato says truly, 'I will not cross the bridge'. As a truth-teller he will cross the bridge; but as a truth-teller of the negative proposition he will not cross the bridge. Although medieval professors of logic were expected to have worked out solutions to these problematic sentences and their students would have studied those solutions, it was normally sufficient for a student to know how to detect an insoluble proposition in order to avoid conceding it in a dialectical exchange. Insolubles and sophisms of all of these kinds challenged students to think much more carefully about the truth-conditions of everyday statements and helped them deal effectively with truth-conditions of statements in scientific and technical contexts.

    The sophism (*sophisma*) is aporetic in structure. It is the conjunction of two epicheiremes.

? (q or not-q).

With 'p', 'q' and '→' defined as previously, one of two dialectical propositions is chosen by the answerer, and replies to a series of questions yield the desired conclusion:

$$q \,/\!/\, [?\, p_1, ?\, p_2, ...?\, p_n] \rightarrow \text{not-q}$$

Paradox ensues when dialectical reasoning is applied to both alternatives in the original question and the results of these procedures are combined. The sophism differs from the basic aporeme in two ways: formally, the sophism appears valid but is not; materially, the sophism contains premises which appear to be, but are not in fact, plausible or credible.

Discovery of the *Sophistical Refutations* (the ninth book of Aristotle's *Topics*) corresponded with the rise of university education in the thirteenth century, and sophisms came to play an important part in required logic courses. For the student who knew how to argue they challenged his ability to discriminate between valid and invalid arguments. A ready supply of sophisms provided an opportunity to sharpen one's skills at fallacy detection (Jean Buridan, 1966). Finally, for those attracted to purely logical analysis semantical puzzles like the Liar opened up one of the great theoretical areas of medieval logic, namely, study of the logic of punctuation and of differences between meaning and the uses of language.

Mixed modes of argumentation

The forms of argumentation examined thus far are often found independently as the controlling or principal form of argumentation for a particular work. At times, however, the forms are combined to produce a much more powerful treatment of a subject than could be accomplished by any one of them taken alone. Here are some examples of how medieval thinkers integrated the basic forms of argumentation.

From the twelfth century Anselm of Canterbury's *Monologium* and *Proslogion* illustrate how dialectical argumentation may complement scientific argumentation (Anselm, 1965, 1986). The former work mounts a series of dialectical arguments that support the thesis that God exists. The latter adopts one thesis proved in the *Monologium*, viz. the definition of God as 'that than which none greater can be conceived', and develops a single scientific proof or demonstration (*philosophema*) that such a being exists. Objections to this conclusion by the monk Guanilo 'on behalf of the fool' (who says in his heart that there is no God) are duly answered by Anselm. This exchange exemplifies dialectical argumentation (*epicheirema*) in *Proslogion*.

Thomas Aquinas' *Summa Theologica* is another example of the integration of two forms of argumentation examined above (Thomas Aquinas, 1945). The work is divided into various questions on particular topics. Each question is further divided into two or more articles that deal with particular aspects of the question. Finally, each article has a definite format. For example, the article devoted to the question: Whether God exists? has three parts (Aquinas 1). First, arguments called 'objections' are presented against the thesis that God exists. Next, after a brief reply stating the author's own conviction (often embellished with a quotation from Scripture or from another respected authority), the author presents his own demonstrative reasoning on the topic. Finally, the author replies to the objections set forth initially. It is easy to discern in this format a combination of two kinds of argumentation that we have discussed. The initial objections and the final replies are plainly examples of epicheiremic argumentation. The so-called 'body' of the article consists in the author's scientific demonstration (*philosophema*) of conclusions relevant to the question. *Summa Theologica* maintains a balance between dialectical and scientific forms of argumentation. The *Disputed Questions* exhibit a much richer dialectical component (objections and replies) in comparison to their scientific component (Thomas Aquinas, 1949).

No survey of medieval argumentation-forms would be complete without some discussion of the late medieval exercises called 'obligations' (*obligationes*), as they appear, for example, in Paul of Venice's *Logica parva* (Paul of Venice, 1984). In general, an obligation is an exchange between two parties wherein one consents to respond to statements proposed by the other; and both agree to do this relative to an original thesis and within a set time limit. The goal of the questioner (*opponens*) is to try to get the answerer (*respondens*) to concede or deny some proposition so as to contradict the original thesis; that of the answerer is to concede or deny each statement proposed to him so as to avoid such contradiction. Obligations are of two types: positions (*positiones*) where the original thesis is regarded as accepted by the answerer; depositions (*depositiones*) where the original thesis is regarded as rejected by the answerer. In either case, however, the goal of the questioner is to try to trip the answerer into self-contradiction; that of the answerer is to avoid self-contradiction. Later medieval logic manuals included elaborate rules to help answerers decide whether to concede, deny or doubt a proposition tendered by a questioner.

Here is an example of a simple obligational exchange.

1. Questioner: I pose to you, 'Every man runs'.

2. Answerer: I admit and I concede, 'Every man runs'.

3. Questioner: I propose to you, 'Every man sits'.

4. Answerer: I concede, 'Every man sits'.

5. Questioner: I propose to you, 'Every man runs and every man sits'.

6. Answerer: I concede, 'Every man runs and every man sits'.

7. Questioner: I propose to you, 'Some man does not run'.

8. Answerer: I concede, 'Some man does not run'.

9. Questioner: You respond poorly (*male*).

Rules of obligations told answerers how to reply to particular kinds of propositions. Each step in the above exchange follows one of the standard rules. For example, (2) is required by a rule, 'Everything possible which is posited to you initially is to be admitted by you'. Occasionally, a questioner would pose initially an impossible or paradoxical proposition, and the answerer would have to decide how to reply to it. (4) follows from a rule for responding to irrelevant propositions, i.e. those which neither follow from nor are inconsistent with the starting thesis. Simply, the answerer is to respond according to the quality of the proposition: If it is true, it is to be conceded. If false, denied. If doubtful, doubted. (6) follows from a rule that requires concession of the conjunction of two or more propositions previously conceded. (8) is an erroneous step by the answerer; for it violates a rule that requires denial of any proposition inconsistent with what has been conceded. Although this example of an *obligatio* is greatly simplified, it shows how the *obligatio* format could be used to instruct and exercise students in dialectical reasoning and to train students in basic principles of inference.

With respect to the forms of argumentation examined earlier the *obligatio* format exposes an answerer to a range of possibilities. If the answerer completes the exercise successfully, i.e. he responds without contradicting either the starting thesis or any other propositions that have been conceded or denied, the exchange is a simple dialectical argumentation or epicheireme. If the respondent should grant a proposition that contradicts one previously entered in the exchange, the argumentation may appear to be valid but is in fact formally or materially invalid, thus degenerating into sophism. Hence, the *obligatio* format affords an opportunity to learn how fallacious reasoning can occur in dialectical argumentation. Once a student has mastered the *obligatio* form, it is clear that the starting theses and subsequent propositions tendered by the questioner could be propositions from any area of inquiry that the student was presumed to know. Hence, the format could be used to test a student's understanding of a particular subject-matter.

The purpose of the *obligatio* has been a point of controversy among historians of logic. Some have claimed that its aim is to explore highly theoretical problems in formal logic and possible worlds semantics (Boehner, 1952; Hamblin, 1970; Spade, 1977). Others have claimed that it offers a format for training and exercising students on skills of dialectical reasoning and basic inference. Still others that it is a format for examining students on specific subject-matters (Perreiah, 1982). Suffice it to say that the *obligatio* was one of the most original and interesting inventions in the field of dialectical argumentation in the Middle Ages.

Conclusion

Each century of the modern era has pictured the medieval period from its own intellectual perspective. To the Renaissance humanist it was a wasteland of intellectual and literary decadence when a barbaric tongue replaced classical Latin eloquence. To the sixteenth century religious reformer it was an age of excessive papal power, diminished personal freedom and spiritual regression. To the seventeenth century scientist it was a period of dogmatism when slavish devotion to Platonism and Aristotelianism thwarted scientific discovery. To the eighteenth century enlightenment thinker it was an time of superstition and political repression. To the nineteenth century romantic it represented an ideal of elevated spirituality where humans transcended the natural world for communion with the supernatural. Twentieth century scholarship has stressed the study of medieval texts themselves in an effort to understand the Middle Ages on its own terms.

This approach to the sources has been especially fruitful in recovering the contributions of the medievals to western literature, science, philosophy, theology, education and the professions. As the present study has attempted to show, the attitude of medieval thinkers toward intellectual work was neither random nor haphazard nor, as some humanists were wont to suggest, mindless. In all rational inquiry they were guided by models of argumentation well-articulated in the ancient world: scientific demonstration (*philosophema*), dialectical argumentation (*epicheirema*), aporetic argumentation (*aporema*) and sophistical argumentation (*sophisma*). The medievals transformed these models and adapted them to their own circumstances, needs and purposes.

In the transitional period between the late scholastic and early humanistic period (roughly, 1375-1425), a great deal of confusion was created about the nature and value of argumentation in the scholastic tradition. Lorenzo Valla's *Dialectica* which may be regarded as a paradigm of humanistic attacks on scholasticism trivializes dialectic in comparison with rhetoric. 'What else is dialectic than a kind of confirmation and confutation the various sorts of which are part of discovery (*inventio*)?' (Valla, 1982). Despite Valla's representation of dialectic as merely a refutational art, the argumentation forms that we have distinguished are alive and well in his works. His polemical works, dialogues, disputed questions and disquisitions on various topics exhibit the epicheiremic form of argumentation.

In the sixteenth century Philip Melanchthon's reforms at Wittenberg set new academic standards for major European universities during the Reformation (Spitz, 1984). Despite initial objections by Martin Luther to traditional training in dialectic for theology students, Melanchthon established at Wittenberg a curriculum that included the *disputatio* as well as a considerable body of Aristotelian materials in the sciences. Although Aristotle was excluded from the study of religion and Holy Writ, the modes of argumentation that we have examined continued to be a formative influence on the methods of learning cultivated during the Reformation.

In the seventeenth century the writings of Francis Bacon and Rene Descartes were highly critical of earlier philosophical and scientific traditions. Bacon's *Novum Organon* and *The Advancement of Learning*, just as Descartes' *Discourse on Method* and *Rules for Direction of the Mind*, offered new rhetorical defenses of science and expounded new methods of empirical investigation and conceptual analysis (Bacon 1900, 1974; Descartes, 1955). Nonetheless, the methods of argumentation advanced by these authors confirm the durability of the forms that we have elucidated. What are Bacon's criticisms if not epicheiremic arguments against the views that he opposes? What are Descartes' skeptical problems if not a battery of aporetic arguments concerning the possibility of human knowledge? What are Descartes' scientific treatises if not exercises in scientific demonstration (philosophema)? It is hardly accidental that Benedict Spinoza's *Ethics* that epitomized these trends is written in the classic form of axiomatized science (Spinoza, 1951).

Allowing for innovations in literary and rhetorical style, similar evidence for the survival of classical argumentation forms in the philosophical literature of the eighteenth, nineteenth and twentieth centuries could be developed; but that would take us well beyond the limits of this study. Suffice it to say that the methods of argumentation cultivated by the dialecticians of the Middle Ages built durable bridges not only between rhetoric and science and between formal and informal logic, but also between the Ancient and Modern worlds.

References

Anselm, Saint (1965), *St. Anselm's Proslogion*, translated by M. J. Charlesworth, Clarendon Press: Oxford.

Anselm, Saint (1986), *A New Interpretative Translation of St. Anselm's Monologion and Proslogion*, translated by Jasper Hopkins, Arthur J. Banning Press: Minneapolis.

Aristotle (1984), *The Complete Works of Aristotle*, edited by J. Barnes, Princeton University Press: Princeton, NJ.

Aurelius Augustine, Saint (1948), *Basic Writings of Saint Augustine*, edited by W. J. Oates, Random House: New York.

Bacon, Francis (1974), *The Advancement of Learning and New Atlantis*, edited by Arthur Johnston, Clarendon Press: Oxford.

Bacon, Francis (1900), *Advancement of Learning and Novum Organum*, Colonial Press: New York.

Bird, Otto (1960), 'The Formalizing of the Topics in Medieval Logic', *Notre Dame Journal of Formal Logic*, Vol. 1, pp. 138-149.

Bird, Otto (1962), 'The Tradition of the Topics: Aristotle to Ockham', *Journal of the History of Ideas*, Vol. 23, pp. 307-323.

Bird, Otto (1969), 'Topic and Consequence in Ockham's Logic', *Notre Dame Journal of Formal Logic*, Vol. 2, pp. 65-78.

Bochenski, I. M. (1961), *A History of Formal Logic*, translated by I. Thomas, Chelsea: New York.

Boehner, P. (1952), *Medieval Logic: An Outline of its Development from 1250 to circa 1400*, University Press: Manchester.

Boethius (1929), *Commentary on Porphyry's Isagoge*, in *Selections from Medieval Philosophers*, edited and translated by R. McKeon, Charles Scribner's Sons: New York.

Boethius (1978), *Boethius' De topicis differentiis*, translated by E. Stump, Cornell University Press: Ithaca, NY.

Boethius (1988), *Boethius' In Ciceronis topica*, translated by E. Stump, Cornell University Press: Ithaca, NY.

Boethius (1969), *The Consolation of Philosophy*, translated by V. E. Watts, Viking Penguin: New York.

Camporeale, Salvatore (1972), *Lorenzo Valla Umanesimo e teologia*, Nella sede Dell'istituto Palazzo Strozzi: Firenze.

Clagett, Marshall (1961), *Science of Mechanics in the Middle Ages*, University of Wisconsin Press: Madison.

Cuetius, Ernst A. (1953), *European Literature and the Latin Middle Ages*, translated by W. R. Trask, Routledge and Kegan Paul: London.

Descartes, Rene (1955), *Discourse on the Method of Rightly Conducting the Reason and Rules for the Direction of the Mind*, in *Philosophical works of Descartes*, translated by E. S. Haldane and G. R. T. Ross, Vol. 1, Dover Publications: New York.

Erickson, K. V. (1974), *Aristotle: The Classical Tradition in Rhetoric*, Scarecrow Press: Metuchen, NJ.

Giles of Rome (1944), *Errores philosophorum*, translated by J. Koch and J. O. Reidl, Marquette University Press: Milwaukee, WI.

Grant, Edward, ed. (1974), *A Source Book in Medieval Science*, Harvard University Press: Cambridge, MA.

Green-Pedersen, Neils J. (1984), *The Tradition of the Topics in the Middle Ages*, Philosophia Verlag: Munich.

Hamblin, C. L. (1970), *Fallacies*, Methuen and Company: London.

Hugh of St. Victor (1961), *The Didascalicon of Hugh of St. Victor*, translated by J. Taylor, Columbia University Press: New York.

Hyman, Arthur (1989), 'Demonstrative, Dialectical and Sophistic Arguments in the Philosophy of Moses Maimonides', in *Moses Maimonides and His Time*, edited by E. L. Ormsby, Catholic University of America Press: Washington, D.C.

Jean Buridan (1985), *Jean Buridan's Logic*, translated by P. King, D. Reidel Publishing Company: Dordrecht.

Jean Buridan (1966), *Sophisms on Meaning and Truth*, translated by T. K. Scott, Appleton, Century Crofts: New York.

John of Salisbury (1971), *Metalogicon*, translated by D. McGarry, Peter Smith: Gloucester, MA.

John Scotus Eriugena (1853), *Periphyseon* or *The Division of Nature*, in *Patrologia Latina*, ed. J. P. Migne, Vol. CXXII.

Kneale, William, and Martha Kneale (1962), *The Development of Logic*, Clarendon Press: Oxford.

Kretzmann, N., A. Kenny, and J. Pinborg (1982), *The Cambridge History of Medieval Philosophy*, Cambridge University Press: Cambridge.

Laurentii Valle (1982), *Repastinatio dialectice et philosophie*, edited by G. Zippel, Antenore: Padua.

Lindberg, D. (1978), *Science in the Middle Ages*, University of Chicago Press: Chicago.

Moody, E (1953), *Truth and Consequence in Mediaeval Logic*, North Holland Publishing Company: Amsterdam.

Moses Maimonides (1963), *The Guide of the Perplexed*, translated by S. Pines, University of Chicago Press: Chicago.

Murphy, James J. (1974), *Rhetoric in the Middle Ages*, University of California Press: Berkeley.

Paul of Venice (1984), *Paulus Venetus: Logica Parva*, translated by A. Perreiah, Catholic University of America Press: Washington, D.C.

65

Peter Abailard (1976), *Sic et Non*, edited by C. Boyer and R. McKeon, University of Chicago Press: Chicago.

Peter Abelard (1970), *Dialectica*, edited by L. M. DeRijk, Van Gorcum: Assen.

Peter of Spain (1947), *Summulae Logicales*, edited by I. M. Bochenski, Marietti: Rome.

Pinborg, Jan (1984), *Topik und Syllogistik im Mittelalter*, in *Medieval Semantics*, edited by S. Ebbesen, Variorum: London.

Plotinus (1962), *The Enneads*, translated by S. McKenna, Faber and Faber: London, First Ennead, Tr. III.

Robert Kilwardby (1988), *De ortu scientiarum*, In *The Cambridge Translations of Medieval Philosophical Texts*, edited by N. Kretzmann and E. Stump, Cambridge University Press: Cambridge.

Spade, Paul (1975), *The Mediaeval Liar*, a catalogue of the insolubilia-literature, Pontifical Institute of Mediaeval Studies: Toronto.

Spade, Paul (1977), Roger Swyneshed's *Obligationes*, edition and comments, in *Archives d'histoire doctrinale et litteraire du moyen age*, Vol. 44, pp. 243-285.

Spinoza, Benedict de (1951), *Ethics*, in *Works of Spinoza*, translated by R. H. M. Elwes, Vol. 2, Dover Publications: New York.

Spitz, L. W. (1984), 'The Importance of the Reformation for the Universities: Culture and Confessions in the Critical Years', in *Rebirth, Reform and Rresilience, Universities in Transition 1300-1700*, edited by J. M. Kittelson and P. J. Transue, pp. 42-67, Ohio State University Press: Columbus.

Stump, E. (1989), *Dialectic and its Place in the Development of Medieval Logic*, Cornell University Press: Ithaca.

Thomas Aquinas (1945), *Basic Writings of Saint Thomas Aquinas*, edited by A. C. Pegis, Random House: New York.

Thomas Aquinas (1949), *Quaestiones Disputatae*, Marietti: Rome.

Vance, Eugene (1987), *From Topic to Tale: Logic and Narrativity in the Middle Ages*, University of Minnesota Press: Minneapolis.

William Ockham (1974), *Summa logicae*, edited by P. Boehner, G. Gal, and S. Brown, Franciscan Institute: St. Bonaventure, NY.

William of Sherwood (1966), *William of Sherwood's Introduction to Logic*, translated by N. Kretzmann, University of Minnesota Press: Minneapolis.

6   The *Port Royal Logic*

Russell Wahl

The work that came to be known as the *Port Royal Logic* was probably the most influential logic book of its time. It was first published, anonymously, in 1662 as *La Logique ou l'art de penser*,[1] and was pretty much continuously in print both in France and in England well into the second half of the nineteenth century. It appeared in England in 1664, being published first in French, then in Latin, and then in English translation in 1685. New translations, based on later editions, appeared in 1717 and 1818. The work was influential not only insofar as it was a standard textbook, but also in that it became a model for other such works. A glance at the tables of contents of logic books from the eighteenth century will confirm this. John Locke was also very much influenced by the *Port Royal Logic*, adopting some of its organization and terminology in his own work, despite the fact that it opens with an attack on what was to become one of Locke's most cherished dogmas, that all our ideas come entirely from sense experience.

While there are portions of the *Port Royal Logic* which are rooted in traditional scholastic logic, the tone of the work is that of a break with the old. The authors suggest in their introductory remarks that previous logic books were quite dry and easily forgotten. They say that part of the remedy for this problem will be the use of new examples, many of them taken from classical literature, which was enjoying a revival, and many of them taken from contemporary works in science. The work is firmly allied with seventeenth-century developments in philosophy and science, and the references to philosophical works prior to Descartes are in general negative, with the important exception of those of St. Augustine.

What is perhaps most revolutionary (or, some might say, confused) about the work is its attitude toward the point of logic: According to the Port Royalists, the focus of logic should not be on argument, disputation or the systematic presentation of things already known, but on a method of discovering new truths and clearing the mind of false prejudices. The Port Royalists expressed this attitude often by suggesting that their logic, unlike those that came before it, is practical. A constant theme of their criticisms of scholastic logic is not that it is wrong, but that it is of little use in discerning the true from the false. A present-day reader of the *Port Royal Logic* might well see in it anticipations of criticisms that current advocates of informal logic or 'critical thinking' level at their colleagues who emphasize formal logic. While there is some justification in this judgment, it is also an over-simplification.

By the seventeen century, the abbey at Port Royal des Champs[2] had become a center of religious and political controversy. The nuns and retreatants of Port Royal were associated with the Jansenist movement,[3] which held an extremely anti-Pelagian attitude toward original sin and God's grace. Their doctrines had political ramifications which were rightly seen as a threat by the Jesuits and the court. This book and the *Grammaire générale et raisonnée*, also known as the *Port Royal Grammar*, were based in part on courses taught at the *petites écoles de Port Royal*, which were closed in 1661. While the work was published anonymously, it was written by Antoine Arnauld (1612-1694) and Pierre Nicole (1625-1694), both of whom were associated with Port Royal. Although there is still some dispute as to how much each one contributed, Arnauld is generally credited with having written most of the work.

Among those associated with Port Royal at this time were, in addition to Arnauld and Nicole, the Duc de Luynes, who, in 1647, translated Descartes' *Meditations* from Latin into French and for whose son the *Port Royal Grammar* was ostensibly composed; Claude Lancelot, who along with Nicole taught at the schools and who co-authored with Arnauld the *Port Royal Grammar*; and Blaise Pascal, famous as a mathematician, scientist, and author of *les lettres Provinciales* and *les Pensées*. Pascal was an early innovator of probability theory and may have had something to do with the four chapters on probability in Book Four of the *Port Royal Logic*.[4]

Besides the *Port Royal Logic* and *Grammar*, Antoine Arnauld is best known for his defense of Jansenism; for the fourth set of objections to Descartes' *Meditations*, where he was the first to articulate the 'Cartesian circle'; for his dispute with Nicolas Malebranche over the nature of ideas, published in his *Des vraies et des fausses idées*; and for his correspondence with Leibniz over the latter's doctrines of individual substance, freedom, and necessity. His other philosophical works make very clear his debt to Descartes, and this debt is also quite apparent from a glance at the *Port Royal Logic*, which was heavily influenced by Descartes' *Discourse on Method* and the earlier *Rules for the Direction of the Mind*, which had not been published, but which had been made available to Arnauld and Nicole.

The attitude toward logic

This Cartesian influence is present in the whole work, particularly the sections on conception and method, and it underlies much of the criticism of traditional syllogistic logic, in addition to being a source of the new conception of logic. One aspect of this criticism had been around as early as Sextus Empiricus, and would later be taken up by John Stuart Mill, namely, the criticism of syllogistic logic as useless in the discovery of new truths. If we understand the syllogism to be a method of discovering new truths, then it does appear to have a very limited utility. Given the Cartesian account of knowledge, we would draw the stronger conclusion that the syllogism is entirely useless for this purpose. Indeed, Descartes himself drew this conclusion in the *Rules*:[5]

> . . . we should realize that, on the basis of their method, dialecticians are unable to formulate a syllogism with a true conclusion unless they are already in possession of

the substance of the conclusion, i.e. unless they have previous knowledge of the very truth deduced in the syllogism. (Rule X, AT X, 406, CSM I, 36-7)

As several commentators have pointed out, though,[6] Aristotle had not intended his logic to be a method of discovery. In fact, he and his followers had intended the syllogism to serve primarily as a method of presentation or of instructing, or convincing others concerning what was already known.

Descartes, then, took the syllogism to be something it was not intended to be. However, he was also suspicious of the method of disputation or dialectic. The view that dialectic was the foundation of inference was closely associated with Aristotle and the syllogism, and with Peter Ramus, who defined logic as the art of disputing well and who comes up for criticism in the *Port Royal Logic*. One major reason Descartes was suspicious of dialectic was that it involved general agreement on fundamental matters as its starting point. This was unacceptable to Descartes for two reasons: On the one hand, he felt that in the past many falsehoods had been generally agreed to, and on the other hand, his disagreements with the Aristotelians on matters of physics were disagreements about fundamentals.

In their rejection of disputation, Arnauld and Nicole followed in Descartes' footsteps. There is some irony in this, as, in contrast to those of Descartes, Arnauld's best philosophical works were composed as disputations with other philosophers.

Despite its belittling of the value of traditional logic, the *Port Royal Logic* does include a discussion of the rules for determining which syllogisms are valid (part three), and also a discussion of the Aristotelian categories (part one, ch. 3), and of the 'topics' (*les lieux*), or 'places', discussed in part three, chapters 17-18. These are included as useful classificatory devices and, in the case of the syllogism, as useful for exercising, or training, the mind. However, the discussion is always sprinkled with words of caution, counseling the reader not to make more of these than this, and denigrating them as of little use in the discovery of new truths, or, in the case of the topics, of new arguments (DJ 237, F 295).

Descartes himself did not dismiss logic as a method of presentation. He distinguished what he called *analysis*, which was the method of arriving at truths, from *synthesis*, which was the best method of presenting them to others. These terms are used in the Cartesian way in the *Port Royal Logic*, particularly in part four. Descartes illustrated his method of analysis in his *Meditations* and in the mathematical and scientific works which were included in the *Discourse on Method*: the *Optics*, the *Meteorology*, and the *Geometry*. He illustrated the method of synthesis in the appendix to the *Replies to the Second Set of Objections* and in the *Principles of Philosophy*. I will say more about analysis and synthesis in the section discussing Part Four of the *Port Royal Logic*.

There is another aspect of the conception of logic as understood by the Port Royalists which also has its roots in Descartes' work. This aspect should be distinguished from the general concern for a logic of discovery as opposed to a method of presentation, although it is related to that concern. It is an aspect not to be found in the work of Mill,[7] who otherwise shared the critical attitude toward the syllogism. A twentieth-century reader, not aware of the Cartesian view of logic, may well be surprised at some of the things included as 'logic' in the *Port Royal Logic*, and may well conclude, as I. M.

Bochenski did, that the whole enterprise is tainted with psychological considerations which do not properly belong to logic at all.[8]

We are accustomed to thinking of logic, including the informal variety, as primarily concerned with arguments and reasons. Logic is not taken to be concerned with the truth or falsehood of individual propositions. In general, their truth or falsehood is taken to be the concern of the sciences rather than of logic.

However, when one turns to the *Port Royal Logic*, it looks as though this fundamental distinction is not respected. In the first discourse, which serves as an introduction to the work, the goal of the book is stated as being to train the judgment so that it is better able to discern the true from the false (DJ 7, F 35). In the second discourse, which was added in 1664 in response to criticisms of the work, Arnauld and Nicole defended the title, 'Art of Thinking', as opposed to 'Art of Reasoning Well', by asserting that 'the purpose of logic is to give rules for all activities of the mind, as much for simple ideas as for judgements and reasonings' (F 47). The view that 'logic' should include anything which might aid the thinking process is also expressed in the opening section of the first chapter of part two, on judgement. This chapter and the next one on the verb were added in 1683 and taken pretty much directly from the *Port Royal Grammar*. Arnauld and Nicole set aside the question whether this material belongs more to grammar than to logic with the following comment: 'The goal of logic is to think well. Clearly, then, an understanding of different functions of words – that is, of sounds which are used to express ideas – is useful to logic' (DJ 99, F 143).

This attitude toward logic demands some remarks. On the one hand, the vision of logic as including anything that helps one think well, when this is explicitly characterized as discerning the true from the false, may well seem so broad as to include almost any kind of learning as logic. Such a concern, along with the specific concern that some scientific principles (including some contentious ones) were being included as logical principles, may well have been behind some of the criticism of the *Port Royal Logic*, as indeed it would be among current logicians were they to read this work. On the other hand, it should be stressed that this view of logic as 'clear thinking' in the wide sense enabled Arnauld and Nicole to include and emphasize many things that would, otherwise, not have been included in a logic text. Many of these topics are the sorts of things which one finds today in informal logic, critical thinking, or composition textbooks. There is much emphasis, for example, on such semantic concerns as the problem of ambiguity, the treatment of exclusives and exemptives, and the pragmatic discussion of the relevance of the falsity of relative clauses to the truth or falsity of a whole statement (part two, ch. 7). This broad view also enabled Arnauld and Nicole to talk about fallacies which are not interesting from a formal standpoint but are psychologically compelling. These 'faulty arguments advanced in public life and everyday affairs' are given extensive treatment. No doubt Arnauld and Nicole, given their Jansenist concern for the problem of *amour-propre* which they see as lurking behind most of these fallacies, were especially sensitive to these sorts of fallacies. However, their discussion is first rate, surpassing that of most logic textbooks today. These are the kinds of fallacies probably most often committed, though usually not in the blatant form they are here revealed to have, even by people who should know better. Here are a few examples of these fallacies of 'public life and everyday affairs' which also serve to capture the flavor of the *Port Royal Logic*:

I am a native of country X.
Therefore, I must believe that Saint so-and-so
preached in country X. (DJ 266, F 325)

I belong to the Y order.
Therefore, I must believe that Y order has
such-and-such privileges. (DJ 267, F 325)

I love him.
Therefore, he is the cleverest man in the world. (*Ibid.*)

I did not write that book.
Therefore, it is a bad one. (DJ 270, F 328)

Taking logic in this wide sense also allowed Arnauld and Nicole to include discussions of statements which were 'morally universal', which they characterize as those which are true for most of the extension of the subject term, though not all, such as 'All old people praise the good old days' (DJ 148, F 198). More significantly, it allowed them to include the final four chapters on probabilistic reasoning, including useful suggestions concerning when to accept past-tense statements and future contingent statements. This latter part includes among other things a discussion of games of chance and the irrationality of fearing thunderstorms.

While those who think logic should be concerned with critical thinking in a larger sense would welcome these discussions, few today would characterize logic as including the determination of the truth of simple judgments or ideas, as Arnauld and Nicole do. Their remarks concerning simple judgments do appear to justify the charge that the Port Royalists were confusing epistemological, scientific, and psychological elements with logical ones. While there is some truth to this charge, at least concerning epistemological questions, we should be careful not to confuse the Port Royalists and other early Cartesians with later advocates of psychologism who were to become Frege's target. The authors of the *Port Royal Logic*, like their contemporaries, viewed logic as the study of the laws of thought. Given that they understood ideas to be the units of thought, which things they chose to include in their logic would naturally be related to their views concerning ideas. The Port Royalists appear confused about the scope of logic only if we ignore or distort their account of ideas, which is quite different from that of Hume, Kant, or Mill, and if we ignore the Cartesian theory of inference, which not only allows, but requires that logic be concerned with simple mental apprehensions. In the next section, I will examine the Port Royalists' discussion of ideas and simple judgments, and, in the following one, their account of inference.

71

Conception and judgement

The *Port Royal Logic* is divided into four parts, starting with ideas, or the operation of conceiving, moving on to judgments, then on to reasoning, and finally to method. This way of organizing such treatises was to become standard. The organization follows the Cartesian maxim that one should begin with the simplest elements and move from there to the more complex. Judgments are defined as a uniting or separating of two ideas; reasoning is characterized as a series of judgments; and the proper method of demonstrating, the authors say, will involve a series of reasonings.

Many logic or critical thinking texts include sections on definitions and the clarification of concepts and also discussions of warrant which are more epistemological than logical. These are generally seen as preliminaries to the major goals of formulating and analyzing arguments. As I have suggested, though, more recent textbooks would not go along with the view expressed in the *Port Royal Logic* that logic should focus primarily on the formulation of correct ideas and judgements. In the First Discourse, Arnauld and Nicole made it clear that this was their major concern:

> Most of man's errors derive not from his being misled by wrong inferences but rather from his making inferences from premises based on false judgments. Previous writers on logic have searched but little for a remedy of this failing; to supply such a remedy is the principal object of the new reflections scattered throughout this book. (DJ 12, F 41)

The second discourse (F 47) makes clear that logic should be concerned not only with judgements, but with simple ideas, i.e. with the determination of which ideas we should use in building judgements.

It is this point which will appear most confused to a twentieth-century reader. This is especially the case as it is natural, when reading a work like this, for us to think of ideas along the lines of such critics of rationalism as Hume and Kant, both of whom held that all the content (though not necessarily the form) of ideas is provided by sense experience, and is therefore outside the province of logic. The British Empiricists likened ideas to sense impressions and complexes of sensory images based on sense impressions. If we think of ideas in this way, the Port Royalists' claim that logic should be concerned with the formation of simple ideas and simple judgments looks very confused. To make sense of their claims, we need to look at their account of ideas.

Despite their claim (DJ 31, F 65) that the word 'idea' is so clear that it cannot be explained by others without distortion, there is a difficulty understanding exactly how the Port Royalists thought about ideas. They strongly rejected the empiricist account sketched above, particularly in the first chapter of part one. While they characterize an idea as anything in the mind, they distinguish the mind from what they – following Descartes February 21, 1997 – call the corporeal imagination, where, according to their view, sensory images are stored. Arnauld held that if I am thinking of a chiliagon or the sun, then this act of thinking is my idea. In his later work, Arnauld made it clear that ideas should not be thought of as little pictures or images, and he made explicit what is perhaps only implicit in the *Port Royal Logic*, namely that an idea is not the object of

72

mental awareness but is the actual mental perception. Like Descartes, Arnauld and Nicole rejected the view that images derived from sense experience should be thought of as paradigms for ideas; they are at pains to give examples of ideas of 'pure intellect' such as those of a chiliagon and of God, and are harshly critical of Hobbes and Gassendi, who followed Aristotle in stating that all our ideas have their origins in the senses.

These ideas, then, should not be thought of as little mental pictures of things. But how should we think of them? They are, I believe, better thought of as discursive concepts, although that is not the way either Arnauld or Descartes would have expressed it. What would now be expressed as beliefs about a chiliagon, such as that its angles add up to 1,996 right angles, is expressed by Arnauld and Nicole as a property contained objectively within the idea of a chiliagon, or at least within a clear and distinct idea of it. Where we would speak in terms of deriving consequences from truths about a figure containing a thousand angles, Arnauld and Nicole speak in terms of clearly and distinctly perceiving what is contained within the idea of a chiliagon.

We can better understand some of the things Arnauld and Nicole say about ideas (and thus ultimately what they conclude is logic) if we understand these ideas to have what today would be called a 'propositional content'. Arnauld and Nicole followed Descartes in holding that our minds are in some sense structured to reality in that we are capable of being aware of, or 'perceiving', the correct natures of things. The mark of an accurate perception is its clarity and distinctness. It is on the basis of these clear and distinct perceptions of natures that we can form fundamental judgments. Thus, Descartes, in the fifth meditation, says that contained objectively in his idea of a triangle are such properties as *that its angles add up to two right angles*, and *that its greatest side subtends its greatest angle* (AT VIII, 64, CSM II, 45). It is on the basis of perceiving these properties within the mind's perception that the mind is able to form true judgments about triangles.

Seeing ideas in this way can help us understand the Port Royalists' discussion of clarifying concepts and the sense in which Descartes and the Port Royalists would say an idea is true. This latter point is a little puzzling, as most current logicians would rightly reserve the words 'true' and 'false' to propositions, judgments or assertions, rather than ideas. Descartes was not very clear on this matter, saying first in the third meditation that, strictly speaking, ideas cannot be false (AT VII, 43, CSN II, 28), but then going on to say that ideas can be 'materially false' (a notion which he ties to confused and obscure ideas) while, at several points, he indicates that clear and distinct ideas are true. Arnauld and Nicole, unfortunately, follow this pattern, using 'true' with respect to ideas,[9] but then going on to say that properly speaking only propositions and judgments can be said to be false, although they allow that a complex term can be false in that it may either express or implicitly assume a false judgment (DJ 121-2, F 170).

A clear and distinct idea is a perception of a genuine or true nature. These are the ideas which the Port Royalists, following Descartes, sometimes call true. Part one of the *Port Royal Logic* is devoted primarily to a discussion of these ideas and to suggestions as to how to clarify the obscure and confused ones. Examples of clear ideas are those of existence, duration, order, body (extended substance), and also a person's idea of himself as a thinking being. These are ideas on which someone could base a true judgment. Ideas of what were later called secondary qualities are given as examples of obscure and confused ideas: colors, sounds, tastes, hot and cold (DJ 66, F 102). When explaining why these are obscure, Arnauld and Nicole ultimately have to explain them in terms of false beliefs or erroneous judgments (DJ 67, F 103). The false beliefs they may have in mind involve attributing the sensed quality, or something similar to it, to an external object. Arnauld and Nicole give as their most detailed example the idea of weight (DJ 69, F 105). In this passage, they say that 'the idea of a thing which falls' is 'true', presumably because it is very clear and distinct. The idea of the cause of the fall, they say, is true also. However, the inattentive mind moves beyond this and forms the idea of an internal principle within the object which causes the downward motion. Presumably, this aspect is then included within the idea of weight, and it is this idea which is said to be confused. The confused idea appears to be the result of a false judgment.

Clarifying a concept will involve stripping away what has been rashly assumed to be entailed by it and focusing on what is seen as essential to it. By such a procedure, one can come to see that 'being extended' and 'being capable of motion' are contained within the idea of a body, and thus one can form the true judgements 'Bodies are extended' and 'Bodies are capable of motion', while avoiding false ones, such as 'Bodies have within them an internal principle which pulls them downward'. The properties contained within the idea are also called the 'comprehension' of the idea, which, in the case of general ideas such as this one, Arnauld and Nicole distinguish from the 'extension' of the idea, those objects which fall under the concept, in this example are bodies. This distinction had certainly been recognized before, but is here put in terms of the new philosophy.

This view of ideas also forms the framework for the distinction between real and nominal definitions – their words are *définitions des choses* and *définitions des noms*. Arnauld and Nicole discuss this distinction in chapters 12 through 14 of part one and chapter 16 of part two. Their opening remarks on nominal definitions have a surprisingly Leibnizian or Russellian flavor. These definitions, they say, are useful in avoiding ambiguities, which are the result of confused and obscure ideas. Such ambiguities can be avoided by the construction of a new language by means of nominal definitions. They have in mind such meaning postulates as 'By 'heat' I mean the sensation' or 'By 'heat' I mean what causes the sensation'. These, they point out, are arbitrary in the sense that they cannot be disputed or be false. But, of course, some will be more useful than others, in that some might not apply to anything at all. Real definitions, on the other hand, are what explicitly capture what is contained within a clear and distinct conception of something, that is, the essential characteristics of the thing. The most clear and simple conceptions cannot have real definitions in this sense. Arnauld and Nicole allow as a kind of real definition a definition by what they call 'proper accidents', or accident which, though not part of the essence, picks out just those things in question. These definitions they call 'descriptions'.

Thus we can see why Arnauld and Nicole took logic to be concerned with the clarification of simple concepts and elementary judgments based on those concepts: they saw ideas not as bundles of sense impressions but as complex concepts whose components were logically related to the whole. To a modern reader, their remarks on what is contained within a perception of the mind certainly appear to justify the charges that psychological elements have been mixed with logical ones and that what should properly be regarded as scientific discoveries are being put forth as matters of logic. These charges will appear to be even more justified when we turn to the conception of inference held by Descartes, and which is behind the method of part four, namely the view that inference boils down to a clear and distinct perception of the relation between two propositions.

However, we should be careful not to confuse this view with later psychological accounts of logic. Neither Descartes nor Arnauld thought that a property was contained within a concept because people believed it was, or were psychologically such that they could not help believing it was or because of an observed connection in nature. They thought that when the mind attended to (had a clear and distinct perception of) a genuine nature, it could, aided by the natural light of reason, perceive necessary containments and connections. They thus thought that human beings have a special faculty which enables us to reason and see logical connections among concepts. This certainly brings an epistemological element into their logic, but makes their logic no more psychologistic than that of Bertrand Russell, who at one time thought that to do logic we had to have a special sort of awareness of logical entities.[10]

While including the question of the truth or falsehood of simple judgments as matters to be treated in a logic book may well seem wrongheaded by contemporary lights, there is a sense in which Arnauld and Nicole, again following Descartes, thought that those foundational judgments which were based on clear and distinct perceptions have the status which later philosophers gave to logical or analytic truths. However, the very notion of an analytic truth belongs to a later period and is not very helpful for understanding Cartesian logic. In fact, it is quite distorting.[11]

The Cartesians would include among these foundational judgments geometrical truths, which they would say can be seen to be true in virtue of what is contained within clear and distinct perceptions. However, they would give the same status to the fundamental principles of Cartesian physics, for example that bodies are extended and move but do not have internal motivating principles, and to such judgments as 'I am a thinking thing'. There is a sense in which the Cartesians thought that Aristotelian physics was not just false, but impossible, and that this impossibility could be discerned by a careful examination of the concepts involved.

The conception of logic we have here is certainly different, and much wider, than that of twentieth-century formalists. However, this is not because logic is being confused with empirical or psychological matters, but rather because the notion of what can be determined by reason alone was held to be considerably greater than had been earlier thought, or than what would later be thought, especially after Hume and Kant.

Reasoning and method

Expanding on a theme running throughout the book, Arnauld and Nicole opened the section on reasoning (part three) with the following disclaimer:

We treat next that part of logic which contains the rules of reasoning, the part deemed most important and the only aspect of logic traditionally treated with any care. But there is reason to doubt whether this part of logic is as useful as is generally believed. Man is more likely to err by drawing inferences from false principles than by inferring incorrectly from true principles; rarely are we led astray by an argument whose conclusion is incorrectly inferred from the premises. If any man is unable to detect, by the light of reason alone, the invalidity of an argument, then he is probably incapable of understanding the rules by which we judge whether an argument is valid – and still less able to apply those rules. (DJ 175, F 231)

Behind this overstatement is the Cartesian theory of inference, with which I shall deal shortly. But despite the belittling of the rules of reasoning, Part Three of the *Port Royal Logic* is quite thorough. Given the attitude expressed in the above quotation, it is not surprising that this part does not contain any genuine innovations in formal logic. Nevertheless, the rules for all the figures of the traditional syllogisms are given, including a version of the verse used by students to help remember the valid forms, which begins, 'Barbara, Celarent, Darii, Ferio, Baralipton . . .' (DJ 202, F 259). There is also a discussion of more complex syllogisms and enthymemes. Furthermore, there is an interesting reduction of the various rules of validity for the syllogism to one rule (Part Three, Ch. 10). This discussion will appear to those trained in formal logic yet again to confuse questions of fact with questions of logic. The rule they give is that a syllogism is valid if one of the premisses (not necessarily the major) contains the conclusion, and the other premiss makes this containment explicit (DJ 211, F 267). To illustrate this principle, Arnauld and Nicole used the following example (DJ 213, F 269): 'Some saint is poor, every saint is a friend of God, therefore some friend of God is poor'. They say that the first premiss here contains the conclusion, and that this containment is made explicit by the second premiss. A modern logician would object that in most cases, it is a question of fact, not logic, whether the conclusion is 'contained' within the premiss.
The rule enables Arnauld and Nicole to deal with complex arguments, such as:

> The duty of a Christian is to refrain from praising criminals.
> Duelers are criminals.
> Therefore, the duty of a Christian is to refrain from praising duelers. (DJ 214, F 271)

without having to order the premisses, rephrase the argument, and determine its mood and figure.[12]
The part on reasoning also includes a discussion of the rules of propositional logic (called 'compound syllogisms') and, as I have already mentioned, an excellent discussion of informal fallacies.
Part four of the *Port Royal Logic* is an attempt to set forth the Cartesian method in a systematic way. The bulk of the discussion from the first two chapters of part four is based on Descartes' *Rules for the Direction of the Mind*, which was written around 1628, but not published until 1701, except for a Dutch translation which appeared in 1684. Other points are borrowed from the *Discourse on Method* and Pascal's unpublished *De*

l'Esprit géométrique. Chapter 2, which was the opening chapter of the first three editions, was taken directly from rule thirteen.

The starting point of the Cartesian view, as I have already mentioned, is the clear and distinct perception. Descartes called these 'intuitions' in the *Rules*. The account of intuition which is given in the *Rules* appears, at first, to be extremely psychological: it is given in terms of what we are able to conceive by attending to what is in our minds. A reader versed in the late nineteenth- and early twentieth-century critiques of psychologism would, quite understandably, hold the suspicion that the Cartesians were unabashedly reducing whether a given proposition is necessary as opposed to contingent to our ability to conceive or imagine whether the proposition could be false, and that they were reducing whether a proposition follows from another to our ability to conceive whether the one could be true without the other. This sort of reduction would make logic a branch of psychology and reduce its certainty to that of an empirical science. As I have already emphasized, reading the Cartesians this way is a mistake. It is true that Descartes and the Port Royalists saw the clear and distinct perception as the criterion for determining whether a proposition is true or whether one proposition follows from another, but it is not true that they thought that this *constituted* its truth or validity. Logic for them was normative rather than descriptive as much as it was for the later critics of psychologism.

The method outlined in part four, chapter 2, is the method of analysis or the method of resolution. This was the method Descartes held to be the true method of discovery. It involves taking the various propositions involved in a problem, ordering them in terms of their simplicity, breaking the more complex into simpler elements, then examining these to determine which of them are known, and then proceeding from the known to the unknown by means of entailments. Descartes stressed this method in the *Meditations* and *Replies*, giving his fullest explanation of it in the replies to the second set of objections. With regard to the *cogito*, Descartes made the following remark:

> When someone says 'I am thinking, therefore I am', he does not deduce existence from thought by means of a syllogism, but recognizes it a something self-evident by a simple intuition of the mind. This is clear from the fact that if he were deducing it by means of a syllogism, he would have to have had previous knowledge of the major premiss 'Everything which thinks is'; yet, in fact, he learns it from experiences in his own case that it is impossible that he should think without existing. It is the nature of our mind to construct general propositions on the basis of our knowledge of particular ones. (AT VII, 140-1, CSM II, 100)

Analysis comes first in the order of discovery, and proceeds from the particular to the general. While many of Descartes' examples are taken from geometry, he gives two examples in rule thirteen which are reproduced in part four, chapter 2 of the *Port Royal Logic*. One of the examples involves the cup of Tantalus, which consists of a figure of Tantalus within a cup in such an arrangement that whenever the figure is bent close to the water, the water drains out of the cup. The other example involves a conjuror who makes it appear as though one stream of water changes into six different colors in his mouth (DJ 303-4, F 370-1).

77

The method of synthesis or composition is given in part four, chapters 3 and 4. It is here also called the 'geometers' method' and the method of explanation. Descartes was critical of this method as used by mathematicians in the past, in particular, arguing that it did not yield genuine understanding. Descartes' criticisms are echoed in chapter 9 of part four, as are his remedies in chapters 6 through 8. These are blended with a further discussion of real and nominal definitions taken from Pascal in chapter 5. The method for the sciences, as outlined in chapter 11 of part four, involves both analysis and synthesis, although Arnauld and Nicole do not put it this way. Analysis will be involved in clarifying definitions, determining which propositions are certain and which immediate inferences are correct. Synthesis will be involved in the rules 7 and 8 for method, which involve the proper order of explanation (DJ 336, F 408).

Descartes did not think that we can just examine any proposition and see whether it is true or not, but he did think we could do this for the simplest and clearest propositions, concerning, for example, body and extension and simple geometrical figures. We then proceed from these evident propositions to less evident ones by what he called *deduction*. This was not a process of fitting propositions into valid patterns, but one of reducing chains of propositions to simple inferences. The deduction relation between these reduced to intuition in that a simple deduction involved an intuition of the relation between two propositions. It is for this reason that Descartes and the Port Royalists did not think the general inference patterns and rules of validity of syllogisms were so important. The individual inference, perceived with the aid of the natural light to be valid, is what is at the foundation of them.

After such a deduction, we are in a position to grasp the truth of the deduced proposition. We see, Descartes would claim, not only that it is true, but why it is. Descartes' problem with the syllogism and what he saw as an abuse of the method of synthesis was not that he didn't think the conclusions didn't really follow from the premises, but that these arguments do not yield any genuine understanding. For that to occur, one would need to see why the premises are true, what is contained within them, and what therefore follows from them. The rules given in part four, chapters 6 and 7 of the *Port Royal Logic* are supposed to insure just this.

Given their view of ideas and inference as outlined above, it was not so unreasonable for the Port Royalists to think of what would later be thought of as metaphysical assumptions as having the status which is now reserved for purely formal truths. It was Kant, building on what was, essentially, Hume's view of ideas, who argued for a more limited view of the domain of conceptual truths. As this eighteenth-century view of ideas, which was also fashionable in the early twentieth century, has again come under criticism, the methodology of the Port Royalists does not appear as confused as it once did. A reader of the *Port Royal Logic* is struck by the fact that while the discussion here of the classification of concepts and the clearing out of the prejudices of the mind do not look like what we would classify as purely logical investigations, nevertheless, they are more like logical investigations than empirical ones. It is perhaps better to say that here, as with the work of Leibniz, which is often contrasted with that of the Cartesians, what is blurred is the distinction among logical, semantical and metaphysical truths.

With the new emphasis on critical thinking and the logic of 'real' as opposed to 'formal' arguments, the authors and readers of contemporary critical thinking texts might also wonder if their inquiry, too, involves a metaphysics and a blurring of this metaphysics and semantics with logic.

The infamous Cartesian emphasis on certainty

There is another concern which I would like to deal with finally which contemporary readers, particularly those concerned with the logic of 'real' arguments, might have which is almost the direct opposite of the concern I have been dealing with. I have in mind here the emphasis on complete understanding, and on deducing conclusions only from propositions known with certainty. These emphases are characteristic of Cartesian works such as this, and may strike a reader as a method which works only for mathematics. This suspicion might be reinforced by the fact that Arnauld and Nicole, like Descartes before them, spend quite a bit of time talking about geometry, particularly the geometric method. In other matters, it might seem as though the dialectical method, which the Port Royalists disdained, is a better way to make progress, given a world filled with contingent truths and fallible knowers.

There is no doubt that the Cartesians held that geometry and arithmetic should be paradigms for knowledge and that they hoped to extend the method of these disciplines to other areas. They also emphasized certainty and not employing propositions which are doubtful in the course of a demonstration. In the *Port Royal Logic*, the little discussion that occurs on observation and induction is mostly cautionary.

However, when one looks at the examples Descartes gives in his scientific works and those which are reproduced in the *Port Royal Logic*, it is fairly clear that they allow an important role for experiment and observation. The problems the Cartesians were explaining were generally problems from experience. The method Descartes actually used did not ignore observation, but required an analysis of the problem to determine what observations are necessary. Hypotheses are formed on the basis of the initial observation and in accordance with the fundamental principles (thus no occult properties are hypothesized). In his famous discussion of refraction in the *Optics* (AT VI, 93-101, CSM I, 156-161), Descartes constructs a thought experiment employing tennis balls to get at the core of the problem and to determine the amount of deflection. He then talks about confirming the results and determining the particular constants of refraction by means of observations. The picture one gets is not (as is often presented) that of reason as opposed to experience, but rather of reason as a guide and corrective to experience.

The concern with certainty is primarily at the foundational level, concerning the basic concepts and principles. In the *Port Royal Logic*, a distinction is made between those propositions which can be seen to be true without a great deal of effort and the others. Only the first are to be taken as axioms. The others, even though they may be just as necessary, need to be demonstrated. The demonstration should employ only propositions previously demonstrated or seen to be true on their own. Some propositions, though, can be demonstrated only as a matter of faith, and others can be shown to be probably true. In the discussion of testimony of others and belief in historical events in part four, chapters 13 and 15, Arnauld and Nicole make it clear that there are propositions which should be believed, but about which there is still reason for doubt. In chapter 15, they discuss the question of whether one should believe that a contract which has been signed by two notaries is postdated or not. Their conclusion (DJ 351, F 424) is that the circumstance of its being signed is sufficient reason to believe it has not been postdated, but that this belief can be overridden by further information. The further information could be such as to make one withdraw the belief, or (as in evidence of bribery), make one believe the contract to be false. They are quite clear that the beliefs they have been discussing are fallible: 'The above are remarks about judgments made concerning belief in events. It must not be thought that these remarks will always insure us against error' (DJ 353, F 426).

Notes

1. The title of the first English edition was also *Logic; Or, The Art of Thinking*, although it soon became popularly known as the *Port Royal Logic* and this latter was used as the title by Thomas Spencer Baynes in his translation of 1851. For the citations from the work, I have chosen the most recent translation by Dickoff and James, 1964 [hereafter DJ]. Unfortunately, this work is no longer in print. For the French, I have chosen the still available Flammarion, 1970 [hereafter F]. The critical edition by Clair and Girbal, 1981 is no longer in print. The Dickoff and James translation is more readable than earlier ones, but is not sensitive to some of the philosophical issues which bothered Arnauld, and so should be used by scholars only with caution. Scholars should consult one of the French editions or the Baynes translation. This caution is not meant to fault Dickoff and James, who consciously updated the work to make it more accessible and relevant to the contemporary reader. See their opening remarks (DJ, xiv). (This essay was written before the publication of the translation by Jill Buroken: *Logic or the Art of Thinking*, Cambridge University Press, 1996. This translation is far superior to that of Dickoff and James).

2. The original abbey was founded in 1204 at Porrois (the name evolved into 'Port Royal'), roughly ten kilometers southwest of Versailles. By 1626, the abbey had deteriorated and the residents moved to what became known as Port Royal de Paris. The original abbey then became known as Port Royal des Champs. In 1637 the '*Solitaires*' moved back to Port Royal des Champs. The abbess, Mère Angélique, who was Arnauld's sister, returned to Port Royal des Champs in the 1640's.

3. The Jansenists were those who defended the work of Cornelis Jansen (Latinized to 'Cornelius Jansenius') (1585-1638), Bishop of Ypres, whose book *Augustinus* was published in 1640. The controversy, though, between those who held what were later called Jansenist views concerning the doctrine of original sin, grace, and the related doctrine of contrition, and those such as the Jesuits and Cardinal Richelieu who opposed them, antedated this work.

In fact, the Jansenist controversy was a continuation of the dispute between the Abbé de Saint-Cyran (1581-1643), who was the spiritual director of Port Royal, and Cardinal Richelieu and the Church hierarchy. The dispute was a long and bitter one. In 1653, Pope Innocent X condemned five propositions which were alleged to be contained in Jansen's *Augustinus* and, in 1656, when Arnauld was removed from the Sorbonne, a 'Formulary' denouncing Jansen and the five propositions was drawn up. Arnauld refused to sign the Formulary, claiming that while the five propositions were heretical (given that the Pope said they were), they were not to be found in Jansen's work. Except for a respite between 1669 and 1679, those associated with Port Royal were in the eye of a great storm. Arnauld exiled himself to Belgium from 1679 until his death in 1694, and Louis XIV had Port Royal des Champs razed in 1709.

4. For more on Pascal and probability see Hacking, 1975. On page 74, Hacking suggests that Arnauld did not write the chapters on probability.

5. Reference to this and all other works by Descartes will follow the standard procedures, using the pagination from Adam and Tannery, 1964-76 [hereafter AT] and the translation by Cottingham, Stoothoff and Murdoch [hereafter CSM]. While the *Rules for the Direction of the Mind* was not published until much later, Arnauld and Nicole had seen the manuscript before writing the *Port Royal Logic*.

6. See, for example, the excellent discussion in Gaukroger, 1989, ch. 1.

7. See Mill, 1973, 7: 6-7, where, after praising the *Port Royal Logic*, Mill goes on to say that logic is concerned with inferences, not with intuitive truths.

8. Bochenski sums up the logic of this period as 'poor in content, devoid of all deep problems, permeated with a whole lot of nonlogical philosophical ideas, psychologistic in the worst sense' (1961, 258).

9. DJ 41, F 76. The Dickoff and James translation is misleading here. They translate 'A true idea is an idea whose object is an existing object. If the object of an idea is not an existing object, then the idea is false . . .' This position is at variance with the Cartesian view, but also with Arnauld and Nicole's original French: 'Que si les objets représentés par ces idées . . . sont en effet tels qu'ils nous sont représentés, on les appelle véritables: que si ils ne sont pas tels elles sont fausses . . .'

10. This account was developed in *Theory of Knowledge*, now published in Eames, Vol. 7.

11.   Kant was the first to formulate the analytic/synthetic distinction as it is applied to propositions. While Kant initially formulated the distinction in terms of whether the predicate is 'contained within' the subject (analytic) or not (synthetic), the claims he makes about these judgments involve his distinction between intuitions and concepts, a distinction quite alien to these early Cartesians. Kant held that synthetic judgments, unlike analytic ones, always involve an intuition. See his 'highest principle of all synthetic judgements' (1965, A154, B193). For an excellent discussion of Kant's analytic/synthetic distinction and its relation to the distinction between intuitions and concepts, see Coffa, 1991, ch. 1, esp. 17ff.

12.   The point is that, superficially, this argument may look like a second figure syllogism with an undistributed middle term ('criminals').

References

Arnauld, Antoine and Pierre Nicole, [1662] (1970), *La Logique, ou L'art de penser*, Flammarion: Paris.
Arnauld, Antoine and Pierre Nicole (1851), *The Art of Thinking*, translated by Thomas Baynes, Edinburgh.
Arnauld, Antoine and Pierre Nicole [1662] (1964), *The Art of Thinking*, translated by James Dickoff and Patricia James, Bobbs-Merrill: Indianapolis.
Arnauld, Antoine and Pierre Nicole [1662] (1981), *La Logique, ou L'art de penser*, critical edition by Pierre Clair and François Girbal, J. Vrin: Paris.
Arnauld, Antoine and Pierre Nicole [1683] (1986), *Des vraies et des fausses Idées*, Fayard: Paris.
Bochenski, I. M. (1961), *A History of Formal Logic*, translated by Ivo Thomas, University of Notre Dame Press: Notre Dame, IN.
Coffa, Alberto (1991), *The Semantic Traditions from Kant to Carnap*, Cambridge University Press: Cambridge.
Descartes, Rene (1964-76), *Oeuvres de Descartes,* edited by Charles Adam and Paul Tannery, J. Vrin: Paris.
Descartes, Rene (1984-85), *The Philosophical Writings of Descartes*, translated by John Cottingham, Robert Stoothoff, and Dugald Murdock, Cambridge University Press: Cambridge.
Gaukroger, Stephen (1989), *Cartesian Logic*, Clarendon Press: Oxford.
Hacking, Ian (1975), *The Emergence of Probability*, Cambridge University Press: Cambridge.
Kant, Immanuel [1781] (1965), *Critique of Pure Reason*, translated by Norman Kemp Smith, St. Martins: New York.
Mill, John Stuart (1973), *A System of Logic Ratiocinative and Inductive,* in *The Collected Works of John Stuart Mill*, edited by J. M. Robson, University of Toronto Press: Toronto.

Russell, Bertrand (1984), *The Collected Papers of Bertrand Russell*, edited by Elizabeth R. Eames, Unwin: London.

7 The *Logick* of Isaac Watts

Alan Brinton

Introduction

The first of many editions of Isaac Watts' *Logick: Or, The Right Use of Reason in the Enquiry after Truth, with a Variety of Rules to Guard against Error, in the Affairs of Religion and Human Life, as well as in the Sciences* was published in London in 1725. The most notable among historians of British logic and rhetoric, Wilbur Samuel Howell, says that 'it is probably fair to say that in the English-speaking world more eighteenth-century students and serious general readers learned their lessons about logic from Isaac Watts than from any other source' (Howell 1971, 342). The success of the *Logick* and its adoption as a text at Cambridge and Oxford is all the more remarkable in the light of the fact that Watts was a nonconforming minister.[1]

Watts was born in July of 1674 at Southampton. He was graduated at age twenty from the rather notable dissenting academy of Thomas Rowe at Stoke Newington, where, as is reported in his life in the *Dictionary of National Biography*, 'The teaching in classics, logic, Hebrew, and divinity was excellent' (20: 979). In 1696 he began a five year period of service as tutor to the son of Sir John Hartopp, to which period and activity the origins of his *Logick* are traceable. By March of 1702 he was appointed to the pulpit of the dissenting chapel at Mark Lane, which had at one time been occupied by the famous Puritan preacher and scholar John Owen. Ill health prevented Watts from fulfilling most of the duties of his position – in which, however, he remained at the insistence of his admiring congregation, eventually with the assistance of a co-pastor. In 1712 he was invited to live in the home of Sir Thomas and Lady Abney, whose generous support enabled him to devote most of his remaining thirty-six years to intellectual activity and to writing. He died in November of 1748.

Watts is best known as a poet and hymnist; but he wrote a large number of philosophical and theological works, which were widely read, and among which some others than the *Logick* are worthy of the attention of students of informal logic and critical thinking. We will have occasion to take note of two in particular, *The Improvement of the Mind: Or, A Supplement to The Art of Logick: Containing a Variety of Remarks and Rules* (1741) and *A Plain and Particular Account of the Natural Passions, With Rules for the Government of Them*, which was prefixed to his *Discourses of the Love of God and the Use and Abuse of the Passions in Religion* (1729) and was published separately in later editions as *The Doctrine of the Passions Explained and Improved* (1732, etc.).

The most conspicuous influences on the *Logick* are Arnauld and Nicole's *The Art of Thinking* (the so-called '*Port Royal Logic*' of 1662), Descartes' *Discourse on Method* (1637) and *Rules for the Direction of the Mind* (1628), and Locke's *Essay Concerning Human Understanding* (1690). The *Port Royal Logic* is clearly the model for Watts' *Logick*, both in its structure and in its conception of the subject matter. The *Logick* follows the *Port Royal Logic* in its division into four main parts:

The First Part: Of Perception and Ideas.

The Second Part: Of Judgment and Proposition.

The Third Part: Of Reasoning and Syllogism.

The Fourth Part: Of Disposition and Method.[2]

This division already gives us a sense of how different a conception of the nature and scope of logic Watts (and, of course, Arnauld) had from that of late twentieth century logicians. Only about thirty-five of the *Logick*'s 174 pages (in the *Works*) are devoted to formal logic (I.4.ii-vi, II.2.i-vi, III.1, and III.2.i-vii). The subtitle, 'The Right Use of Reason in the Inquiry after Truth' reinforces this impression. The scope of the subject matter is widened yet further in the initial sentence of the Introduction: 'Logick is the art of using Reason well in our enquiries after truth, and the communication of it to others'. Logic is conceived of by Watts as concerned with 'the principal operations of the mind, which are put forth in the exercise of our reason', namely *perception* ('the simple contemplation of things offered to our minds, without affirming or denying any thing concerning them'), *judgment* ('that operation of the mind, whereby we join two or more ideas together by one affirmation or negation'), 'argumentation or *reasoning*' (the operation 'whereby we infer one thing, that is one proposition, from two or more propositions premised'), and *disposition* (the operation of the mind which effects the 'ranging of our thoughts in such order, as is best for our own and others conception and memory') (I.1).

Watts conceives of the study of logic, then, as ranging *inward*, to the psychological processes involved in reasoning, *forward* in the process of inquiry toward the discovery of truth, and *outward*, toward its presentation or communication to others. Ideas, propositions, syllogisms, and method (or arrangement) are the effects or the *products* of these operations. As such, they enter into his treatment; but the principal emphasis is on operations of the mind rather than on the analysis and evaluation of certain among their productions.[3]

While the *Logick* takes its structure and conception of the subject matter from the *Port Royal Logic*, it is conspicuously Cartesian in its pedagogical approach, which is preceptive. This is a characteristic which it shares with *The Doctrine of the Passions*, *The Improvement of the Mind*, and other of Watts' works. Roughly forty percent of the text of the *Logick* (seventy of 174 pages in the *Works*) is explicitly devoted to precepts and logical advice to the reader. It abounds with sets of 'rules' and 'directions', whose preceptive contents are periodically, and whose formulations are consistently, reminiscent of those of Descartes' *Rules for the Direction of the Mind*.

It is in Part One that the *Logick* owes the most to Locke's *Essay*, especially in what Watts has to say about language. But it should also be observed that *The Improvement of the Mind* is a work of the same genre as, and bears some significant resemblances to, Locke's *The Conduct of the Understanding*, as is noted in a comment made in Samuel Johnson's *Life of Dr. Watts*:

> Few books have been perused by me with greater pleasure than his *Improvement of the Mind*; of which the radical principles may indeed be found in Locke's *Conduct of the Understanding*; but they are so expanded and ramified by Watts, as to confer on him the merit of a work in the highest degree useful and pleasing. Whoever has the care of instructing others may be charged with deficiency in his duty if this book is not recommended. (383-84)

Each of the two works mentioned by Johnson is aptly describable as a practical treatise on critical thinking. Consistently with Watts' *Logick* and with Locke's *Essay*, both *The Improvement of the Mind* and *The Conduct of the Understanding* focus their attention on the intellectual operations of the mind. And both share the avowed purpose of the *Logick*, whose 'design', says Watts, is 'to teach us the right use of our reason, or intellectual powers, and the improvement of them in ourselves and others' (I.1).

From an informal logician's point of view, the two most distinctive features of Watts's *Logick* are its conception of the subject matter and its preceptive approach. In what follows, there will be ample occasion to illustrate the latter. My own opinion (and my own experience, I should add) is that precepts of critical thinking are of somewhat greater pedagogical value than is generally supposed. But it is in its wider conception of the subject matter of logic that I believe the *Logick* has the most to offer to our own study of informal logic and critical thinking.

So, in what follows, after an identification and brief review of parts of the *Logick* whose topics are likely to be of interest to readers of this volume, I will turn more seriously to what appears to me to be a most important and insightful way in which its conception of the subject matter is brought to bear on matters which are especially nettlesome to contemporary theorists and pedagogues of argumentation.

Part one - perception and ideas

'The first part of Logick', writes Watts at the outset of its treatment, 'contains observations and precepts about the first operation of the mind, perception or conception . . .' (I.1). Perception and conception are the mental operations; *ideas* (including conceptions) are the *products* of those operations. Watts accepts the definition of an *idea* as 'a representation of a thing in the mind' (I.1). The 'things' represented are 'beings'. The first three chapters of part one are devoted to the theory of ideas and to a discussion of various distinctions with regard to modes and substances and with regard to kinds of ideas. These chapters of part one are more likely to be of interest to historians of philosophy, especially to students of Locke (whose views are mentioned) and of Descartes and Arnauld (who are also important early modern theorists of ideas) than to informal logicians. Chapter 4, 'Of words and their several divisions, together with the advantage and danger of them', is likely to be of more interest to students of informal logic, especially in terms of the sensitivity Watts shows to various confusing aspects of natural language, such as disparities between negation in terms and negation in ideas. 'Terms', he writes, 'are either positive or negative'. 'But so unhappily are our words and ideas linked together, that we can never know which are positive ideas, and which are negative' (I.4.ii). 'Dead' he gives as an example of a positive term which represents a negative idea, while 'immortal' is a negative term which represents a positive idea. The negative and positive terms 'unhappy' and 'miserable' signify (in his view) one and the same idea.

In section iii of chapter 4, 'Of simple and complex terms', there is a clear recognition of the significance of what we would now call the 'emotive meaning' or 'emotive force' of terms:

> Among the terms that are complex in sense, but not in words, we may reckon those simple terms which contain a primary and secondary idea in them; as when I hear my neighbor speak that which is not true, and I say to him, this is not true, or this is false, I only convey to him the naked idea of his error; this is the primary idea: But if I say it is a lie, the word lie carries a secondary idea in it, for it implies both the falsehood of the speech, and my reproach and censure of the speaker. On the other hand, if I say it is a mistake, this carries also a secondary idea with it; for it not only refers to the falsehood of his speech, but includes my tenderness and civility to him at the same time.

Watts' treatments of negation in terms and ideas and of secondary (or 'emotive') meanings are cursory; but they are indicators of his attempt to bring the sorts of insights offered in part four of Locke's *Essay* ('Of Words') to bear as part of a course of studies in logic (which is, of course, further indication of his conceiving of logic as concerned with the operations of the understanding). Chapter 4 involves a more extended discussion of *equivocity* in Sections vi-viii – of its character, its abuses ('. . . when persons use such ambiguous words, with a design to deceive, it is called equivocation'), and its causes.

The remaining chapters of part one are devoted to the giving of precepts, 'general directions relating to our ideas' (ch. 5) and 'special rules to direct our conceptions of things' (ch. 6). The general directions relating to ideas are, in brief, (1) 'Furnish yourselves with a rich variety of ideas', (2) 'Use the most proper methods to retain that treasure of ideas which you have acquired', (3) Be selective in your intellectual pursuits, and (4) 'Learn to acquire a government over your ideas and your thoughts', i.e. to develop habits of attentiveness and resistance to distractions. The 'special rules' for conception are more interesting (and more Cartesian sounding). They enjoin conceiving of things (1) 'clearly and distinctly in their own natures'; (2) 'completely in all their parts'; (3) 'comprehensively in all their properties and relations'; (4) 'extensively in all their kinds'; and (5) 'orderly, or in a proper method' (44).

Several sets of yet more specific rules are given as well, for example rules for 'definitions of things', which require that a definition be (1) 'universal', agreeing 'to all the particular species or individuals that are included under the same idea'; (2) 'proper and peculiar to the thing defined'; (3) 'clear and plain'; (4) 'short [though not unduly so], so that it has no tautology in it, nor any words superfluous'; and (5) not involving use of 'the thing defined nor a mere synonymous name . . .' (I.6.v). A distinction between *definitions of things* and *definitions of names* (i.e., of substantive terms) is also an important feature of Watts' treatment of conception and definition. The directions for 'definition of names' are essentially warnings to avoid confusion arising out of the irregularities of language or the differences between words or ideas and things. In this context, he again takes up the problem of emotive meaning and the employment of euphemism (to use more recent terminology): 'It has been a frequent practice . . .', he complains, 'to put new favorable names upon ill ideas, on purpose to take off the odium of them. But notwithstanding all these flattering names and titles, a man of profuse generosity is still a spendthrift; a natural son is a bastard still; a gallant is an adulterer; and a lady of pleasure is a whore' (I.6.3).

I have given only a sampling of listings of more specific rules and directions in part one; better than half of it is preceptive.

Part two - judgment and propositions

'When the mind has got acquaintance with things by framing ideas of them', Watts writes at the start of Part Two, 'it proceeds to the next operation, and that is, to compare these ideas together, and to join them by affirmation, or disjoin them by negation, according as we find them to agree or disagree. This act of the mind is called judgment '. . . The mental operation of *judgment* has as its product *propositions*. Chapter 1 and sections i-vi of chapter 2 of part two are devoted to scholastic doctrines of the nature and kinds of propositions. The remaining sections (vii-ix) are mainly of epistemological interest and provide the grounding for the lists of 'general directions' and specific rules of chapters 4-5 (which conveniently repeat most of the significant content of these earlier sections). The epistemology of vii-ix is openly Cartesian. Clearness and distinctness (in discerning agreement or disagreement of ideas) are advanced in section vii as providing 'a certain criterion of truth' in judgment. Section viii contains the clear expression of the commonplace (often now associated with W. K. Clifford's 1877 essay 'The Ethics of Belief') that in believing 'the degree of assent ought to be exactly proportional to the degree of evidence'. Watts' comments with regard to what is now referred to as 'the ethics of belief' are brief; but the fact that he thinks it has a place in a logic textbook is suggestive and is a further indication of theoretical and pedagogical implications of a wider conception of the subject matter of logic.

Chapter 3 is also Cartesian in its concern with sources of error in judgment. I set it aside for the moment, however, to be treated in more detail as illustrative of the significance of conceiving of logic as concerned with operations of the mind.

Chapter 4 proposes 'General directions to assist us in judging aright', which may be briefly stated as follows: (1) Philosophical inquirers should re-examine the grounds of old opinions and cast aside those which were 'formed without due examination'. (2) All ideas of objects concerning which we pass judgments should be 'clear and distinct, complete, comprehensive, extensive, and orderly'. (3) Affirmation of any proposition should be subsequent to and determined by careful comparison 'with the utmost attention' of subject and predicate ideas. (4) We are to 'Search for evidence of truth with diligence and honesty, and be heartily ready to receive evidence, whether for the agreement or disagreement of ideas'. (Under this rule, Watts also enjoins an expending of effort in the search for truth 'in due proportion to the importance of the proposition'.) (5) In the absence of a clear preponderance of evidence, we ought to suspend judgment. (6) Evidence for propositions must come through 'those proper and peculiar mediums or means' suited to the kind of proposition (e.g. sounds, colors, odors by the evidence of the senses, the specifics of religion by the evidence of divine revelation). (7) We should have ready at hand settled general principles 'whose evidence is great and obvious' with regard to whatever subject matter is in question, to aid us in judging particulars. (8) The degree of assent to propositions ought to 'bear an exact proportion to the different degrees of evidence'. (9) We should keep an open mind, ever receptive to objections to our opinions.

Noteworthy about these 'grand principles of belief and practice' is the extent to which the concern is with *inquiry* (as opposed to justification) and with the ethics of belief (specifically, in directions (4), (5), (8), and (9)). Both of these aspects of Watts' directions for 'judging aright' are consonant with the directive or preceptive approach itself, and I shall have more to say with regard to both in later further comments about his conception of the subject matter.

In the sections of chapter 5, sets of 'special rules' are proposed for judging with regard to matters of (1) sense, (2) reason and speculation, (3) morality and religion, (4) prudence, (5) human testimony, (6) divine testimony, and (7) the course of human and natural events. The division here is not entirely felicitous, some of the heads referring to differences of subject matter, others to sources or types of evidence. Nevertheless, there are a number of useful insights in this chapter, and, more significantly, an appreciation of the importance of having due regard to differences in subject matter as well as an attempt to identify relevant subject-matter-specific (or medium-specific) principles of inquiry or inference. The special rules of chapter 5 may be seen as further elaborations upon general directions (6) and (7) of chapter 4: *Acquire evidence through 'proper and peculiar mediums or means'* and *Have ready at hand appropriate settled principles.*

By way of illustration, the special rules for *testimony* advise us to consider (1) 'whether the thing reported be in itself possible', (2) whether there is concurring non-testimonial evidence, (3) whether the testifier has the capabilities and has been positioned so as to know the truth of the matter, (4) 'whether the narrator be honest and faithful', (5) whether there is concurring testimonial evidence from other witnesses (with consideration of *their* credentials as well), (6) 'whether the report were capable of being easily refuted at first, if it had not been true', (7) 'whether there has been a constant, uniform tradition' of belief in the reports of ancient witnesses, (8) to what extent the report has been doubted, tested, and confirmed by 'considerable persons' (*credible persons*, I take it), (9) whether 'there be anything improbable in the thing itself'; further rules direct us to keep in mind (10) that the absence of testimony to a happening may be evidence that it did not occur (a principle which might occur to us to be of interest in connection with the supposed fallacy of *argumentum ad ignorantiam*), (11) that testimony often bears within itself the marks of truth or falsehood (or of veracity or the lack thereof), and (12) that testimony typically contains a mixture of truth and falsehood, the sorting out of which is incumbent upon its recipients.

Part three - reasoning and syllogism

It is of some interest that, while roughly sixty-five pages are devoted (in the *Works*) to each of the first two 'parts of logick', only twenty-eight pages are given to the third. Though chapter 1 and sections i-vi of chapter 2 are given over to formal matters – to the idea of a formal argument, to kinds of syllogisms, mood, figure, implication, disjunction, and the like – Watts has a notable lack of enthusiasm for the study of formal logic. He observes, for example, that 'the true light of nature, a good judgment, and due consideration of things, tend more to true reasoning than all the trappings of mood and figures'. 'But lest this book be charged with too great defects and imperfections', he continues, 'it may be proper to give short hints of that which some logicians have spent so much time and paper upon' (III.2.iii). Generally, his view seems to be that formal logical errors are easily detected by sensible persons. At the close of his brief discussion of what we now call 'propositional arguments', Watts observes (echoing a dark misgiving that occasionally sweeps over the proceedings in the modern standard logic course) that:

> These conjunctive syllogisms are seldom deficient or faulty in the form of them; for such a deficiency would be discovered at first glance generally by common reason, without any artificial rules of logick: The chief care therefore is to see that the major proposition be true, upon which the whole force of the argument usually depends. (III.2.v)

Toward the use of schemes of rhetorical invention (such as the employment of 'topics' or 'commonplaces' in finding middle terms) Watts expresses a similar opinion:

> But when a man of moderate sagacity has made himself master of his theme, by just diligence and enquiry, he has seldom to run knocking at the doors of all the topics, that he may furnish himself with argument or matter of speaking. (III.2.vii)

III,2,viii, 'Of several kinds of arguments and demonstrations', is especially of interest in its division of arguments in terms of whether their middle term is drawn from judgment, faith, ignorance, past professions, authority, or passions. These are arguments *ad judicium* (which take their middle term from 'the nature or existence of things'), *ad fidem* (appealing to testimony), *ad ignorantiam* (drawn from the insufficiency of evidence on some question), *ad hominem* (involving an 'address to our professed principles'), *ad verecundiam* ('an address to our modesty'), and *ad passiones* ('or if it be made publicly, it is called *ad populum*, or an appeal to the people'). 'Middle term' in this context is used rather loosely for whatever it is in terms of which the inferential connection is to be made. For example, the structure of *argumentum ad fidem* might be representable (though it is not so represented by Watts) as:

> Person S bears witness (under thus-and-so conditions, etc.) to the truth of proposition P (that so-and-so occurred). Witness by person S (under thus-and-so conditions, etc.) provides grounds for belief. Therefore, there are grounds for belief that P.

in which S's bearing witness provides the middle term. *Argumentum ad fidem* and the others are, then, *syllogisms*, 'syllogism' being also used rather loosely, having been defined earlier as 'an argument whereby we are wont to infer something that is less known, from truths which are more evident' (III, intro.). Just as Watts regards propositions as typically involving the comparison of two ideas, so he regards reasoning and syllogism as typically involving the connecting of two ideas by way of a mediating idea expressed in a middle term.

It is worthy of note that Watts does not treat the modes of argument under discussion in section 8 as inherently fallacious. '*Argumentum ad ignorantiam*', '*argumentum ad passiones*', etc. are not given as names of fallacies or sophisms, but rather as names of argument types. There is no indication that Watts even considers any of these modes of argument to be inherently problematic. Their discussion does, however, provide the transition to the treatment of modes of argument which are.

> If a syllogism agree with the rules which are given for the construction and regulation of it, it is called a true argument: If it disagree with these rules, it is a paralogism or false argument: But when a false argument puts on the face and appearance of a true one, then it is properly called a sophism or fallacy, which shall be the subject of the next chapter. (III.2.viii)

Unfortunately, with regard to arguments *ad ignorantiam* and *ad hominem* the *Logick* fails to provide any rules or directions. The aforementioned treatment of testimony does have *some* implications with respect to these and does provide precepts which are directly applicable to arguments *ad fidem* and *ad verecundiam*, while the treatment of prejudices in part two provides useful insights (to which we will attend later) in relation to argument *ad passiones*.

The presentation of the Doctrine of Sophisms in chapter 3 of part three is brief, consisting in an identification and short characterization of 'the most remarkable springs of false argumentation' which have been named by previous logicians. These are *ignoratio elenchi* ('a mistake of the question'), *petitio principii* ('a supposition of what is not granted'), arguing in a circle ('very near akin to the *petitio principii*'), *non causa pro causa* ('the assignation of a false cause'), *fallacia accidentis* ('a sophism wherein we pronounce concerning the nature and essential properties of any subject according to something which is merely accidental to it'), *a dicto secundum quid ad dictum simpliciter* ('when we argue from that which is true in particular circumstances, to prove the same thing true absolutely, simply, and abstracted from all circumstances'), composition and division, equivocation, and false induction ('when from a few experiments or observations men infer general theorems and universal propositions'). Two general tests for 'solving' sophisms are proposed in the following section, which are, first, that the premises must 'at least implicitly contain the conclusion', and, second, that the same term must be taken in precisely the same sense in all occurrences. The first of these rules is not at all clearly explained by Watts, and the second seems applicable only to composition, division, and equivocation.

The discussion of these sophisms is on the whole unremarkable. Watts himself observes that the treatment of the Doctrine of Prejudices in part two 'has anticipated a great deal of what might be said on the subject of sophisms' (III.3.1). Our own (postponed) examination of part two, chapter 3 will show, I believe, that it is in the treatment of the Doctrine of Prejudices that the *Logick* has the most to offer to the theory of informal fallacies.

The closing chapter (4) of part three proposes some general rules with regard to reasoning. These are akin to the general directions of part two and again show the Cartesian influence. They are (1) 'Accustom yourself to clear and distinct ideas, to evident propositions, to strong and convincing arguments'; (2) 'Enlarge your general acquaintance with things daily, in order to attain a rich furniture of topics, or middle terms, whereby those propositions which occur may be either proved or disproved . . .'; (3) 'In searching the knowledge of things, always keep the precise point of the present question in your eye'; (4) 'When you have exactly considered the precise point of inquiry, . . . then consider what, and how much you already know of this question, or of the ideas and terms of which it is composed'; (5) 'In choosing your middle terms, . . . always take such topics as are surest and least fallible, and which carry the greatest evidence and strength with them'; (6) 'Prove your conclusion, as far as possible, by some propositions that are in themselves more plain, evident, and certain, than the conclusion . . .'; (7) 'Labour in all your arguings to enlighten the understanding, as well as to conquer and captivate the judgment'; (8) '. . . learn to distinguish well between an explication and an argument, and neither impose upon yourselves, nor suffer yourselves to be imposed upon by others, by mistaking a mere illustration for a convincing reason'; and (9) 'In your whole course of reasoning, keep your mind sincerely intent on the pursuit of truth; and follow solid argument wheresoever it leads you'.

There is, then, a continuation, in similar veins, of the preceptive approach, of which I have again taken note by means of a rather long listing, without which, however, it is hard to get a clear sense of what Watts is up to. In this case, as in the others (especially in the giving of general directions), what we are presented with is, in effect, a list of *truisms* of opining or inference making. But they are not necessarily (and, sadly, not commonly) truisms or operative principles of judgment or reasoning in society at large or for many undergraduate students who register for introductory logic courses. Whether an overtly preceptive approach such as we find in the *Logick* is the best (or even a useful) pedagogical strategy in getting students to regard such principles as truisms is debatable. But it is a virtue of Watts's approach in the *Logick* that he gives a central place to the inculcation of the truisms of careful thinking and reasoning.

Part four - disposition and method

The treatment of the 'fourth part of logick' is remarkably short, too short for division into sections. One has the sense of a project going down hill, from the sixty-four and sixty-five pages of parts one and two, to the twenty-eight of part three, to a mere thirteen in part four. Chapter 1 includes a cursory discussion of the nature and kinds of method, chapter 2 the presentation of seven rules of method. Watts defines *method* in logic as 'the disposition of a variety of thoughts on any subject, in such order as may best serve to find out unknown truths, to explain and confirm truths that are known, or to fix them in the memory' (IV.1). Method is divided into *natural* and *arbitrary*. Natural method or arrangement follows the order to be found in things; arbitrary proceeds or arranges artificially for special purposes such as those of memory, persuasive communication, or amusement. A further division of natural method is made into *synthetic* and *analytic*, the treatment of which is clearly derived from that of the *Port Royal Logic*, to which it is very much inferior. In general, part four of the *Logick* has the appearance of having been hastily thrown together. In contrast with the Cartesian emphasis on inquiry in the treatment of method in the *Port Royal Logic*, the emphasis in the *Logick* is on the role of method in *communication*. The precepts of chapter 2 require that method be such as to ensure that discourse is secure from error, 'plain and easy', distinct 'and without the perplexing mixture of things that ought to be kept separate', full, short 'or without superfluity', 'proper to the subject and the design', and 'connected'. Chapter 2 is addressed mainly to speakers and writers rather than to inquirers and derives its precepts from rhetorical rather than from logical sources.

The *Logick* closes with the following observations:

> The particular means or method for a farther improvement of the understanding, are very various, such as meditation, reading, conversing, disputing by speech or by writing, question & answer, &c. And in each of these practices some special forms may be observed, and special rules may be given to facilitate and secure our inquiries after truth. But this would require a little volume by itself, and a treatise of logick has always been esteemed sufficiently complete without it.

This short paragraph is a rough sketch of the *Logick's* sequel, *The Improvement of the Understanding*, a work which is almost entirely preceptive. It has two main parts. The first part, on 'the Attainment of useful knowledge', takes up such topics as reading, the hearing of lectures, learning a language, improvement by conversation and by Socratic and forensic disputation, habits of study, improvement of memory, and inquiry concerning causes and effects. The second part, on 'the Communication of useful knowledge', takes up topics such as methods of teaching, style, persuasion, the use and abuse of appeals to authority, instruction by preaching, and writing for the public. Most likely to be of interest to informal logicians are chapter 18 of the first part, 'Of determining [i.e. deciding] a question', and chapters 3-5 of the second part, on convincing others of a truth or delivering them from error, on authority, and on dealing with other person's prejudices. As already noted, *The Improvement of the Understanding* is a significant treatise on what we would now call 'critical thinking', one worthy of closer attention than our brief treatment of the *Logick* allows for.

The Doctrine of Prejudices[4]

I said earlier that the two most distinctive features of the *Logick*, from an informal logician's point of view, are its preceptive (prescriptive) pedagogical approach and its conception of the subject matter. The former has been profusely illustrated. The latter, which is a feature more widely shared with other logics of the seventeenth and eighteenth centuries, is now more specifically the object of our attention.

The Doctrine of Prejudices is concerned with sources of error in judgment (or reasoning), as is indicated by the title of chapter 3 of part two, 'The Springs of False Judgment, Or the Doctrine of Prejudices'. 'Prejudice' has, for Watts, a number of distinct though related meanings. 'Prejudice' literally means 'prejudgment', as is reflected in his comment that 'Rash judgments are called prejudices' (II.3.intro.). In this sense, a prejudice is a particular judgment made prematurely, 'a judgment that is formed concerning any person or thing before sufficient examination' (II.3.intro). It was Descartes' view that *all* errors in judgment are the result of the Will's choosing to assent to propositions concerning which the Understanding is inadequately informed. 'From what source, therefore, do my errors arise?', he asked himself, who gave the answer, 'Solely from the fact that, because the will extends further than the intellect, I do not contain the will within the same boundaries; rather, I even extend it to things I do not understand' (Descartes, 1971, fourth meditation, 38). There is every indication in II.3 (and in the 'directions' of II.4) that Watts shares this Cartesian view and that Descartes is one of his sources for the Doctrine of Prejudices.

But Descartes was himself concerned not so much with errors in judging particular things or persons as with more general assumptions and 'foundational' beliefs, which he regarded as typically underlying and being the main source of particular surface-level mistakes, for example the general belief that the world is as it appears to sense perception to be. From our point of view, it is such general principles of which it seems more appropriate to speak as 'prejudices'. The same appears to be true for Watts and his contemporaries, for whom 'prejudice' is much more frequently used to denote a general belief which is itself rash in the sense of being ill-founded and which in turn 'prejudices' more specific judgments for which it provides spurious grounding. 'Prejudice' is sometimes taken by Watts in this second sense, for example when he observes that 'we are nursed up in many silly and gross mistakes about domestic affairs' which 'must be cured by calling all the principles of our young years to the bar of more mature reason'.

> And what is it but custom that has for past centuries confined the brightest geniuses, even of the highest rank in the female world, to the business of the needle only, and secluded them most unmercifully from the pleasures of knowledge, and the divine improvements of reason? But we begin to break all these chains, and reason begins to dictate the education of youth. May the growing age be learned and wise! (II.3.iv)

The general belief that the female sex is suited only for such occupations of kitchen, nursery, and needle suits our modern conception well as an example of prejudice. But for Watts the belief that the world is as it appears to our senses to be is equally a prejudice in this sense.

But there is yet a third sense of 'prejudice' to be found here which there is reason, I believe, to regard as the most fundamental sense in the *Logick*. The real 'springs of false judgment', whether of more general ill-founded assumptions or of particular erroneous opinions, are logically offending *tendencies of the mind*.

Prejudices of the mind are divided by Watts into four classes, depending upon whether they arise from *things*, *words*, *ourselves*, or *other persons*. In some sense, all prejudices in this sense arise from ourselves, so that those in the third class may be regarded as in a way primary. Some are occasioned by the nature of things (external objects and events), for example by their being obscure, by their appearing 'in a disguise', by their containing a mixture of qualities some of which are more striking than is indicative of their relative importance, by their appearing differently from different perspectives, by their lending themselves to accidental associations, and so on. Other prejudices are occasioned by the nature of individual words or terms – for example, from the vacuity of certain substantive terms, from equivocity, and from synonymity – or by the rhetorical force of words in combination. Yet other prejudices are occasioned by the influence of other persons through education, custom, and authority. But the prejudices themselves are principles of the mind, such as the tendency to take the reports of our senses at face value, the tendency to take a word in whichever among its possible senses suits our purposes, and the tendency to mistake custom for nature and as a result to set up the customs of our own country as a standard by which foreigners are to be judged.

Among prejudices identified as having special reference to *ourselves*, the most striking are those arising from *the passions*, from *love of self*, and from peculiarities of *individual temper*. Our passions 'disguise every object they converse with, and put their own colours upon it, and thus lead the judgment astray from truth'.

> It is love that makes the mother think her own child the fairest . . . And envy represents the condition of our neighbor as better than it is, that there may be some pretence for her own vexation and uneasiness. Anger, and wrath, and revenge, and all those hateful passions, excite in us far worse ideas of men than they deserve, and persuade us to believe all that is ill of them. (II.3.iii)

Fondness for self, he observes, might be included under the passions, but looms so large as a source of prejudices as to merit treatment under a separate head. 'We are generally ready', he writes,

> to fancy every thing of our own has something peculiarly valuable in it, when indeed there is no other reason but because it is our own . . .
> We set up our own opinions in religion and philosophy as the tests of orthodoxy and truth; and we are prone to judge every practice of other men either as a duty or a crime, which we think would be a crime or a duty in us . . . This humour prevails sometimes to such a degree, that we would make our own taste and inclination the

standard by which to judge every dish of meat that is set upon the table, every book in a library, every employment, study and business of life, as well as every recreation. (II.3.iii)

Individual 'tempers, humours, and peculiar turns of mind' lead one person to be inclined to credulity, another to 'a spirit of contradiction'; one to be dogmatical, another skeptical; some to be fickle and ever changing their opinion; some to think always in extremes; some to revere whatever is ancient, others to take novelty as a mark of truth.

Now when Watts says that the Doctrine of Prejudices anticipates much of what might be said about sophisms, it appears to be because he regards particular surface-level logical errors (of the kind we now identify as 'informal fallacies') as being rooted in deeper principles – some natural, some acquired – of the human mind. His prescriptions with regard to prejudices of the mind are likely to strike us as more suited to a therapist than to a logician. For example, in the case of prejudices arising from the passions, he advises as follows:

The cure of these prejudices is attained by a constant jealousy of ourselves, and watchfulness over our passions, that they may never interpose when we are called to pass a judgment of any thing: And when our affections are warmly engaged, let us abstain from judging. It would also be of great use to form our deliberate judgments of persons and things in the calmest and serenest hours of life, when the passions of nature are all silent . . . (II.3.iii)

and he refers the reader to further 'sentiments and directions' to be found in his *Doctrine of the Passions*, whose directions for the government of the passions effectively constitute a cognitive *therapia* with regard to human emotion and motivation. So far removed is his conception of the scope of logic from that of our own time.

Conclusion

There is a great deal to be said for the late nineteenth century 'de-psychologizing' of the study of logic. At the same time, it may very well be the case that a de-psychologized logic is seriously disadvantaged in its confrontation with some important issues which are now regarded as falling under the purview of the informal logician. It may be, for example, that the problems which standard logic texts have tried to address in chapters on informal fallacies can be at best addressed very superficially without attention to underlying psychological tendencies and proclivities of the sort identified by Watts as 'prejudices of the mind'. Works such as the *Logick* and *The Improvement of the Mind* are likely to strike some students and teachers as more insightful and of greater practical value than most late twentieth century works on informal logic and critical thinking. Because of that possibility, as well as on account of their insights on a variety of particular topics in which there is in our own time renewed interest, these works are well worth the attention of modern informal logicians.

Notes

1. The fullest recent treatment of the *Logick*, together with a critical discussion of the influences on it, its own historical significance, and its contents is to be found in Howell, 1971. Howell also provides relevant facts about the life and career of Watts.

2. Of other logics following the division and approach of the *Port Royal*, a work which is especially worthy of mention (though more obscure) is the *Systeme de Reflexions qui peuvent contribuer a la nettete et a l'entendue de nos connaissances, ou Nouvel Essai de Logique* (1712) of Jean-Pierre de Crousaz, which appeared in English translation a year before the publication of Watts' *Logick*. Crousaz explicitly acknowledges the influence of Descartes and Francis Bacon as well as that of the *Port Royal Logic*.

3. Compare Hume's comment in the Introduction to his *Treatise of Human Nature*: 'The sole end of logic is to explain the principles and operations of our reasoning faculty, and the nature of our ideas . . . ' (xv).

4. Prejudice has, of course, been widely written about and discussed by social scientists and social critics in our own time, most commonly with regard to ethnic prejudice. Prejudices as *logical* phenomena, or those which are peculiarly deserving of the name 'logical prejudices', have been discussed to some extent in twentieth century works on critical thinking and informal logic.
   They are treated seriously in Robert Thouless' *How to Think Straight* (1939, Simon and Schuster: New York), in Susan L. Stebbing's *Thinking to Some Purpose* (1939, Pelican: New York), in Giles St. Aubyn's *The Art of Argument* (1957, Christophers: London), and in *Fallacy: The Counterfeit of Argument* by W. W. Fearnside and W. B. Holther (1957, Prentice-Hall: Englewood Cliffs, NJ). A number of other works deal with the topic briefly, for example Anthony Flew's *Thinking Straight* (1977, Prometheus Books: Buffalo, NY) and Richard Purtill's *Logical Thinking* (1972, Harper and Row: NY).
   In my own opinion, the best recent treatment of logical prejudices, though still inferior to that provided in the *Logick*, is given by Thouless. In general, the preoccupation of late seventeenth and early eighteenth century writers with the subject of *self-knowledge* seems to have encouraged a greater emphasis on identifying and dealing with prejudices of the mind.

References

Arnauld, Antoine, and Pierre Nicole [1662] (1964), *The Art of Thinking*, translated by James Dickoff and Patricia James, Bobbs-Merrill: Indianapolis.

Bacon, Francis [1620] (1969), *The New Organon*, in *The New Organon and Related Writings*, Bobbs-Merrill: Indianapolis.

Clifford, W. K. (1947), *'The Ethics of Belief' and Other Essays*, edited by Leslie Stephen and F. Pollock, Watts: London.

Crousaz, Jean-Pierre de [1712] (1724), *A New Treatise of the Art of Thinking*, translated from the French, London.

Descartes, Rene [1628] (1911), *Rules for the Direction of the Mind*, in *The Philosophical Works of Descartes*, translated by Elizabeth S. Haldane and G. R. T. Ross, Vol. 1, Cambridge University Press: Cambridge.

Descartes, Rene [1641] (1971), *Meditations on First Philosophy*, translated by Donald A. Cress, Hackett: Indianapolis.

Howell, Wilbur Samuel (1961), *Logic and Rhetoric in England, 1500-1700*, Russell and Russell: New York.

Howell, Wilbur Samuel (1971), *Eighteenth Century British Logic and Rhetoric*, Princeton University Press: Princeton.

Hume, David (1978), *A Treatise of Human Nature*, edited by L. A. Selby-Bigge with revisions by P. H. Nidditch, Oxford University Press: Oxford.

Johnson, Samuel (1906), *Lives of English Poets*, Oxford University Press: Oxford.

Locke, John [1690] (1975), *An Essay Concerning Human Understanding*, edited by P. H. Nidditch, Oxford University Press: Oxford.

Locke, John (1754), *Some Thoughts on the Conduct of the Understanding in the Search of Truth*, Glasgow.

Watts, Isaac (1971), *The Works of Isaac Watts*, edited by G. Burder, AMS Press: New York. Reprint of the London edition of 1810-11.

8 Whately and the study of fallacious reasoning

Raymie E. McKerrow

Whately's *Elements of Logic* emerged as one of the most important texts on logical reasoning in the early part of the nineteenth century. In essence, the study of logic had become moribund and was a target of criticism from students and academics alike. The text, from its first edition in 1826 through its many editions in England and America (it was in its ninth English edition by 1848), became *the* source of introductory information on the art and science of logical reasoning. As part of his discussion, Whately included a section on fallacious reasoning. In focusing on that portion of the text, this chapter will examine his orientation toward the study of what has since become known as informal logic, discuss his classification and treatment of various forms of fallacious reasoning, and consider the merits of his contribution to the study of fallacies. Before embarking on these themes, an understanding of who Whately was and his approach toward teaching and writing on rhetoric and logic needs to be briefly discussed.

Archbishop Richard Whately (1787-1863)

The eighth and youngest child of an Anglican cleric was born in London on 2 February 1787. He matriculated at Oriel College, Oxford University in 1805, at the age of eighteen. While a competent undergraduate student, he only earned what was termed 'second class honors' (a step above merely 'passing' required exams and a step below the coveted 'first class honors') in mathematics and humanities, the two broad classifications in which examinations were held. Having graduated in 1808, he remained at Oriel as a masters student, and received his second degree in 1812 and spent the next decade as a College Tutor. Between 1822 and 1825 he served as the pastor of a rural parish in Halesworth, and then returned to Oriel to teach. In late 1831, Whately was appointed by the Prime Minister, Lord Earl Grey, to the Church of England's Archbishopric of Dublin, Ireland. Whately accepted and remained the Archbishop of Dublin until his death on 8 October 1863.

As a lecturer at Oxford (1812-22, 1825-31) Whately taught rhetoric, logic, and, for a brief time, political economy. He published the *Elements of Logic* in 1826 and followed that with the *Elements of Rhetoric* in 1828. In addition, he published collections of his sermons and other essays on religion, including *The Use and Abuse of Party Feeling in Matters of Religion* (1822), *Letters on the Church by an Episcopalian* (1828), and *Essays on the Errors of Romanism, having their Origin in Human Nature* (1830). As a teacher, 'he was neither markedly popular nor unpopular with the students generally' (Akenson, 64). The following reminiscence, published in *McBride's Magazine* in 1872, is instructive (cited in Akenson, 63-64):

> The logic class is assembled. The door by which the Principal is to enter is exactly opposite to the foot of the stair which descends from his own apartment. It stands open, and presently a kind of rushing sound is heard on the staircase. In the next instant Whately plunges head foremost into the room, saying, while yet in the doorway, 'Explain the nature of the third operation of the mind, Mr. Johnson'. But as none of the operations of Mr. Johnson's mind are so rapid as those of the energetic Principal, the latter has had time to fling himself into a chair, cross the small of one leg over the knee of the other, balance himself on the two hind legs of the chair and begin to show signs of impatience before Mr. Johnson has sufficiently gathered his wits together.
>
> While that process is being accomplished, the Principal soothes his impatience by the administration of a huge pinch – or handful rather – of snuff to his nose, copiously sprinkling his waistcoat with the superfluity thereof. Then at last comes from Mr. Johnson a meagre answer in the words of the text-book, which is followed by a luminous exposition [from Whately] of the rationale of the whole of that part of the subject, in giving which the lecturer shoots far over the heads of the majority of his hearers, but is highly appreciated by the select few who are able to follow him.
>
> Now, Mr. Jackson, examine this syllogism: All men are dogs, all philosophers are men; therefore all philosophers are dogs. Is that a correct conclusion?' Poor Mr. Jackson incontinently falls into the trap, and simperingly opines that such a conclusion is not altogether correct.
>
> 'On the contrary, sir, the conclusion is drawn from the premises with perfect logical correctness. You fancy that the logic is bad because the conclusion is false in fact. When shall I succeed in making you understand that logic has nothing to do with the accuracy or inaccuracy, the truth or falsehood, of the statement of facts contained in the premises? . . .'
>
> As the lecture proceeds, the lecturer takes the matter more and more into his own hands, and ends by giving a masterly elucidation of that part of the subject which is occupying the class. And during the whole of the time the lecture lasts – somewhere more than an hour, probably – the reverend lecturer continues to throw himself about on his chair into the strangest attitudes, very frequently balancing himself on one of the hind legs of it.

While, admittedly, not all lecturers during this period of education at Oxford were this 'odd' in their personal behavior in class, the above does suggest the kind of interaction Whately sought with his students as he endeavored to teach them the principles of sound reasoning.

Whately's approach in his own writing was characterized by a similar practical sense of what students needed to know, and the most efficient means of organizing and conveying that information. As a cleric and a professor, he was not a scholar: 'Content with what he considered to be the fundamental components of ethics, religion, metaphysics, grammar, logic, rhetoric, and political economy, he was satisfied to remain on the periphery of each subject's deeper content' (McKerrow, 1975, v). Thus, he was at his best when expressing the fundamental nature and implications of ideas and principles in clear and comprehendible terms for his audience. In later years, he wrote a series of 'easy lessons' on such topics as money matters, Christian evidences, and reasoning for the education of the young. Many of these were heavily used in classrooms throughout England and Ireland in the 1830s-1860s.

Whately's *Elements of Logic*

Drafted initially with the assistance of his student, John Henry Newman, as notes for the use of students, the *Logic* first appeared as an essay in *Encyclopedia Metropolitana* in late 1823 (Jongsma, 1982; McKerrow, 1978; Whately-Hawkins Correspondence). Published in book form in 1826, the text went through nine editions between 1826 and 1850. While it grew in size as new examples were added, it did not change substantially in its overall orientation toward logic. While John Stuart Mill's championing of inductive logic and Augustus DeMorgan's foray into symbolic logic occurred during the same period of time, Whately steadfastly ignored both these new developments and his critics in revising the work. Nonetheless, it was heralded in its own era by such writers as Sir William Hamilton, John Stuart Mill, Alexander Campbell Fraser, George Boole and Augustus DeMorgan as responsible for the revival of logical studies in England in the early nineteenth century (see Lindsay; Jongsma, 1982; McKerrow, 1987; Van Evra, 1984). As Lindsay noted in 1871, Whately's text 'awakened a real study of Logic, and was the forerunner of a host of logical textbooks, which, if they added little to the science they profess to expound, at least showed the national zeal for the study' (557).

The historical setting in which Whately studied and later taught prompted a renewed study of reasoning. The utility of syllogistic reasoning had undergone significant attack over the last few centuries. Bacon, Descartes, the Port Royalists, Locke, Watts, Duncan, Reid, Campbell, and Stewart had each taken their turn in disparaging the syllogism as a serious focus of study. As the rhetorician George Campbell observed in the late seventeen hundreds, 'there is no reason to wish its [logic's] revival, as eloquence seems to have been very little benefitted by it, and philosophy still less' (70). While logic had its defenders (for example Gillies in 1797, Kirwan in 1807, Copleston in 1809), none had produced works which replaced the by now dated work by Dean Aldrich (*Artis Logicae Compendium*, 1691). As other studies have noted, there was a favorable climate at Oxford for introducing an updated version of Aldrich's work (Howell, 42-60; Jongsma, 1983; McKerrow, 1987; 176-77).

The nature of fallacies

Whately's treatment of logic, and consequently of fallacies as well, is premised on his nominalist interpretation of language. As he notes in the *Logic*, 'No 'common terms' have, as the names of Individuals ('singular terms'), *any real thing existing in nature* corresponding to each of them' (1857, 147-48). What this suggests is that universal terms (as in 'chair' to represent all varieties of chairs) do not denote real features of the world; they are but the construction of our mind. This perspective on language leads him to constantly remind the reader of the *meaning* of the words being used, as contrasted to simply being aware of the *form* in which they appear. As he takes pains to note, our minds may be easily misled by inappropriate language use, as it applies to both our own reasoning and the reasoning of others. In fact, in an observation that prefigures later experimental research on syllogistic reasoning, he accurately notes 'there is no absurdity so gross which men will not readily admit, if it appears to lead to a conclusion of what they are already convinced' (1857, 191). Whether listening to others or creating our own rationale for a belief, if we truly are convinced of the belief, violations of formal rules of reasoning will little hinder our reasoning process. His interest in the potential abuses of language in the context of reasoning improperly or unfairly is thus prompted by the possibility that a scientific, principle-based understanding of the kinds of fallacies one might either fall into or be subjected to will form an appropriate habit of mind immune to such errors (1857, 168-69).

In defining fallacies, Whately readily admits what appears an acceptable truism: it is impossible to develop rules 'the mere learning of which will enable us to *apply* them with mechanical certainty and readiness' (1857, 168). In addition, he notes that the classification scheme he will introduce does not resolve all problems with respect to learning the fallacies themselves: '[I]t must of course be often a matter of doubt, or rather, of arbitrary *choice*, not only to which genus each *kind* of fallacy should be referred, but even to which kind to refer any *one individual* Fallacy' (1857, 174). This does not mean that just any classification scheme is appropriate. Whately objects that other writers on logic have consistently abandoned logical principles once they embark on a treatment of fallacies. Contrariwise, his classification scheme is premised on a single principle drawn from his earlier discussion of logical reasoning: 'In every Fallacy, the Conclusion either *does*, or *does not follow from the Premises*' (1857, 175). Improper reasoning is termed a material fallacy in the former case, and a logical fallacy in the latter case. What is unique in terms of contemporary treatments of fallacious reasoning is that the discussion is clearly couched in terms of deductive reasoning. Whately was not an exponent of inductive logic, as that form was characterized by Mill and others. Hence, he saw deduction as the only form of serious reasoning and treated fallacies within that context. Schmidt (63) has argued that Whately correctly infers that fallacies may be differently named, but that he is incorrect in assuming that the genus to which individual fallacies belong is equally indeterminate. However, the same logic Whately uses to suggest that any argument may be labeled differently depending on how one interprets it applies to the genus/species indeterminacy. As he implies in several places in the discussion of fallacies, the interconnectedness between fallacies is such that they may be realigned under different labels, depending on how one sees the fallacy in question. Given the variations in classification schemata since Whately's time, with the same fallacy appearing under quite different genus headings, it would seem that Whately's observation is accurate (see Carney & Scheer, Fearnside and Holther).

Before moving into an analysis of fallacies, Whately advances some general observations about the importance of the subject matter and the need to examine words carefully. As one might expect in a text, Whately implores the reader to recognize that improper reasoning is not the sole province of the 'skillful sophist' (1857, 181). Rather, anyone can be subject to the ambiguities of language in practical use. He gives the example of the young preacher who, in striving to keep his language 'plain' when addressing the lower classes (thereby rendering it simple and easy to comprehend) also avoids the use of metaphor or other figurative language with which to adorn the discourse. This, Whately notes, extends the application of 'plain' language into an arena which is not conducive to instructing the lower classes. In a veiled criticism of contemporary preaching he adds 'the above instance is not drawn from mere conjecture, but from actual experience of the fact' (1857, 182). Nonetheless, taking Plato's criticism of orators to heart, Whately cautions against the deliberate use of erroneous argument by those whose principles are suspect and whose ends are so unworthy as to win arguments only by subterfuge. Thus, while there is room for the honest and principled rhetor who unwittingly errs in reasoning, the sophist is the target of harsh criticism. The concern is that sophistry may win the day if listeners are not careful in their assessment of language which appears pleasing and convincing, yet is founded on invalid argument or errors in ambiguity or relevance.

While it is difficult to detect fallacies, once clear to the analyst, the absurdity of the logic employed is obvious. To make this point, Whately offers the analogy of the difficulty of ascertaining the guilt of a criminal: once known, it is easy to convict and punish. In a passage which stresses the importance of language, Whately cites with approval Francis Bacon's maxim that language, instead of being at man's command, is instead often the rule of the mind. As an illustration of 'the influence of words on thoughts' Whately notes the response of a moralist to the issue of suicide: presuming that God has outlawed murder, the moralist proceeds to use that commandment as a reason to negate suicide as a moral act. Whately argues that the error is to see suicide as a species of murder, when it has none of the effects usually associated with that term (injury to others). Finally, he offers some rather sound advice for the contemporary age as well as for his own: it is easier to hide fallacious reasoning in a long discourse, with premises separated in time from one another, thereby making it more difficult to assess the weakness inherent in the argument. In other words, if one desires to dissemble, being long-winded is an advantage.

Logical Fallacies: The following division simplifies Whately's discussion of logical fallacies (Whately is not always specific or consistent with respect to labeling fallacies discussed, hence liberties have been taken in constructing the list):

I. Logical

    A. Violations in form of reasoning: Undistributed Middle; Illicit Process; Negative Premises; Three Terms

II. Semi-logical

A. Ambiguous use of middle term: Equivocation; Paronymous Terms; Origin/Custom; Interrogation; Amphiboly; Accident; First/Second Intention; Primary/Secondary; Time/Place

B. Contextual: Composition/Division; Thaumatrope; Accident

Whately does not spend much time on the first category, reasoning that he already has fully discussed the problems inherent in rule violation in the preceding discussion of deductive reasoning. He notes, however, that a sound strategy in evaluating your own arguments is to place yourself in the opponent's position, and then review your case. As he suggests, popular applause is not a very solid ground on which to assess the adequacy of your arguments from the perspective of their soundness, hence it is important to consider their effectiveness in removing doubts in an opponent's mind.

As the text went through multiple editions, the classification scheme was not altered, but the discussion was somewhat revised to reflect new examples, and to analyze additional forms of mistaken reasoning. This is particularly true in the discussion of ambiguous language used in the 'middle term' of a syllogism. Changes from edition to edition are not of significance for the present purposes; the following discussion is based primarily on the ninth edition, which includes the most complete discussion of fallacies (the above list is based on the ninth edition).

The *semi-logical* fallacies are those which utilize ambiguous middle terms (in all but the case of an 'undistributed middle term' as that is a formal error) and context in an improper fashion. The fallacies listed under this heading are clearly explained, but readers then and now would be hard pressed to derive a convenient set of names for all of those discussed. As noted earlier, the discussion is framed by the rules of syllogistic construction. Thus, all of the examples are presented in the regular syllogistic pattern, with illustrations of ambiguity with respect to the 'middle terms' clarified in reference to particular fallacies. Of those discussed, two that are familiar to students studying contemporary logic and argument are *equivocation* and *amphiboly*.

The key to a fallacy of equivocation is not simply that a term admits of more than one meaning, but that it is in fact used in two different senses each time the middle term appears in the syllogism. This much is obvious, but Whately goes on to validate the need for precision in fixing the meaning of terms. Consistent with his use of analogy in other instances, he suggests that just as burglars do not batter down the front door but come in a window that was left unlocked, arguers do not make glaring mistakes in using language, but shade meanings ever so slightly to take advantage of a listener's carelessness. Thus, taking care of '*minute* points' (1857, 194) in reasoning is essential. Unfortunately, he neglects to provide a clear example of what is intended by 'minute' differences in the senses of terms. The remainder of the discussion is devoted to more easily discernible variants of an equivocal use of language. The second fallacy discussed (listed above as 'paronymous') concerns those terms which share the same root, and hence are mistakenly thought to be the same. To say someone who murders is therefore a murderer makes perfectly good logical sense, but to say that '*projectors* are unfit to be trusted; this man has formed a *project*, therefore he is unfit to be trusted' (1857, 195) errs in assuming the two key terms are equivalent in meaning and application. A second example is more to the point: Whately notes the difference between 'presumption' which has both a strong and weak force, and 'presume', which implies strong reason to believe. He suggests that moving from presumption of guilt to presumed guilt may suggest two very different senses of the degree of guilt. In moving the discussion forward, Whately examines differences in language that occur when a word's original meaning and its customary use are employed to produce an equivocation (listed as 'origin/custom' above). As he notes, a person may employ the term 'representative' to argue that a legislator must merely represent the wishes of constituents (origin), when ordinary use (custom) demands no such restriction on a legislator's ability to act on their behalf.

The placement of the fallacy of interrogation within this general set is not as clear, as it is less an ambiguity of middle terms than a case in which several questions are raised in the context of asking one. Discussed in terms similar to the better known 'complex question' fallacy, the error fits better under the heading of 'undue assumption' of an unproven premise: 'Have you stopped beating your child' assumes the fact of beating, which may be yet unproven. Nonetheless, Whately defends his choice, noting that the fallacy fits under this head due to an equivocal meaning in a key term employed in the question. Depending on the response, the person asking can employ one or the other of the meanings as benefits the argument being advanced. Seeing this kind of equivocation as equivalent to asking two questions in one is a stretch, and Whately seems to admit as much in referring the reader to later discussions where undue assumption is central to the argument's error.

In a discussion that is poorly developed, Whately suggests that equivocation also may occur when either the term's intrinsic significations differ or the context in which it is used permits more than one meaning. His only examples refer to the context being understood by the user and listener, in which case there is no confusion as to the term's meaning. His discussion of amphiboly, on the other hand, is more clearly connected to ambiguity. In this instance the problem lies in the construction of a sentence, thereby allowing for two meanings to be derived. While ambiguity is possible in this sense, it is not a logical extension of the previous discussions of terms and premises. An amphibolous sentence is simply unclear as to its meaning; amphiboly has little direct relation to the general heading under which it appears. Whately's examples are of little help to most twentieth-century readers, as they are either in Latin (from Aldrich), depend on historical context that may well be unfamiliar to a reader, or are minor lapses in which the referent of a clause is unclear. Words also are potentially ambiguous through accidental equivocation, as in the case of a term that can be opposed to two or more very different concepts, for example 'light'/'heavy', 'light'/'darkness' (1857, 202). Although not indicated by Whately, the fallacy would occur only when one confounds the senses in a syllogism. Another sense of equivocation occurs when what Whately refers to as 'first' and 'second intention' of terms are involved. Terms which are in general usage also are employed within disciplines or communities in more specific, often technical senses. In fact, the same term may be used in a variety of disciplines to refer to very different concepts: 'line' may refer to the configuration of troops or a string used in fishing. Instead of indicating a specific fallacy associated with this usage, Whately notes the importance of being careful 'to avoid confounding together, either the first and second intentions, or the different second intentions with each other' (1857, 204).

Words also may be connected to each other by direct resemblance or by analogy. In these cases, Whately suggests that one of the terms is primary, and its application in another context is secondary: '*sweet* is originally and properly applied to *tastes*; secondarily and *improperly (i.e.* by analogy) to sounds' (1857, 205). The problem arises in believing that the referent's analogous terms are themselves always similar or that the analog covers more ground than the terms would suggest. Whately refers, in keeping with his discussion of ambiguous terms, to the analogous use of 'servant' in biblical and other classical texts (primary) to contemporary servants in one's household (secondary). What people forget, he argues, is that the servants of classical times were often slaves and hence possessions; the servants of the present day are not. Thus, the analog only suggests a similar relationship of service to another, not that the remainder of the relations between people are the same. Strictly speaking, the only time resemblance and analogy fit under ambiguity is when single terms are used in a way that relies on confusion over their primary and secondary applications; presumably, a speaker could shift meaning as needed, or could imply that what was true in the primary sense of the term's application, is equally true under the secondary application.

Time and place also figure in the ambiguity of expression. In taking note of metonymy, Whately notes that 'door' may signify an entryway and an object that closes it. Similarly, 'smell' may signify either an attribute in an object which produces an odor, or one's sensation of the odor. Whately relates these examples to part/whole and to cause/effect ambiguities, and ties them to their proximity in time or place. Exactly how either time or place affects the attribution of equivocal meanings is not clarified by Whately.

Whately's sensitivity to the conventional use of language underscores his discussion of ambiguity. Towards the end of this section, he suggests how the ordinary use of language may invite common errors of thinking. Whately observes that to say 'punishing a criminal deters others' misses the actual impact of the event: what deters action is one's own apprehension of being punished. That is, the deterrence is effective not from the punishment itself, but from the salience it has for other individuals. If one is not affected by the punishment, it will do little to deter the commission of a similar act. What is needed in order to overcome these and other abuses is clear definition of the particular terms in question. While it is a fair criticism to say that Whately's treatment of ambiguous terms is at times unclear, and includes illustrative fallacies which do not appear to fall under the heading as defined, his discussion does represent a careful working out of the various ways in which precise terms can be misunderstood.

The fallacies of division and composition are examined under the general heading of semi-logical fallacies arising from the context in which they occur. Once again, Whately returns to the form of reasoning, observing that both fallacies occur in misusing middle terms in the major and minor premises of a syllogism. In one premise, the term is used in a collective sense, while in the other, it is used in a singular sense. Whately observes that 'there is no Fallacy more common, or more likely to deceive' than that which establishes 'some truth, *separately*, concerning *each single* member of a certain class, and thence to infer the same of the *whole collectively*' (1857, 215-16). The discussion proceeds to an analysis of what Whately refers to as a 'thaumatrope fallacy'. In this instance, the fallacy occurs when two incompatible goals are being advocated by a speaker. The adroit speaker transfers back and forth between the goals so rapidly as to create the impression that they are in fact seen as compatible:

> The fallacious belief thus induced bears a striking resemblance to the optical illusion effected by that ingenious and philosophical toy called the Thaumatrope; in which two objects painted on opposite sides of a card, - for instance a man, and a horse, - a bird, and a cage, - are by a quick rotary motion, made to impress the eye in combination, so as to form one picture, of the man on the horse's back, the bird in the cage. (1857, 216)

In a contemporary vein, the fallacy can be seen in the combination of such seemingly incompatible propositions as 'downsizing the institution' and 'improving the quality' of the programs offered. The sense in which this is a composition fallacy is admittedly somewhat forced; nevertheless, Whately could argue that it fits, as what is true of the particulars is taken to be true of the illusory picture created by the rapid transition between topics. The fallacy of division, on the other hand, occurs when the language used obscures reference to the individual particulars (what is true of the whole is true of its parts). As Whately observes, the loose reference to 'all' may divert attention from the critical assessment of particulars. Unfortunately, Whately's discussion is imprecise, noting that 'this is a fallacy' (1857, 217) in seeming reference to division, and then offering a fallacy of composition as an illustration.

The fallacy of accident is the final semi-logical fallacy considered. The error occurs when one premise assumes the term in its essential nature or attribute, while the other implies its further significations: 'what is bought in the market is eaten; raw meat is bought in the market; therefore raw meat is eaten' confounds substance and circumstance (1857, 219). On the whole, the fallacies of composition, division, and accident are clearly related to the logical scheme advanced as they can be expressed in terms of ambiguous middle terms. The thaumatrope fallacy, on the other hand, violates the organizing principle as it is unrelated to middle terms being confounded or ambiguously utilized. In treating that fallacy, Whately further confounds the incompatibility with its manner of presentation: it only occurs in the instance of rapid transition between topics so as to obscure the incompatibility.

Material Fallacies: The following list identifies the topics Whately discusses under this general heading:

I. Begging the Question (*petitio principii*): Arguing in a circle; Oblique expression.

II. Undue Assumption: Sign/Cause confusion; Experience misused; *Post hoc* fallacy; Indirect Assumption; Fallacy of Reference; Calculation of probabilities; Irrelevant conclusion *(ignoratio elenchi)*.

III. Argument Strategies: Objections; Prove part of proposition; Maintain too much; Jests.

The discussion of material fallacies proceeds on the premise that these arguments are deficient by virtue of the propositional content of the premises being advanced. Thus, Whately remains within the deductive model in analyzing the errors that are made. With respect to the various forms of 'begging the question', Whately advises students to be wary of confusing what has been demonstrated with what must be demonstrated. When the premise advanced is dependent on the conclusion for its own truth value, instead of promoting the conclusion as a logical consequence of what has been argued, the argument is fallacious. This form of circular reasoning is difficult to detect when there are several intervening claims or observations; one does not notice the dependence relation as easily as when the argument is stated in compressed, syllogistic form. The only way to ascertain this is to understand the content of the premise and as Whately suggests, 'narrow the Circle, by cutting off the intermediate steps' (1857, 222) thereby exposing its relation to the conclusion. Another way the sophist may confuse the listener or reader is to assert a claim that implies the acceptance of what is at issue without ever acknowledging its role in the argument. Oblique language thus talks around the issue while never raising it to a level of scrutiny.

Assuming a premise that is false or 'undue' also is an example of fallacious reasoning. Whately examines various argument strategies which may mislead the hearer. Arguing from either a cause or an effect that has not been sufficiently supported, or erroneously treating a sign of a condition or event as the cause is to engage in unsound reasoning. Similarly, arguing from conclusions drawn from experience can be equally unsound, as in the case of the person who assumes a cure from having taken medication when the only thing known 'is that he took the medicine, and that he recovered' (1857, 225). Arguing that a change in direction, while not harmful in itself, will lead to disastrous consequences mistakes the power of a single cause to produce calamity. Although Whately highlights this last example as a *post hoc ergo propter hoc* fallacy (after this, therefore because of this), the label fits the argument from experience as well, at least insofar as he illustrates it. While the change in direction implies a 'slippery slope' argument (the action begins a downward trend toward bigger problems), Whately does not consider that aspect of the sort of inference in question.

Whately also introduces a 'fallacy of reference' which, while an appeal to authority, has a special twist: the appeal is to works which the audience is unlikely to actually consult, and which if consulted would be found inadequate as support. With respect to this category, what is fallacious is not so much the undue assumption of a premise, as the creation of an argument in which the presence of its status '*shall not be perceived*'. Thus, the error admits, as Whately implies, of multiple transgressions whereby audiences may be misled by an assumption that has the appearance of proof.

The calculation of probabilities also may engender fallacious argument. The key to Whately's treatment of this kind of reasoning lies in his emphasis on the relative degree of dependence or independence of the various reasons being assessed. In a chain of reasoning, where the reasons are dependent on one another, Whately observes that the calculation of probabilities produces a result that is *weaker* than the individual reasons taken alone: if two reasons are assessed as 2/3, the resulting conclusion will be 4/9 or little more than 1/3. In the converse case, where the reasons are independent, Whately assesses the chances the reasons are false (in this case, 1/3 each). By multiplying the 'negative' probability and subtracting from one, he arrives at the cumulative probability of the independent reasons: $1/3 \times 1/3 = 1/9$; $1 - 1/9 = 8/9$, hence the conclusion is stronger than the reasons alone. A fallacy occurs when one incorrectly attributes to a conclusion a greater degree or lesser degree of probability than it in fact enjoys. Whately suggests that this commits a fallacy of either composition or division (which was discussed under the heading of 'ambiguous middle term') as it presents the impression that what is true of the whole or parts is likewise true of the other. The important point is that it is a fallacy, irrespective of whether it belongs to one category or the other. Thus, while the genus may change depending on how you define the fallacy, it is nonetheless a kind of reasoning to avoid, and to be aware of when others are calculating probabilities.

The final major category of 'undue assumption' fallacies is that of irrelevant conclusions. Within this discussion, Whately includes such well-known fallacies as *ad hominem* (to the person), *ad verecundiam* (to the authority), and *ad populum* (to the people). In analyzing the psychological impact of irrelevancies such as these, Whately observes that 'it will very often happen that some *emotion* will be excited – some sentiment impressed on the mind – . . . such as shall bring men into the *disposition* requisite for your purpose though they may not have assented to, or even stated distinctly in their own minds, the *proposition* which it was your business to establish' (1857, 233). In effect, the argument is presented in a way that diverts attention from the actual claim, and seeks to establish its value by advancing claims that are independent from it. While he admits that not all instances where one appeals to the person or the people are groundless, they are fallacious when unfairly applied to the situation. Thus, 'the fallaciousness depends upon the . . . attempt to deceive' (1857, 239) the audience into believing that what has been proven is more general or universal than it is in fact.

The conception of *ad hominem* argument, as Hitchcock notes, is developed by Whately in a manner that is unusual by today's textbook standards (also see Hansen, 1995; Johnstone, 1996; van Eemeren & Grootendorst, 1993; Walton, 1985). Rather than limiting it to the case in which one abuses another by name calling or other strategies, Whately, following Locke's lead, 'finds this form of argument quite legitimate in proving that the adversary is bound to admit the conclusion which follows from his principles, but fallacious if used to prove the proposition absolutely and universally' (Hitchcock, 268). As Walton (1985, 55) indicates, Whately's introduction of this analysis, and the shift from circumstantial premise to universal conclusion is 'seminal'. One of the examples used in discussing this form of circumstantial *ad hominem* argument that has attracted attention concerns the reply of a sportsman who, having been attacked for killing for sport, replies 'why do you feed on the flesh of the harmless sheep and ox?'. The burden of proof is thereby shifted to the accusers, who may then reply that such killing is needed lest the animals overrun the planet. Whately avers that the true reason, 'gratification of the palate' is one which the accusers would rarely admit (1857, 238). In this case, the sportsman is alluding to an inconsistency between the accusation and the action of the persons bringing it forward. To disprove the alleged inconsistency, the accusers must bring forward their own claims and thereby assume a burden of proof. In recent treatments of the example, Walton (1985, 1987) notes that Boole objected on the ground that there is no proven inconsistency between eating meat and accusing a hunter of killing for sport, and that hence the rejoinder is not an adequate response to a personal attack. While the analysis is more detailed than is necessary to review here, the conclusion Walton draws is instructive:

> So who really committed the *ad hominem* fallacy, the sportsman or the critic? The answer is that it all depends on how you describe the propositions that go together to make up the alleged inconsistency. Described one way, the sportsman comes out right, described another, the propositions make the critic's argument come out right. What you have to do in order to untangle the disputation . . . is to formulate precisely the propositions. (1985, 57)

While Whately might not agree with the criticism of his example, he would applaud the procedure recommended for determining the right answer. Given his nominalist bias towards precise understanding of terms, he would do no less in a similar circumstance.

Whately includes 'shifting ground' as a fallacy within the category of irrelevant conclusions. In his view, this is one of the most frequent 'dodges' of an advocate who finds himself faced with giving up his position. Rather than admit the weakness in the argument, the advocate merely offers another rationale that shifts attention away from the original point. A variant of this fallacy occurs when a person shifts from an attack on one premise to another, without completing the initial refutation: '*And besides*', is an expression one may hear from a disputant who is proceeding to a fresh argument, when he cannot establish, and yet will not abandon, his first' (1857, 240-41). Similarly, advocates often mistake what it is that should be proven with respect to a claim's possibility, probability, or necessity. Showing something to be possible when it should be argued that it is probable, or arguing that something should be necessary when probability will suffice leads audiences astray. These issues are more properly discussed as errors in strategy, rather than discrete errors in reasoning from a premise to a conclusion. Thus, it is difficult to maintain 'shifting ground' in its various guises as a specific fallacy. While Whately is correct in suggesting that this kind of argument frequently occurs, and that it often is more successful than it should be, his classification of the strategies as fallacies is inappropriate.

The 'fallacy of objections' is a clearer instance of drawing an irrelevant conclusion from the mere presence of objections against a specific claim. In offering advice to young Christians (and it should be noted that most students were Christians), Whately cautions his readers to be wary of 'anti-Christians' who raise objections for which there is no satisfactory answer. What should, in his view, be recalled is that the weight of objections lies in the opposite direction: 'there are infinitely more, and stronger objections against the supposition that the Christian Religion is of *human* origin' (1857, 242). In a comment that has relevance for our present-day, Whately goes on to observe that this fallacy is the province of 'bigoted anti-innovators, who oppose all reforms and alterations indiscriminately' (1857, 243). Recognizing the contingent nature of many claims, Whately notes that objections may be raised on either side of a policy. In the instance of the policy of transporting prisoners to Australia (and Whately cannot resist adding a political observation based on his own negative response to the policy), he notes that those who defend the policy typically raise objections to any substitute plan that is offered, without considering that while no plan is perfect, theirs may be least perfect of them all: 'the *best* must be open to *some* objections, though the very *worst* is much *less* objectionable than Transportation' (1857, 243).

An advocate who raises objections, however, also may be correct. That is, to object is not the fallacy, but to reason from that process to a conclusion that is not supported by the argument is fallacious. An astute advocate may mislead an audience by showing that an objection is correctly raised, and thereby conclude that an entire project or work is worthy of rejection. Whately suggests that this is valid only in the instance of probable reasoning, wherein weakening one of the links in a chain, or in a set of circumstances being added together, will thus weaken the conclusion. In an illustration that fits within the fallacy of composition as well, Whately suggests that an objection that answers to only a part of the whole does not necessarily mean the whole is therefore unworthy and to conclude otherwise is to err in reasoning. He cautions advocates against 'maintaining too much' as many of their points may be open to refutation, and hence jeopardize the value of the argument as a whole: 'The Quakers would perhaps before now have succeeded in doing away with our superfluous and irreverent oaths, if they had not, besides many valid and strong arguments, adduced so many that are weak and easily refuted' (1857, 246). He also cautions advocates against misleading an audience by suppressing the conclusion of an argument. He notes that audiences normally will follow the speaker's assertion that a particular premise leads to a conclusion, and if there is a long chain of reasoning in between, the audience may be less able to detect whether that conclusion has in fact been reached. Not presenting the conclusion or illustrating the connection between premise and conclusion gives the dishonest advocate an advantage, as the audience is more likely to assume that the conclusion is fairly arrived at. The major value in the discussion of objections, as suggested above, is not in their connection with fallacies in reasoning. Whately takes a broader view of fallacy in considering material fallacies than he does in his consideration of logical and semi-logical fallacies. Instead, the value lies in his general advice about how disputants may deceive and mislead, even unintentionally, their audiences.

Assessing Whately's contribution

Whately did advance the study of logical, semi-logical and material fallacies. As noted, his *Logic* was responsible for a reinvigoration of interest in the subject. Thus, as a general resource for scholars and students alike in the nineteenth century, Whately's treatment stood the test of time. However uneven and ill-considered some of his examples and types are, Whately offers to his students a sound introduction to the typical kinds of illicit arguments they will encounter. He is realistic enough to know that his classification scheme is not perfect, but he defends it as at least grounded in the principles of logic, rather than simply offering a laundry-list of fallacious argument types. Schmidt has argued that Whately's account is flawed in one significant respect: the indeterminacy of 'to which genus each *kind* of fallacy should be referred' (Whately 1857, 174) is not supported by clear reasoning (Schmidt, 62). On the contrary, as suggested in the discussion of calculation of probabilities, Whately does offer a sound

111

rationale for his claim that an argument may be assigned arbitrarily to one genus or another. The calculation process, which is treated as a material fallacy, also can be considered as a semi-logical fallacy of composition or division. Thus, fallacies may be not only subject to arbitrary reclassification in terms of the various kinds within a genus, but also may be seen as associated with more than one genus. Whately also, as Hamblin suggests, advances the discussion in listing 'logical fallacies' as the initial genus (Hamblin, 195). This is a product of systematizing the classification scheme as one grounded in the principles of logic. If one starts from valid reasoning as that which follows accepted rules, then invalid reasoning represents a departure from that principle. Hamblin (173-75) also credits Whately for recognizing the relevance of material fallacies such as the *ad hominem* and *ad verecundiam* in relation to the shifting of the burden of proof. As Hamblin (175) and Walton (1992, 10) suggest, and the above analysis confirms, the implications of this connection are not worked out in any detail.

While it would not be fair to say that Whately was the most significant writer on fallacies in the nineteenth century, it is fair to suggest that his treatment is generally sound and merits the attention of any scholar wishing to extend the definition of specific fallacies or their overall classification. The more recent recasting of informal reasoning in dialectical terms (for example, by van Eemeren and Grootendorst) moves the analysis away from the perspective Whately offers. While the jury is still out with respect to this shift in emphasis, Whately's contribution remains a valuable resource for students of argumentation.

References

Akenson, Donald H (1981), *A Protestant in Purgatory: Richard Whately, Archbishop of Dublin*, Archon Books: Hamden, CT.

Campbell, George [1776] (1963), *The Philosophy of Rhetoric*, edited by Lloyd F. Bitzer, Southern Illinois University Press: Carbondale, IL.

Carney, James D., and Richard K. Scheer (1964), *Fundamentals of Logic*, Macmillan Company: New York.

Copleston, Edward (1809), *The Examiner Examined or Logic Vindicated*, Oxford University Press: Oxford.

Eemeren, Frans H. van, and Rob Grootendorst (1992), *Argumentation, Communication, and Fallacies: A Pragma-Dialectical Perspective*, Lawrence Erlbaum: Hillsdale, NJ.

Eemeren, Frans H. van, and Rob Grootendorst (1993), *The History of the Argumentum ad Hominem since the Seventeenth Century*, in E. C. W. Krabbe, R. J. Dalitz, and P. A. Smith (eds.), *Essays in Honor of Else M. Barth*, Amsterdam and Atlanta, GA.

Evra, James van (1984), 'Richard Whately and the Rise of Modern Logic', *History and Philosophy of Logic*, Vol. 5, pp. 1-18.

Fearnside, W. Ward, and William B. Holther (1959), *Fallacy: The Counterfeit of Argument*, Prentice-Hall: Englewood Cliffs, NJ.

Gillies, John (1797), *Aristotle's Ethics and Politics, Comprising his Practical Philosophy Translated from the Greek: Illustrated by Introductions and Notes; The Critical History of his Life; and A New Analysis of his Speculative Works*, London.

Hamblin, C. L. (1970), *Fallacies*, Methuen & Co.: London.

Hansen, Hans V. (1995), 'Whately and the Burden of Proof', paper presented at the Ontario Philosophical Society, University of Windsor.

Hansen, Hans V. (1996), 'Whately on the *ad Hominem*: A liberal exegesis', *Philosophy and Rhetoric*, Vol. 29, pp. 400-415.

Hitchcock, David (1992), 'Relevance', *Argumentation*, Vol. 6, pp. 251-70.

Howell, Wilbur Samuel (1971), *Eighteenth-century British Logic and Rhetoric*, Princeton University Press: Princeton, NJ.

Johnstone, Henry W., Jr. (1996), 'Locke and Whately on the Argument *ad Hominem'*, *Argumentation*, Vol. 10, pp. 89-97.

Jongsma, Calvin (1982), *Richard Whately and the Revival of Syllogistic Logic in Great Britain in the Early Nineteenth Century*, Ph.D. diss., University of Toronto.

Jongsma, Calvin (1983), 'Richard Whately's role in Great Britain in the Early Nineteenth Century', Birth of Mathematical Logic conference, Fredonia, NY.

Kirwan, Richard (1807), *Logick: or An Essay on the Elements, Principles, and Different Modes of Reasoning*, London.

Lindsay, Thomas (1871), On Recent Logical Speculation in England, in *System of Logic and History of Logical Doctrines*, edited by Friedrich Ueberweg, translated by T. Lindsay, Longmans, Green: London.

McKerrow, Raymie E. (1975), Introduction, Whately R. [1827], *Elements of Logic*, Scholars' Facsimiles and Reprints: Delmar, NY.

McKerrow, Raymie E. (1978), 'Method of composition: Whately's Earliest Rhetoric', *Philosophy and Rhetoric*, Vol. 11, pp. 43-58.

McKerrow, Raymie E. (1987), 'Richard Whately and the Revival of Logic in Nineteenth-Century England', *Rhetorica*, Vol. 5, pp. 163-85.

Schmidt, Michael F. (1986), 'On the Classification of Fallacies', *Informal Logic*, Vol. 8, pp. 57-66.

Walton, Douglas N. (1985), *Arguer's Position: A Pragmatic Study of Ad Hominem Attack, Criticism, Refutation, and Fallacy*, Greenwood Press: Westport, CT.

Walton, Douglas N.(1987), 'The ad Hominem Argument as an Informal Fallacy', *Argumentation*, Vol. 1, pp. 317-31.

Walton, Douglas N. (1992), *The Place of Emotion in Argument*, Pennsylvania State University Press: University Park, PA.

Whately-Hawkins Correspondence, Oriel College, London, IV, BPD 6813, # 343.

Whately, Richard [1826] (1827), *The Elements of Logic*, 2nd ed., J. Mawman: London.

Whately, Richard (1857), *The Elements of Logic*, 9th ed., Boston: James Munroe and Company: Boston.

9   Jeremy Bentham's *Handbook of Political Fallacies*

Rob Grootendorst

Introduction

In this chapter, I will discuss Jeremy Bentham's contribution to the study of political fallacies.[1] The subject of 'political fallacies' is a neglected area in the professional literature on argumentation.[2] Except for Bentham's *Handbook of Political Fallacies (Handbook)*, no monograph treats political fallacies systematically as a topic in its own right.[3] Bentham's book did not receive the attention and appreciation it deserves. In some respects, it is a misinterpreted and misunderstood book, even by people who praise it. One of the main mistakes is that Bentham's book is taken to be a rhetorical treatise. I will argue that it is essentially dialectical in nature and try to show that, from a pragma-dialectical perspective, it is a valuable contribution to the study of political fallacies.

The history of the *Handbook of Political Fallacies*

The English philosopher Jeremy Bentham (1748-1832) was born in London and studied at Queen's College in Oxford. He is known as the 'Father of Utilitarianism', a theory influenced by the ideas of David Hume and inspired by Joseph Priestley's principle of 'the greatest happiness for the greatest number'. Bentham's ideas about political, economic, judicial, and educational reform are based upon this principle. As Harald A. Larrabee, the editor of the *Handbook of Political Fallacies*, writes, 'nearly all of the improvements in the social and political life of England between 1825 and 1870 are traceable to him or his followers' (1971, v).[4]

Bentham's *The Book of the Fallacies*, as the *Handbook* was called originally, was written out of dissatisfaction with political practice in late eighteenth and early nineteenth century England. Bentham discovered how very many ways there were by which a clearly beneficial measure could be check-mated in a political assembly, especially by using the sort of specious arguments called fallacies: the unsound, illogical contentions which might nevertheless be easily accepted as sound by the unwary.

Bentham had planned the book since 1808, but the English edition was not published until 1824. First, in 1816, a French edition was published, freely edited and translated from Bentham's unfinished notes by Pierre Étienne-Louis Dumont, a Swiss writer and former Protestant clergyman, and a pupil of Bentham's. The title of the French edition was *Traité des sophismes politiques*. The English edition was prepared under Bentham's supervision from his unfinished papers by Peregrine Bingham the Younger, who was assisted by Francis Place and John Stuart Mill.[5]

In 1826, a twenty eight page summary of *The Book of Fallacies* was published as a 'Prefatory Treatise on Political Fallacies' in *Parliamentary History and Review*, a new and ambitious periodical, edited by Bingham. Bingham believed that he was supplying his readers 'with an instrument which will, we trust, enable them at once to discover and expose those fallacies, the prevalence of which has but too much contributed to retard political improvement'.

In 1952, the *The Book of Fallacies* got its new title *Handbook of Political Fallacies* in the revised edition by Harold A. Larrabee. According to the Preface, apart from the omission of several outdated passages, the revisions are 'only in matters of style: to a language more acceptable to the modern reader'. [6]

Bentham's definition and classification of fallacies

Bentham defines a fallacy as follows:

> . . . any argument employed or topic suggested for the purpose, or with the probability of producing the effect of deception, or of causing some erroneous opinion to be entertained by any person to whose mind such an argument may have been presented. (*Handbook*, 3)

Fallacies are to be distinguished from what Bentham calls 'vulgar error': 'an opinion which, being thought to be false, is considered in itself only, and not with a view to any consequences which it may produce'. The term 'fallacy', on the other hand, is applied to:

> . . . discourse in any shape considered as having a tendency, with or without design, to cause any erroneous opinion to be embraced, or, through the medium of some erroneous opinion already entertained, a pernicious course of action to be engaged in or persevered in. (*Handbook*, 5-6)

In *The Handbook of Political Fallacies*, only fallacies are discussed which relate to 'the adoption or rejection of some measure of government, whether of legislation or of administration' (*Handbook*, 6). The book describes 'the great variety of tactics employed by the defenders of entrenched abuses when confronted with an obviously good piece of legislation proposed by the reformers' (*Handbook*, vi).

Bentham discusses some thirty of these tactics, which he regards as the principal species of political fallacies. They were grouped by Dumont under three main headings; later, Bingham added a fourth category. The four categories are:

1. fallacies of authority,

2. fallacies of danger,

3. fallacies of delay,

4. fallacies of confusion.[7]

Fallacies of *authority* invoke some sort of higher authority in order to rule out all discussion; their object is to repress, on the ground of the weight of such authority, all exercise of the reasoning faculty. The people who are most likely to abuse authority are, according to Bentham, lawyers (in whose interest it is that the law be as complex as possible and that authority be expensive and difficult to discover), judges, and clergymen.

Fallacies of *danger* excite groundless alarms; their object is to repress, on the ground of danger in various shapes, the discussion of a proposed matter. Fallacies of *delay* postpone debate indefinitely; their object is to postpone such discussion, with a view to eluding it altogether. Fallacies of *confusion* resort to sheer confusion of the issue; their object is to produce, when discussion can no longer be avoided, by way of vague and indefinite generalities, such confusion in the minds of the hearers as to incapacitate them for forming a correct judgment on the question at issue.

Bentham's taxononmy constitutes a hierarchy of lines of defense against proposals for change, a sort of *stasis* (though not identical to the classical *stases* of fact, definition, quality, and procedure). The fallacies of authority come first: If an authority says so, it must be so. The fallacies of danger come next: If the fallacies of authority fail, perhaps people can be frightened into inaction by value-laden descriptions of the harm that will follow from the measures suggested. Then the fallacies of delay follow: If the fallacies of authority and danger both fail, delaying tactics can be used to attenuate the force of any suggestion of change. Finally, all else failing, one may have to allow discussion of the issue at hand. The *stasis* of last resort is confusion, a blurring of the issue, the creation of uncertainty about basic definitions, about what is at stake.

The political influence of the *Handbook*

Bentham's *Handbook of Political Fallacies* has a frankly political purpose: It was to be used as an instrument for the logical dissection of legislative debates, and hence as a weapon for parliamentary reform. Its stated aim is to improve government, that is, to facilitate reform. Bentham assumes that reform will bring about the greatest good for the greatest number by the application of reason, directly (by showing how specific measures promote their ends) and indirectly (by destroying the persuasive force of what

116

he calls 'deceptious arguments'. Bentham states his purpose in the Introduction as follows:

> The business of the present work [is] pointing out the irrelevancy, and thus anticipating and destroying the persuasive force of . . . deceptious arguments . . . Sophistry is a hydra of which, if all the necks could be exposed, the force would be destroyed. (*Handbook*, 7)

In the fifth (and final) part, Bentham concludes:

> . . . in proportion as the acceptance and hence the utterance of these fallacies can be prevented, the understanding of the public will be strenghtened, the morals of the public will be purified, and the practice of government will be improved. (*Handbook*, 228)

In the English politics of Bentham's day, a facade of reasonableness had to be presented to the world, with the result that 'civil life was one great and continuous practical lesson in the art of saying one thing and meaning another' (*Handbook*, xxiii). It was upon this issue of hypocritical fictions and fallacies that Bentham the realist and hater of shams declared war. What Bentham kept repeating was that the cure for all the 'persevering propagation of immorality and misery' through deliberately muddy thinking was clear thinking (*Handbook*, xxiv-xxv).

According to Bingham (and Bentham), the principal reasons for the wide prevalence of bad logic in Parliament are: 'Weakness of intellect; imperfections of language; and the sinister interest of erring individuals'. Bingham writes:

> By a sinister interest, we mean an interest attaching to an individual or class, incompatible with the interests of the community . . . we call an interest confined to himself *sinister*, when it operates in a direction contrary to those which attach to him as a member of the community. (*Handbook*, xx)

Bentham's major insight seems to be that the very possession of political power inhibits the exchange of ideas; it is not in the interest of the 'ins' to promote public discussion of their policies. Thus according to Bentham, the moral, social, and political phenomenon of fallacy can be regarded as the consequence of a disequilibrium of power.

According to Bingham, it is only in a country which has a combination of corrupt influences upon government and a relatively free press that we find political fallacies flourishing:

> In countries where freedom of the press and public discussion do not exist, the interests of the many are openly and unhesitatingly sacrificed by force to the interests of the few: the people have it not in their power to require reasons . . . Reasons must be given, and reasons sufficient to satisfy or deceive a majority of the persons to whom they are addressed . . . The member of the British Parliament . . . must have recourse to every kind of fallacy, and address themselves, when occasion requires it,

117

to the passions, the prejudices, and the ignorance of mankind. (*Parliamentary History and Review* I (1826): 1-4, quoted in the Preface of the *Handbook*, xix-xxi)

Bentham and Bingham seem to have hoped to force a drastic reduction in the volume of illogical nonsense uttered on the floors of the House of Commons and the House of Lords by labelling the various kinds of spurious arguments and fallacies and making it possible to recognize them. In what way did they think that this could be done in practice? Bentham mentions, for example, the possibility of pointing out instances of the use of fallacies in the printed reports or debates of legislative assemblies. But he also envisages a more direct possibility:

> . . . it may be that any legislator anywhere who is so far off his guard as through craft or simplicity to let drop any of these irrelevant and deceptive arguments will be greeted not with the cry of 'Order! Order!' but with voices in scores crying aloud 'Stale! Stale! Fallacy of Authority! Fallacy of Distrust!' and so on. (*Handbook*, 258-259)

In spite of Bentham's rather naive optimism about the power of reason, the publication of his book did not end the use of fallacies in politics either in England or in the rest of the world – as was to be expected. Harold Larrabee observes:

> Many of the concrete abuses against which Bentham crusaded have disappeared; but some of them are still in existence, and many of them will continue to thrive as long as there is a discrepancy between government as it is, and government as it ought to be. (*Handbook*, xxii).

At the same time, Larrabee is also more optimistic about the positive effects on social and political life of Bentham's *Handbook of Political Fallacies* in the long run:

> . . . the value of *The Book of Fallacies* . . . remains and will continue to do so, because it rests upon the lasting framework of human nature: upon man's propensity to defend his selfishness with bad logic, and upon reason as ultimately the cure. As long as there continue to be vested interests which are 'sinister' in their devotion to something less than the well-being of all mankind, and which defend themselves with spurious arguments, Bentham's manual of political fallacies will supply the honest citizen with an invaluable counter-weapon of rational exposure. (*Handbook*, xxv)

Bentham's influence on the study of fallacies

Very few modern authors refer to Bentham when discussing the fallacies either in a theoretical or in a practical way. In his well-known book *Fallacies*, Hamblin says about Bentham's *Handbook of Political Fallacies* that it is 'too specialized' to qualify as a book-length study of the subject as a whole (1970, 10). In his survey of the 'Arguments 'Ad'' (Chapter 4), Hamblin devotes four rather critical pages to Bentham's book.

118

Bentham's fourfold classification Hamblin considers to be 'not of great importance: the individual headings are many and weird' (1970, 166). Moreover, he accuses Bentham of perpetually committing his own fallacies (1970, 169).

Rhetoricians have largely ignored Bentham's book. The exceptions are Perelman and Olbrechts-Tyteca (in *The New Rhetoric*) and Burke (in *A Rhetoric of Motives*), who refer frequently to it. Neither Perelman nor Burke, however, treats Bentham's ideas on fallacies systematically. When Perelman, for example, refers to one of Bentham's fallacies, most of the time he adds that what Bentham calls a fallacy is not a fallacy at all, but a highly effective technique – which is, of course, totally in line with Perelman's rhetorical attitude towards fallacies in general.[8]

In an article published in 1989, Marie J. Secor explains the underestimation of Bentham's book by Perelman and Burke, and the total neglect by other rhetoricians, primarily by referring to Bentham's own view that the *Handbook of Political Fallacies* is a contribution to the field of logic, not to the field of rhetoric (83). She argues that the book is truly rhetorical in nature (84). Her main reasons are that Bentham does not define fallacy formally as a violation of syllogistic procedure; that his focus on arguments in parliamentary debate reveals his interest in deliberative rhetoric; that his methods of analysis are more characteristic of rhetoric than of logic; and that his treatment of the fallacies is itself highly rhetorical (84). She concludes:

> Not only is Bentham's approach of the fallacies best described using terms borrowed from rhetoric rather than logic, his treatise itself shows him an effective practicing rhetorician. (88)

If we view Bentham's book as a contribution to logic, according to Secor, it must be regarded as severely flawed, but if we read his book as a rhetorical text, we can appreciate the way he articulates how people actually do argue. As an example, Secor mentions Bentham's explanation of the fallacy of sham distinctions, versus Perelman's discussion of the 'dissociation of concepts'. She observes:

> Bentham describes the same process that Perelman does, but in specifically political terms . . .; he notices it as a tactic of political debate employed by those opposed to reform . . . Perelman attaches no moral judgment to the practice itself; Bentham is angry, labeling the technique as a fallacy. (89-90)

Another explanation for the neglect of Bentham's book is, according to Secor, the fact that several of Bentham's critics have questioned the existence of the very phenomena he describes – (political) fallacies (92). She quotes J. H. Burns (1974) and also Bentham's editor, Harold Larrabee, who both hint at the conclusion that there can be no such thing as a defensible theory of fallacy. Secor adds that what Bentham calls political fallacies may indeed not be fallacies at all in any logical sense. She writes:

> It may be that fallacies can be better described as rhetorical phenomena – not formal errors in reasoning but appeals based on socially and institutionally created assumptions about what arguers need to do in order to change or defend existing

conditions. Bentham . . . shows how fallacious reasoning is grounded in political, social, and institutional contexts rather than in the formal properties of arguments . . . He seems to be describing the ways in which people argue in many cultures, fields, and forums rather than an aberration of a specific political institution. (93)

A dialectical interpretation of Bentham's fallacies

This quotation from Secor raises a very interesting question about Bentham's book and about the study of fallacies in general: Are the techniques, tactics, and tricks he describes really fallacies? For Bentham himself, of course, they are: They satisfy without any problems the characteristics mentioned in his definition of a fallacy. For the true rhetorician, however, such as Perelman, Burke, and also Secor, the answer is clearly 'No', because rhetorically speaking, Bentham describes effective means of persuasion. For the true logician, the answer is also 'No', because the phenomena described by Bentham clearly do not fit the logical standard definition of a fallacy as an argument that '*seems to be valid* but *is not so*' (Hamblin, 12).[9] Most of the time, no arguments – in the logical sense of premises and a conclusion – are to be found in Bentham's examples.

The rhetorical criticism that Bentham's fallacies are no fallacies but effective means of persuasion, is not very strong because exactly the same could be said – and has been said – about all fallacies. In a purely descriptively rhetorical approach, there is no room for a normative concept such as 'fallacy'. The logical criticism that Bentham's fallacies are no fallacies because they do not fit the logical definition of a fallacy, is not very specific: The same is true for many of the traditional categories listed in the 'Standard Treatment' of fallacies, as described by Hamblin (1970).

In several books and articles, van Eemeren and Grootendorst have tried to show that in a pragma-dialectical approach to argumentation it is possible to analyze most of the traditional fallacies, including the informal fallacies, in a theoretically motivated and systematic way (See, for example, van Eemeren and Grootendorst, 1984, 1987, 1992, and Grootendorst, 1987). In my view, it is quite easy to see how Bentham's four main categories can be analyzed pragma-dialectically.

In the pragma-dialectical ideal model, rules for reasonable discourse are specified as rules for the performance of speech acts in a critical discussion which is designed to resolve a dispute. The rules constitute, so to speak, a code of conduct for reasonable discussants.[10] The rules are instrumental to resolving a dispute and specify, for each stage of the resolution process, what sorts of speech acts can contribute to this.[11]

Each discussion rule is meant to represent a necessary condition for the resolution of a dispute. Taken together, the rules are supposed to constitute a sufficient condition. Any infringement of a discussion rule, whichever party commits it and at whatever stage in the discussion, is a possible threat to the resolution of a dispute and must therefore be regarded as a dialectically incorrect move, or a 'fallacy' in the pragma-dialectical sense.

And now, to come back to my main point in this section: How can Bentham's four main categories of fallacies be translated into pragma-dialectical terms? In other words: Of which rules for critical discussion are his categories violations?

Bentham's fallacies of *authority* are very easily identified as various types of the *argumentum ad verecundiam*, which can be analyzed as violations of three different pragma-dialectical rules. As a violation of rule 2 ('A party that advances a standpoint is obliged to defend it if the other party asks him to do so'), the *ad verecundiam* is an attempt at evading the burden of proof by giving a personal guarantee of the rightness of one's standpoint (see van Eemeren and Grootendorst, 1992, 117-118 and 139). As a violation of rule 4 ('A party may defend his standpoint only by advancing argumentation relating to that standpoint'), it is an attempt at defending one's standpoint by parading one's own qualities instead of advancing arguments (see van Eemeren and Grootendorst 1992, 135-137). And as a violation of rule 7 ('A party may not regard a standpoint as conclusively defended if the defense does not take place by means of an appropriate argumentation scheme that is correctly applied'), it is the inappropriate or incorrect use of the symptomatic argumentation scheme by presenting one's standpoint as right because an authority says it is right (see van Eemeren and Grootendorst, 1992, 161-163 and 167).

Bentham's fallacies of *danger* can be seen as a subspecies of the *argumentum ad populum*, which is (also) a violation of rule 4 because a standpoint is defended by playing on the emotions of the audience (see van Eemeren and Grootendorst, 1992, 134-135). And his fallacies of *confusion* can be seen as special cases of misusing ambiguity or unclearness, which is a violation of rule 10 ('A party must not use formulations that are insufficiently clear or confusingly ambiguous and he must interpret the other party's formulations as carefully and accurately as possible') (see van Eemeren and Grootendorst, 1992, 197-204).

Bentham's fourth category, the fallacies of *delay*, appears more difficult to classify in the pragma-dialectical system. It seems that these fallacies are not violations of any given rule for critical discussion but rather a violation of some higher-order rule, presupposed by the pragma-dialectical first-order rules. This higher-order rule requires people to try to resolve their differences of opinion through critical discussion. Postponing discussion indefinitely, with a view of evading it altogether, clearly is a violation of this rule.[12]

A this point, a sceptic might ask whether it really makes sense to analyze Bentham's political fallacies from a pragma-dialectical perspective. The sceptic might argue that the main purpose of a political debate is not to resolve a dispute, but to win the debate or to please potential voters. If this is right, then it is a serious objection. After all, one is justified in applying the pragma-dialectical rules for critical discussion only if the discourse under consideration is actually aimed at resolving a dispute.[13]

However, I do not think that the sceptic's view is correct. First of all, I doubt whether his rather cynical view does justice to the intentions of all politicians. And furthermore, in a democratic society, politicians – whatever their ulterior motives may be – can accomplish their goals only if they stick to the rules of the game, most of the time. This condition requires that they must act as if they really are aiming at resolving a dispute. If, in fact, that is not the case, they still must pretend that it is and keep up their facade as a reasonable human being. So, whether or not the aim of political discourse really is to resolve a dispute, it is useful to apply the pragma-dialectical rules. And, accordingly, if one or more rules are violated, it is justifiable to identify the violations concerned as fallacies.

Conclusion

Some people seem to believe that there is a special relationship between fallacies and politics. They think that there are such things as 'typically political' fallacies, or that there are fallacies which are committed only by politicians or more frequently by politicians than by other people, or that politicians are more inclined than other people to commit fallacies. My discussion of Bentham's *Handbook of Political Fallacies* does not support this sort of view. On the other hand, I have argued that it is possible to analyze the fallacies politicians do commit as described by Bentham, as fallacies in a pragma-dialectical sense.

Bentham's book suggests, however, also another interpretation of the special relationship between fallacies and politics. Even though there is, theoretically, nothing special about the fallacies committed by politicians, it seems to be of special interest to study them systematically. Because of their position, politicians have a greater responsibility than 'ordinary citizens'. This responsibility does not pertain merely to the economic and social well-being of society and its citizens, but also to the quality of politics itself.

Even people who are more sceptical and less naive than Bentham about the power of reason, may agree with him that politicians, of all people, should not commit fallacies in pursuing their objectives. Where they do, this should be critized publicly. Perhaps politicians can be educated in how to avoid fallacies, and, most certainly, the public can be educated in how to recognize fallacies, by whomever they might be committed.

Notes

1. I would like to thank Hans Hansen and John Woods for their useful comments on an earlier version of this chapter.

2. This is not contradicted by the fact that in many textbooks and monographs on fallacies examples of fallacies committed by politicians are discussed (see, e.g., Copi, 1986; Walton, 1987; and van Eemeren & Grootendorst, 1992).

3. Vedung, 1982 discusses a few fallacies in political discourse, but fallacies are not the main topic of his book. For that matter, it is remarkable that very few books have been published about fallacies in special fields, also other than politics. Fischer, 1971 on historians' fallacies is one of the rare exceptions.

4. Throughout, my discussion of the background of Bentham's *Handbook of Political Fallacies* relies heavily on Larrabee, 1971.

5. Bingham's contribution remains anonymous in the 1824 edition. On the title page it says: '*The Book of Fallacies; from unfinished papers of Jeremy Bentham*, By a Friend'.

6. In what follows, the references to Bentham's *Handbook of Political Fallacies* are to the 1971 Apollo Edition of Larrabee's 1952 edition.

7. The second category (fallacies of danger) was added by Bingham.

8. See, for example, Perelman & Olbrechts-Tyteca's remark about Bentham's fallacy of the fear of innovation (1969, 107). It is, by the way, interesting to read Larrabee's strong rejection of a purely descriptive approach to fallacies as neutral tools for the influencing of human behavior àla Perelman & Olbrechts-Tyteca: '. . . this amoral attitude . . . can be devastating in its consequences when it is carried over into the realm of practical politics . . . The men of this generation have seen with their own eyes what political fallacies can accomplish in the hands of a Dr. Goebbles or a Politburo' (*Handbook*, x).

9. Curiously enough, with respect to the study of fallacies, we find Charles A. Willard among the 'true logicians'. Though he does not mention Bentham, in his book *A Theory of Argumentation*, he advocates reserving the term 'fallacy' to designate 'a narrow range of discourse problems, logical mistakes' whose 'source of authority is Logic' (1989, 222 and 237).

10. In formulating the pragma-dialectical code of conduct for reasonable discussants, van Eemeren and Grootendorst, 1984 borrowed many ideas from Barth and Krabbe's formal dialectics (1982).

11. In van Eemeren and Grootendorst, 1992, ten discussion rules are discussed. In fact, these ten rules represent a simplified version of the more elaborated and theoretically motivated rules discussed in van Eemeren & Grootendorst, 1984.

12. For a discussion of first-order, second-order, and third-order conditions for critical discussion, see van Eemeren and Grootendorst, 1988, and van Eemeren, Grootendorst, Jackson and Jacobs, 1993.

13. If it is not clear whether or not the discourse is really aimed at resolving a difference of opinion, applying the 'strategy of maximally dialectical analysis' can provide a solution. See van Eemeren and Grootendorst, 1992, 105.

References

Barth, E. M., and E. C. W. Krabbe (1982), *From Axiom to Dialogue*, Walter de Gruyter: Berlin.

Bentham, Jeremy [1824] (1971), *Handbook of Political Fallacies*, edited with revisions and Preface by Harold A. Larrabee, Thomas Y. Crowell: New York. First published in 1952 by The Johns Hopkins Press.

Burke, K. (1962), *A Grammar of Motives and a Rhetoric of Motives*, The World Publishing Company: New York.

Burns, J. H. (1974), 'Bentham's Critique of Political Fallacies', in Parekh, Bhikhu C. (ed.), *Jeremy Bentham: Ten Critical Essays*, Cass: London.

Copi, I. M. (1986), *Informal Logic*, Macmillan and Collier: New York.

Eemeren, F. H. van, and R. Grootendorst (1984), *Speech Acts in Argumentative Discussions*, Foris/Mouton de Gruyter, PDA 1: Dordrecht/Berlin.

Eemeren, F. H. van, and R. Grootendorst (1987), 'Fallacies in Pragma-Dialectical Perspective', *Argumentation*, Vol. 1, pp. 283-301.

Eemeren, F. H. van, and R. Grootendorst (1988), 'Rationale for a Pragma-Dialectical Perspective', *Argumentation*, Vol. 2, pp. 271-291.

Eemeren, F. H. van, and R. Grootendorst (1992), *Argumentation, Communication, and Fallacies: A Pragma-Dialectical Perspective*, Lawrence Erlbaum: Hillsdale, NJ.

Eemeren, F. H. van, R. Grootendorst, S. Jacobs, and S. Jackson (1993), *Reconstructing Argumentative Discourse*, University of Alabama Press: Tuscaloosa.

Fischer, D. H. (1971), *Historians' Fallacies*, Routledge and Kegan Paul: London.

Grootendorst, R. (1987), 'Some Fallacies About Fallacies', in Eemeren, F. H. van, *et al.* (eds.), *Argumentation: Across the Lines of Discipline*, Foris: Dordrecht, pp. 331-342.

Hamblin, C. L. (1970), *Fallacies*, Methuen: London.

Larrabee, H. A. (1971), Editor's Preface, in Bentham (1971), v-xxv.

Perelman, Ch., and L. Olbrechts-Tyteca (1958), *La nouvelle rhétorique; Traité de l'argumentation*, Université de Bruxelles: Bruxelles.

Perelman, Ch., and L. Olbrechts-Tyteca (1969), *The New Rhetoric: A Treatise on Argumentation*, translated by John Wilkinson and Purcell Weaver, University of Notre Dame Press: Notre Dame, IN.

Secor, M. J. (1989), 'Bentham's Book of Fallacies: Rhetorician in Spite of Himself', *Philosophy and Rhetoric*, Vol. 22, pp. 83-93.

Vedung, E. (1982), *Political Reasoning*, Sage: Beverly Hills, CA.

Walton, D. N. (1987), *Informal Fallacies*, John Benjamins: Amsterdam.

Willard, Charles A. (1989), *A Theory of Argumentation*, University of Alabama Press: Tuscaloosa.

10 Mill on inference and fallacies

Hans V. Hansen

The first intellectual operation at which I arrived at any proficiency, was dissecting a bad argument, and finding in what part the fallacy lay. (Mill, *Autobiography*, ch. 1, para. 12)

Introduction

It is now one hundred and fifty years since the publication of Mill's monumental work, *A System of Logic* (1843). From that time until ten years ago it had gone from being the most widely studied book on logic to being not only out of print, but unavailable in many university libraries. The revolution in formal logic which began with De Morgan, Boole and Jevons, and culminated in Frege, and Russell and Whitehead, has placed Mill's work much further afar conceptually than it is temporally. Still, it richly repays study – not only for philosophers of science but also for those who are interested in the history of logic.

Since informal logic, as a discipline, is still in its infancy compared, say, to formal logic and epistemology, just what its boundaries are and proper subject matter is have not yet been firmly settled. Certain issues, nevertheless, which have proven of perennial interest to informal logicians and argumentation theorists are also of central concern to Mill in the *Logic*. I shall limit myself to discussing only some of these. A complete review of Mill's importance to the history of informal logic would take us beyond the limits of a chapter-length study.

Charles Hamblin's *Fallacies* is the most important historical study on that subject to be published; however, I disagree with his easy dismissal of Mill's work on the fallacies. Accordingly, I spend most of my efforts below in an attempt to show that Mill, as well as being original, was remarkably sensitive to many of the problems of fallacy theory. Since Mill's theory of inference is the key to his discussion of the fallacies, I begin by offering an outline of his views on logic and inference. Readers will find that my purpose is to explain Mill's position in as much detail as space allows rather than to point out inconsistencies and other flaws, of which there are not a few. Some of the recent critical studies are indicated in the notes.

Mill's theory of inference

The proper subject of logic, says Mill, is proof (*A System of Logic*, II,i,1).[1] He means 'proof' to be understood broadly to include not only deduction and generalization, but observation as well (V,iv,1). This conception of logic is wider than most modern conceptions which restrict logic to a study of the premiss-conclusion relation only. For Mill, however, logic is no less than scientific method itself, and this is indicated in the subtitle of the *Logic* which describes the work as being *A Connected View of the Principles of Evidence and the Methods of Scientific Investigation*. Mill did not envision a distinction between the logic of the sciences and the logic of everyday affairs. He thinks that 'a complete logic of the sciences would also be a complete logic of practical business and common life' (III,i,2). Nevertheless, Mill takes as the model of good argumentation what he believes to be correct scientific practice. Keeping in mind Mill's broad notion of logic turns out to be important if we are to understand the charge that the syllogism contains a *petitio*. It is equally important, as we shall see, for understanding his approach to the fallacies.

Kinds of inferences

Whately's *Elements of Logic*, which preceded Mill's own book by less than twenty years, and which Mill had favorably reviewed in 1828,[2] takes the view that there is only one kind of inference, or reasoning.

> In every instance in which we *reason*, in the strict sense of the word, *i.e.*, make use of arguments, whether for the sake of refuting an adversary, or of conveying instruction, or of satisfying our own minds on any point, whatever may be the subject we are engaged on, a certain process takes place in the mind which is one and the same in all cases, provided it be correctly conducted. (Whately, ch. I, sec. 1)

This 'certain process' is syllogistic reasoning: '. . . all reasoning, on whatever subject, is one and the same process', says Whately, 'which may be clearly exhibited in the form of syllogisms' (Whately, Dissertation, ch. I, sec. 1). An interesting consequence of this view is that all correct reasoning involves general propositions since only syllogisms with at least one general premiss can be valid. Early in his career Mill endorsed Whately's deductivism (Ryan, 6) but he rejects it entirely in the *Logic* where he maintains that although there are three discernable kinds of inference in use, at bottom, two of them are analyzable into the third kind, which is reasoning from particulars to particulars. Hence, Mill rejects Whately's position that correct reasoning depends on generalizations.

Logicians now distinguish deduction and induction on the basis of whether the inference is intended to be necessary or probabilistic. Mill, however, adopts a version of the classical distinction which simply said that deduction (ratiocination) is inference from generals to particulars, and induction is inference from particulars to generals. Mill attempts to improve on this by allowing there to be inductions from general propositions to more general propositions, and also deductions to generalizations provided that the conclusion is less general than the most general premiss of the deduction. The third kind of reasoning identified, to which Mill ascribes fundamental importance, is inference from particulars to particulars. The existence and legitimacy of such inferences are defended on two related grounds. First, we 'perpetually' do make such inferences, and second, brutes and infants reason successfully without having access to generalizations (which depend on language); hence, there are inferences from particulars to particulars (II,iii,3). Mill thinks such reasoning 'is not only valid but . . . the foundation of both' (II,i,3) induction and deduction as well; it is a 'fiat of logicians' (II,iii,3) that insists that every inference must involve a generalization.

Let us first see how particulars-to-particular inferences are related to induction. No generalizations are needed for such inferences, but, nevertheless, whenever a set of particular premisses justifies another particular proposition it equally justifies a generalization (III,i,2; II,iii,5). For example, if there is sufficient evidence from observation of particulars for the proposition that Bentham is mortal, the same evidence will support, to the same degree, the generalization that all men are mortal. This claim, that evidence indifferently supports, to the same degree, both particular propositions and their generalizations, allows one to see the proper place for deduction in the overall reasoning process.

An induction from particulars to generals, followed by a syllogistic process from those generals to other particulars, is a form in which we may always state our reasonings if we please. It is not a form in which we *must* reason, but it is a form in which we *may* reason, and into which it is indispensable to throw our reasoning, when there is any doubt of its validity . . . (II,iii,5)

In other words, if a certain particular proposition, C, is justly inferred from other particular propositions, then the generalization of C, C^*, also inferable from the same evidence, will serve as a major premiss in syllogisms from which we may deduce other particular propositions. Should any of these syllogistic conclusions turn out to be false this will show that the inference to the generalization, C^*, was not warranted and, therefore, also show that the inference to the new particular, C, was unwarranted. Deduction has thus been allocated an ancillary function, viz. that of serving to check non-deductive inferences.[3]

Exorcizing the petitio in the syllogism

Early in the *Logic* (I,vi,4) Mill draws a distinction between verbal and real propositions which corresponds roughly to Kant's analytic-synthetic judgment distinction. Accordingly, the inference in an argument may be seen as either verbal (analytic) or real (synthetic) depending on whether the corresponding conditional is a verbal or a real proposition. *Real* inferences have both a semantic and an epistemic component.

Semantically, real inferences are those whose corresponding conditionals are not tautologies. Epistemically, the demand is that the inference lead from old (known) to new truths (III,ii,1). Mill mistakenly took these two requirements to be co-extensional as his discussion of the syllogism reveals.

Mill agrees that on the received interpretation – *not* his – of general propositions, the syllogism, when considered as a proof, contains a *petitio*. To see what he means by this we must consider his account of the *petitio* fallacy. With a qualification, he accepts Whately's definition of *petitio principii*. It is:

> the fallacy 'in which the premise either appears manifestly to be the same as the conclusion, or is actually proved from the conclusion, or is such as would naturally and properly be so proved'. By the last clause I presume is meant, that it is not susceptible of any other proof; for otherwise, there would be no fallacy. (V,vii,2)[4]

The part of the definition that is relevant to Mill's claim that on the received view the syllogism contains a *petitio* fallacy, is the third disjunct which Mill rewords to mean that the premiss could not be proved in any other way than by appeal to the conclusion. This kind of *petitio* has become known as circular reasoning and, in part, its identification involves the claim that, contrary to appearances, the argument depends on but two mutually supportive inferences. It is not denied that the conclusion follows from the premises, but it is claimed that at least one of the premises, to be acceptable, could be inferred (at least in part) only from the conclusion.

The received interpretation of general propositions (e.g., 'All men are mortal') that Mill rejected is that they are conjunctions of singular propositions (e.g., Man *a* is mortal & Man *b* is mortal & . . . etc.). On this interpretation such propositions can be known true only if each of the singular propositions, into which it is analyzable, is known to be true. Thus, a syllogism, for example,

Major:	All men are mortal
Minor:	*Socrates is a man*
Conclusion:	Socrates is mortal

if given as a proof, will be a circular argument. This is because the conclusion ('Man *s* is mortal') is really evidence for the major premiss. In other words, the major presupposes the conclusion. But in a proof the premises must be more certain than the conclusion to be proved; therefore, no premiss may presuppose the conclusion.

This kind of objection against the syllogism has a long history. Whately was familiar with it and tried to meet it by distinguishing what is asserted from what is involved by implication in the premises of a syllogism, thereby allowing that syllogistic reasoning could lead to new knowledge. Mill quickly dismisses Whately's suggestion, saying that it has no 'serious scientific value' (II,iii,2). If Mill had allowed Whately his distinction, the way would be open to saying that there was syllogistic reasoning which satisfied the epistemic dimension of inference and not the semantic one, and the two requirements would be brought into conflict. A second objection, related to the first, is that if general propositions really are correctly analyzed as shorthand for long conjunctions, then the conclusion follows directly, by conjunctive severance, from the major premiss without the aid of the minor premiss. On the received interpretation of general propositions, then, the syllogism is an argument with a superfluous premiss.

Mill's own view of general propositions, when combined with the semantic and epistemic requirements that real inferences must satisfy, attempts to cast the syllogism, and reasoning in general, in an entirely different light. He holds that a generalization is more than a convenient summary of particular observations: it is also a 'process of inference'. 'The results of many observations and inferences, and instructions for making innumerable inferences in unforeseen cases, are comprehended into one short sentence' (II,iii,3). This means that a proposition is not, upon analysis, merely the assertion of a conjunction of singular propositions. It is, rather, several things.

First, a generalization (e.g., 'All men are mortal') is a statement that summarizes observations that some (perhaps a great many) men are mortal; second, it is a claim that one has inferred that all similar things (men, that is) will be mortal as well. The generalization encompasses, for example, President Clinton, but since his demise has yet to be observed his mortality is not claimed as evidence for the generalization. Still, the proposition includes the President's mortality by inference because he is like the others whose mortality has been observed. Third, not only do generalizations *contain* an inference, they are formulae which legitimize further inferences from particulars to particulars. A famous passage deserves repeating:

All inference is from particulars to particulars: General propositions are merely registers of such inferences already made, and short formulae for making more: The major premiss of a syllogism, consequently, is a formula of this description: and the conclusion is not an inference drawn *from* the formula, but an inference drawn *according to* the formula: the real logical antecedent, or premiss, being the particular facts from which the general proposition was collected by induction. (II,iii,4)

If generalizations are understood this way, the *petitio*-in-the-syllogism problem evaporates. The conclusion is inferred from observations that did not include President Clinton and so his mortality cannot be said to be presupposed. Furthermore, the role of the minor premiss is restored and the syllogism now contains a real inference. The real inference is from the singular proposition, 'Socrates is a man', to 'Socrates is mortal', via the generalization.

There is more here than a superficial resemblance to Toulmin's jurisprudential model of argument (Ryan, 32). Toulmin's basic model analyzes arguments into three components: data, conclusion and warrant. Warrants serve to link the data with the conclusion; they provide answers to the question, 'How do you get there?', i.e., from the data to the conclusion.

[T]he warrant is, in a sense, incidental and explanatory, its task being simply to register explicitly the legitimacy of the step involved and to refer it back to the larger class of steps whose legitimacy is being presupposed. (Toulmin, 100)

129

Mill and Toulmin see the generalizations (or warrants) as being inessential to arguments, but they agree that they can be provided to show that the process from data to conclusion is legitimate. There are, of course, substantial differences between the two views. Toulmin does not require that all warrants must be generalizations as does Mill, and Toulmin's theory includes certain unscientific and relativistic ('field dependent', he calls them) elements that would be anathema to Mill.

Mill on the fallacies

Very little has been written about Mill's work on the fallacies, and two recent studies of Mill's philosophy,[5] which otherwise devote considerable space to an examination of the *Logic*, omit discussion altogether of the nearly one hundred pages of Book V, 'Of Fallacies'. One explanation of this lacuna is provided by Hamblin (176) who thought Mill's *Logic* was long-winded and that his discussion of fallacies was not as original as it appeared to be. However, I am inclined to explain it by the disinterest that contemporary philosophers have in fallacy theory, not by any inferiority of Mill's Book V in relation to the rest of the *Logic*.

The importance of the fallacies

Mill defends the inclusion of the book on fallacies in the *Logic* on three separate grounds. First, 'The philosophy of reasoning, to be complete, ought to comprise the theory of bad as well as of good reasoning' (V,i,1). However, there is more than completeness at stake since Mill invokes the traditional maxim that 'we never really know what a thing is, unless we are able to give a sufficient account of its opposite' (V,v,1). We will know more, goes the argument, about reasoning and proof if we can learn something about their opposites. Those who despair the value of fallacy studies because they think the alleged symmetry between good and bad reasoning does not exist, will likely be unpersuaded by this argument.[6]

   The second reason for the inclusion of the book on fallacies is that people actually do commit fallacies with regrettable frequency. Even among the educated, those who know the principles of good reasoning, 'such erroneous inferences, producing corresponding errors in conduct, are lamentably frequent (V,i,1). Knowledge of the fallacies, then, is to serve as a kind of safety valve in our reasoning, not because such knowledge is sufficient for us to reason well but because, despite our best attempts, we have a disposition to err, and familiarity with the fallacies will help us keep this disposition in check. Thus, a study of the fallacies should lead to an improvement in our overall reasoning performance. This is a traditional argument for the importance of the fallacies and it is used, or alluded to, by Aristotle (175a5-17), Arnauld and Nicole (part III, ch. 19) and Whately (ch. III, intro.) among others.

   Mill's third reason for including the book on fallacies is simply that his conception of logic is wider than that of any of his predecessors and so there are new fallacies, especially of induction, to be explained and classified. Mill is not the first to discuss inductive fallacies. The Port-Royal logicians include a version of hasty generalization in their review of fallacies (Arnauld and Nicole, 264), and before that Francis Bacon had announced that 'the doctrine of Idols is to the Interpretation of Nature what the doctrine of the refutation of Sophisms is to common Logic' (Bacon, xl). Nevertheless, Mill is the first philosopher of the modern era to give a systematic discussion of inductive fallacies.

Mill's concept of 'fallacy'

Mill definition of 'fallacy' is not as narrow as the traditional definition of it as an argument 'that *seems to be valid* but *is not* so' (Hamblin, 12). This reflects his wider conception of logic. Although most of the fallacies Mill discusses are bad arguments, bad observations and uncritical belief acceptance are also meant to fit under the definition.

> To examine . . . [i] the various kinds of apparent evidence which are not evidence at all, and of [ii] apparently conclusive evidence which do not really amount to conclusiveness, is the object of that part of our inquiry into which we are about to enter. (V,i,3)

Mill here divides fallacies into two broad classes. In the first class there are only what he calls fallacies of simple inspection, or fallacies *a priori*. These are beliefs rather than arguments and they are fallacies whether or not they are used as evidence for other beliefs. The second class consists of inferential fallacies, i.e., inferences which really have less support than they appear to have.

Mill places two important restrictions on fallacies which makes his treatment of them considerably more sophisticated than most earlier accounts. The first of these restrictions is that casual mistakes – mistakes due to haste or inattention – are not fallacies because they are not the result of using a wrong method or misusing a right method but rather the result of using no method at all. To count as a fallacy, thinks Mill, a mistake must be a failed effort to get things right. Thus, casual mistakes 'do not call for philosophical analysis or classification; theoretical considerations can throw no light upon the means of avoiding them' (V,i,2). The identification of casual errors as distinct from fallacies allows Mill to delimit the class of fallacies; and the basis on which the distinction is drawn – the role of method – indicates that Millean fallacies are mistakes of method; in particular, fallacies in the method of proof.

Mill second restriction on the extension of 'fallacy' is the exclusion of the *moral* causes of error from fallacies. What he means by a 'moral cause' is what we mean by a psychological cause. Such a cause is some state or disposition which influences our reasoning such that we are more likely to commit fallacies. It may be either an indifference to truth which prevents 'the mind from collecting the proper evidences, or from applying to them the test of a legitimate and rigid induction' (V,i,3), or bias, which places 'the intellectual grounds of belief in an incomplete or distorted shape before [our] eyes' (V,i,3). In either case such psychological causes are remote, or *predisposing* causes of the mistake, not the immediate or *exciting* causes in which the fallacy consists. Thus, the explanation of why someone committed a certain fallacy may involve reference to 'moral' causes, but the explanation of what the fallacy is will be given in logical terms, not psychological ones.

Mill's exclusion of psychological causes from the study of fallacies does not come out of nowhere. The *Port Royal Logic* (1662) had introduced a number of sophisms of 'self-love, interest and passion' which resulted from the will's dissoluteness, that is, its negative effect on our judgment of objective matters. Thus, thinking something true (false) because it is to your advantage (disadvantage), or thinking well (ill) of someone because we love (hate) her, count as sophisms for the Port-Royal logicians (Arnauld and Nicole, Part III, ch. 20). Mill's insistence on separating the psychological factors that lead us to make mistakes from the intellectual or logical factors in which the mistakes consist anticipates other late nineteenth century efforts to free logic from psychology.

Classification of fallacies

The problem of classification has dogged fallacy theory since its earliest days. Aristotle admits that more than one classification is possible (168a17-18) and De Morgan began his chapter on fallacies with a sentence that has since become famous: 'There *is* no such thing as a classification of the ways in which men may arrive at an error; it is much to be doubted whether there ever *can be*' (De Morgan, 237). This remark is often taken to be about fallacies in general but, in fact, what concerns De Morgan in this passage is *inferential fallacies*. His point is that actual bad inferences do not, of themselves, suggest any classification in preference to others. Interestingly, Mill does not deny this; he seems to be in complete agreement with De Morgan when he writes,

> The things . . . which are not evidence of any given conclusion, are manifestly endless, and this negative property, having no dependence on any positive ones, cannot be made the groundwork of a real classification. (V,i,3)

Thus, Mill holds that it is only against the background of a theory of proof that classification will be possible. Even so, a fallacious argument may equally well be put in more than one class, and its assignment to a particular class will be arbitrary (V,ii,3). As we will see, Mill's theory of proof presents, almost naturally, his categories of fallaciousness.

For Mill, fallacy can occur in any of the three parts of proof: observation, generalization and deduction.

> [W]e, who profess to treat of the whole process, [not just deduction] must add to our directions for performing it rightly, warnings against performing it wrongly in any of its parts; whether the ratiocinative or experimental portion of it be in fault, or the fault lie in dispensing with ratiocination and induction altogether. (V,i,1)

Accordingly, we would expect that Mill will give us a threefold classification of fallacies corresponding to each of the three elements in the process of proof. In effect, just such a division constitutes the core of Mill's classification, but his inclusion of two other less important categories obscures this basic arrangement.

132

Mill begins by distinguishing non-inferential from inferential fallacies and then pursues further divisions within the inferential category. (In showing Mill's classification I have indicated his placement of familiar fallacies.)

A natural way to discuss these five classes of fallacies is to imitate Mill's process of proof. Thus we begin with fallacies of observation, generalization, and ratiocination. There remain two classes: a catch-all category called 'fallacies of confusion', which also admits the traditional fallacies which have not found a home under any of the three main headings, and the non-inferential fallacies *a priori*.

Fallacies of observation

Those who hold to the standard definition of 'fallacy', or some other purely inferential account of fallacies, will balk at the idea that there are fallacies of observation. But Mill's conception of logic includes observation and, therefore, on his view there will be errors of observation which qualify for fallacy status.

Mill first divides this category into fallacies of non-observation, which consist in overlooking something that should not have been neglected, and fallacies of mal-observation, which occur when 'something is not simply unseen, but seen wrong' (V,iv,1). Non-observation fallacies allow a further distinction between overlooking instances and overlooking circumstances. In the case of instances having been overlooked, Mill admits that such fallacies may equally be considered as inferential fallacies (V,iv,2). His example is that of considering only the successful predictions of a fortune teller and ignoring the erroneous ones. It is an inferential fallacy because it is based on insufficient evidence; but it is also an observation fallacy because there was other evidence that should have been considered. The fallacies of observation which overlook circumstances, however, are cases where at least some of the observations are false; for example, 'observing' that the fortune teller has made a correct prediction when in fact he was working in collusion with someone who provided his information, would make any argument relying on the premiss 'he *predicted* so and so . . .' a fallacy of observation.

The problem with non-observation fallacies is that there is something unseen which renders the data either unrepresentative or false. Fallacies of mal-observation, on the other hand, are characterized not as there being something *unseen* but rather as there being something *seen wrong*. How could this happen? Mill explains as follows:

> Perception being infallible evidence of what is really perceived, the error now under consideration can be committed no otherwise than by mistaking for perception what is in fact inference. (V,iv,5)

Mill's example is of the pre-Copernicans who 'fancied they *saw* the sun rise and set, [and] the stars revolve in circles round the pole' (V,iv,5). They committed a fallacy of mal-observation because what they thought they *saw* was not only something they *inferred* but something they *misinferred*.

Mill is aware that two of his three kinds of observation fallacies could as easily be classified as fallacies of generalization. Why, then, does he bother with the distinction

133

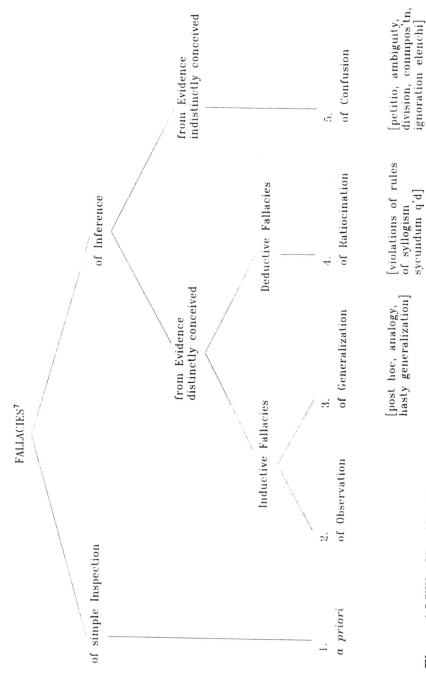

Figure 1 Mill's Classification

FALLACIES[7]

of simple Inspection

of Inference

1.
a priori

from Evidence
distinctly conceived

from Evidence
indistinctly conceived

Inductive Fallacies

Deductive Fallacies

5.
of Confusion

2.
of Observation

3.
of Generalization

4.
of Ratiocination

[post hoc, analogy,
hasty generalization]

[violations of rules
of syllogism
sycundum q'd]

[petitio, ambiguity,
division, conmpos'tn,
ignoration elenchi]

between observation and generalization fallacies? Mill answers that it is convenient 'to make only one class of all the inductions of which the error lies in not sufficiently ascertaining the facts on which the theory is grounded' (V,ii,2). Mal-observation fallacies, for example, really contain two inferences: a main inference which links the avowed evidence with the conclusion, but also an inference which led to the acceptance of that evidence in the first place. The second inference, which leads to the establishment of evidence for a generalization, will count as an observation fallacy.

Whately had maintained that a fallacy could lie either in the undue acceptance of premises, or in the reasoning from those premises, and accordingly introduced a distinction, still used, between material and logical fallacies. A material fallacy is a deductively valid argument which is still a fallacy, either because the premises are unduly assumed or because the argument is an *ignoratio elenchi*. Logical fallacies, on the other hand, consist simply of those arguments which satisfy the standard definition of 'fallacy' (Whately, ch. III, secs. 2 and 3). Broadening Whately's idea suitably to include inductive as well as deductive arguments, we may classify fallacies either as containing an inferential mistake (inductive or deductive) or as arguments whose fallaciousness must be explained as lying outside the inference proper; that is, in the matter or argumentative function of the argument. I think it is plausible that Mill's category of observation fallacies is an adaptation, for perceptual premises, of Whately's broad category of material fallacies. It would be an understandable move on Mill's part. Many modern texts which are less closely wedded to empiricist philosophy of science still retain an analogous category, for example 'premiss acceptability' (Johnson and Blair, 34) and 'dubious assumption' (Freeman, 101).

Fallacies of generalization

Mill speaks of the fallacies of generalization as the largest class of fallacies, and within it he comprehends hasty generalization,[8] false analogy, *post hoc ergo propter hoc*, as well as some others which we will have to pass over. Mill's view is that whereas the fault in the fallacies of observation *could* be seen as lying in the falsity or unacceptability of the premises, the source of error in fallacies of generalization lies more clearly in the inference. However, we shall see that the distinction is difficult for Mill to maintain.

On the surface, a fallacy of generalization is simply an inductive argument wherein, contrary to appearances, the evidence is insufficient for the conclusion. Interestingly, however, this insufficiency is not always accounted for in quantitative terms. Mill distinguishes legitimate generalization from what he calls 'simple enumeration', inferences of the form, 'This, that, and the other A are B, I cannot think of any A which is not B, therefore every A is B' (V,v,4). He volunteers some examples of this kind of reasoning, which, a century and a half later are interesting to recall.

[N]egroes have never been as civilized as whites sometimes are, therefore it is impossible that they should be so. Women, as a class, are supposed not to have hitherto been equal in intellect to men, therefore they are necessarily inferior . . . Bookish men, taken from speculative pursuits and set to work on something they know nothing about, have generally been found or thought to do it ill; therefore

135

philosophers are unfit for business, etc, etc. All these are inductions by simple enumeration. (V,v,4)

What separates simple enumeration from genuine generalization is simply that the latter is a product of the experimental methods[9] and the former is not. Thus Mill refers to simple enumerations as 'the natural Induction of uninquiring minds' (V,v,4) and says that:

Their fallacy consists in . . . that they are inductions without elimination: there have been no real comparison of instances, nor even ascertainment of the material circumstances in any given instance. (V,v,4)

The methods, in fact, are Mill's solution to what he saw as the problem of induction.

Why is a single instance, in some cases, sufficient for a complete induction, while in others, myriads of concurring instances, without a single exception known or presumed, go such a very little way towards establishing an universal proposition? Whoever can answer this question knows more of the philosophy of logic than the wisest of the ancients, and has solved the problem of induction. (III,iii,3)

Mill believes that inductive inferences can only have the strength that they appear to have if the evidence they are based on has been obtained by the use of the experimental methods. The fallacy of hasty generalization is thus not the failure of having insufficient evidence, in the quantitative sense, and leaping to a generalization prematurely, but rather of giving the status 'evidence' to material that has no right to that status.[10]

Let us next consider Mill's discussion of false analogy. His positive account of analogical inference is found in Book III, Chapter xx of the *Logic*. There he writes that such reasoning may be reduced to the following formula (similar to modern accounts): 'Two things resemble each other in one or more respects; a certain proposition is true of the one; therefore it is true of the other' (III,xx,2). Since the conclusions of analogical arguments, as we understand them, are singular propositions it is at first puzzling why they are discussed in the chapter on fallacies of generalization. Mill, however, does not characterize analogical arguments, like we do, as inferences from particulars to particulars. He thinks that analogies can have general conclusions, for example 'The planets are inhabited because the earth is'. Since both inferences from particulars to particulars, and to generalizations are, by Mill's lights, forms of 'generalization', and since Mill's view is that analogies appear to be generalizations, they are appropriately discussed in this section.

The nature of analogies is indicated by comparing them to 'complete' or 'strict' inductions (V,xx,2). A complete, or strict, induction is one in which the methods of difference and agreement have been put into practice. Analogical arguments are thus a kind of imitation induction wherein there is too little available evidence to put the methods of induction to work, and hence too little evidence to warrant a *bona fide* inference. The fallacy of false analogy depends on misidentifying an argument as an

136

induction when it is really just an analogy offering only a 'small increase of probability, beyond what would otherwise exist' (V,v,6).

Another, and more important, way in which false analogy may occur consists in inferring further points of similarity between two objects when the evidence points in the other direction. If it is a necessary condition of a good analogy that the salient positive correlations outweigh the negative correlations, then Mill's view is that the most serious form of false analogy results from failing to see that it is the negative correlations which have the upper hand. But surely this amounts to overlooking evidence that is not to be neglected; thus, Mill's preferred version of the fallacy of false analogy would seem to fit the category of fallacy of observation as well as fallacy of generalization.

Unfortunately, Mill does not elaborate on the idea that the use of analogies is to establish a presumption; however, it is interesting to note that this suggestion is acceptable to some modern argumentation theorists (Walton, 259). Some kinds of dialogues have the object of establishing agreement between two dialoguers rather than establishing truth. In such dialogues analogies would be acceptable forms of argument used either to establish or rebut a presumption. Thus employed, analogies would be fallacious when they are too far-fetched to even accomplish a legitimate shifting of the burden of proof.

Mill's views on *post hoc* reasoning are similar to his account of analogy in that he does not think that all instances of this kind of reasoning are without value. Thus *post hoc* and analogical reasoning can provide *some* support for a proposition. The error lies in overestimating the support they really do furnish. It is not the case that an observation of an event, B, following another event, A, constitutes *no* evidence at all for a causal claim, 'A's cause B's', but singular observations afford only very little evidence for such claims. Mill distinguishes two cases:

(a) if the succession of events is observed in just one instance, and there is no collateral confirmation, then it 'goes scarcely any way at all' towards establishing a causal generalization.

(b) if the succession of events is observed in just one instance, but there is other evidence of the causal connection, then the single observation 'is of some value as a verification by specific experience'. (V,v,5)

Quantity of evidence does matter after all, at least in some cases. It is a mistake to draw a conclusion based on single observations, or to make inductions without the use of comparative instances or the method of elimination.

Fallacies of ratiocination

These are fallacies of deduction and Mill remarks that in 'the common books of logic' the term 'fallacy' is restricted to this class. He does not have much interest in these fallacies and he recommends Whately's *Logic* to the reader saying that he treats the subject 'most satisfactorily'. Mill briefly reviews the most common infractions of the rules of immediate and syllogistic inference, and then turns his attention to *secundum quid* which he takes as belonging to a wider class, viz. those fallacies which consist in changing the premisses in a chain of arguments. *Secundum quid*:

> is committed when, in the premises, a proposition is asserted with a qualification, and the qualification lost sight of in the conclusion; or oftener, when a limitation or condition, though not asserted, is necessary to the truth of the proposition, but is forgotten when that proposition comes to be employed as a premise. (V,vi,4)

This is one of the few places in which Mill remarks on the problems of extended arguments. Here he sees the main problem as one of keeping track of the qualifications of premisses assented to when they are first introduced and then later forgotten. He illustrates with several examples taken from economic theory.

Fallacies of confusion

The fallacies of observation, generalization and ratiocination are the core classes of Millean fallacies. Together they make up that major subdivision of the inferential fallacies in which the evidence is clearly comprehended. The remaining category of inferential fallacies is the one where the evidence is confused, due primarily to ambiguity or vagueness. Not having a firm grip on the evidence can result in:

> forming one conception of our evidence when we collect or receive it, and another when we make use of it; or unadvisedly, and in general unconsciously, substituting, as we proceed, different premises in the place of those with which we set out, or a different conclusion for that which we undertook to prove. (V,ii,2)

The passage shows that there may be confusion either about what the premisses are or about what the conclusion should be (so Mill's classification of these fallacies as being 'from evidence not distinctly conceived' is too narrow). The fallacies included in this category are all as old as the *Sophistical Refutations* and include ambiguity, composition and division, *petitio principii* (which we discussed earlier) and *ignoratio elenchi*.

Heading the list of fallacies of confusion are those due to ambiguity of terms. Here Mill provides several pages of interesting examples. Like Whately, Mill takes composition and division to be due to ambiguity and he thinks there are no fallacies 'more common, or more likely to deceive' (V,vii,1) than these. Fallacious composition occurs when a term is used distributively in one premiss to express a proposition about each member of a class and then the same term is used collectively in the other premiss, or in the conclusion, to express a proposition about the entire class. Division reverses the order of confusion.

In a move reminiscent of Aristotle's claims for *ignoratio elenchi*, Mill suggests that 'almost all fallacies ... might in strictness be brought under ... Fallacies of Confusion' (V,ii,3). He is here remarking on the fact that actual fallacious arguments are often incomplete, and that what the fallacy is will depend on a sometimes arbitrary choice of how one repairs it. In such cases it is unclear what the evidence was intended to be and so the argument is best considered as a fallacy of confusion. Interestingly, Mill thinks that when it is clear what the evidence is, when missing premisses have been supplied and all ambiguities removed, then the argument cannot commit a fallacy of confusion; it must, therefore, fall under one of the remaining four categories (V,ii,3).

One last comparison with Whately is irresistible. Within logical fallacies he distinguished purely logical and semi-logical fallacies. The former are readily identifiable as violations of some syllogistic rule, the latter require additional semantic *savoir faire* to be unmasked. Thus Whately has ambiguous middle term, composition and division, and accident as semi-logical fallacies. Mill's fallacies of deduction match, roughly, with Whately's purely logical fallacies; and the fallacies of confusion are nearly the same as Whately's semi-logical fallacies.

Fallacies of simple inspection

This is Mill's category of non-inferential fallacies. Mill's examples (V,iii) include items from popular superstition ('there are ghosts'), philosophy ('inconceivability implies impossibility') as well as science (the laws of inertia and motion). There is nothing about such propositions which should excuse them from having to undergo the usual process of proof. Purported analytic and synthetic *a priori* propositions also qualify as fallacies in this category since they are 'held for true, literally without any extrinsic evidence' (V,ii,2). Mill's feelings about the *a priori* school of philosophy are strongly expressed in his *Autobiography* (ch. 7, para. 4).

> The notion that truths external to the mind may be known by intuition or consciousness, independently of observation and experience, is, I am persuaded, in these times, the great intellectual support of false doctrines and bad institutions. By the aid of this theory every inveterate belief and every intense feeling, of which the origin is not remembered, is enabled to dispense with the obligation of justifying itself by reason, and is erected into its own all-sufficient voucher and justification. There never was such an instrument devised for consecrating all deep-seated prejudices.

Mill believes that the fallacy can take a more subtle form in which simple inspection creates a *presumption* for a proposition. In itself, a presumption is not enough to support a proposition, but it forestalls the normally required method of proof for the proposition, thus making it seem that there is sufficient evidence for it. The fallaciousness lies not in using the method of proof wrongly but in not using it at all when it should be used.

To count non-arguments as fallacies is, however, a departure from the traditional view. Still it is a practice which is gaining some foothold. Fogelin and Duggan (255) write:

> [A]ssumptions, principles, and ways of looking at things are sometimes called fallacies. Philosophers have spoken of the naturalistic fallacy, the genetic fallacy, the pathetic fallacy, the descriptive fallacy, the intentional fallacy, the affective fallacy, and many more.

These fallacies are all names of supposed philosophical mistakes, i.e, not necessarily arguments but philosophical beliefs. They can creep into arguments but they are considered to be fallacies even when they are just beliefs.

Mill's idea of the fallacies of inspection as propositions which are, but should not be, accepted without the proper backing bears some resemblance to a fallacy identified by van Eemeren and Grootendorst which they describe as 'immunizing the standpoint against criticism'. In their view, treating a proposition as not requiring an argument, and so refusing to assume the burden of proof is a violation of the rule, 'Whoever advances a standpoint is obliged to defend it if asked to do so' (van Eemeren and Grootendorst, 285). It is obvious, too, that Mill's antagonism to the *a priori* defense of a proposition is shared by some modern philosophers of science and, although they may not describe holding a proposition 'immune to revision' (Quine, 43) as a *fallacy*, they do consider it a mistake of scientific method.

Conclusion

Should we agree with Hamblin's negative evaluation of Mill's treatment of the fallacies? There are several reasons to demur.

Mill's contribution to the history of logic and inference is independent of his work on the fallacies, yet it influenced his analyses of individual fallacies and shaped his novel classification. In fact, a consideration of Mill's work clearly demonstrates what we all suspect: that it is conceptions of rationality, or good reasoning, that drive the derivative conceptions of kinds of fallacies. Given that Mill's theory of inference is a sharp break from the tradition he wrote in, this makes his theory of fallacies all the more interesting. Moreover, Mill shows a sensitivity to the problems of fallacy theory when he sees that the same fallacious argument can be classified more than one way, for example, or when he realizes that not all *post hoc* reasonings are fallacies. Mill's examples are hardly ever trite, they are nearly always original, and they are taken from diverse fields including science, religion, politics, economics and philosophy. Given these considerations, it is surprising that Hamblin found so little in Mill's treatment of the fallacies to appreciate. True, Mill's *Logic* is long, repetitive, and sometimes inconsistent. Nevertheless, for the informal logician it is a rich source of original insights, useful analyses and interesting alternatives.[11]

Notes

1.   Hereafter I will simply indicate book, chapter and section of *A System of Logic*; for example, '(II,iii,1)' abbreviates 'book II, chapter iii, section 1'.

2.   In the *Westminster Review*, Vol. 9, January, 1828.

3.   Even though Mill removes syllogistic logic from the central position it
        occupied in nearly all earlier logical theories he still thought it of the utmost
        importance in both science and pedagogy. In his own intellectual development
        he found nothing more valuable than the study of the 'school logic'.

        My own consciousness and experience ultimately led me to appreciate . . .
        the value of an early practical familiarity with the school logic. I know
        nothing, in my own education, to which I think myself more indebted for
        whatever capacity of thinking I have attained. (*Autobiography*, ch. 1, para.
        12)

        Mill believes that 'there is no more important intellectual habit' (II,i,2) than
        being able to discern the exact meanings of assertions. Accordingly, he was
        ready to recommend traditional formal logic as part of the curriculum.

        I am persuaded that nothing, in modern education, tends so much, when
        properly used, to form exact thinkers, who attach a precise meaning to
        words and propositions, and are not imposed upon by vague, loose, or
        ambiguous terms. (*Autobiography*, ch. 1, para. 12)

        Mill's position is here in direct opposition to many who teach informal logic,
        reasoning skills, or critical thinking and who underestimate, and sometimes
        belittle, the value of formal logic. He would undoubtedly have welcomed the
        development of the predicate calculus (and its augmentation to epistemic,
        alethic and deontic modalities) because of the fine grade distinctions it allows
        us to perspicuously represent.

4.   Mill is quoting from Whately, ch. III, sec. 13.

5.   See Ryan, and Skorupski.

6.   Massey argues that there is an asymmetry between showing arguments valid
        and showing them invalid. On the standard definition of 'fallacy' this turns
        into an asymmetry between showing arguments valid (non-fallacious) and
        showing them fallacious. The asymmetry is roughly this. We can, sometimes,
        succeed in showing an argument valid by finding that it instantiates a valid
        form; however, our failure to find a valid form of an argument does not
        convict the argument of invalidity, and hence does not convict it of
        fallaciousness.

7.   This diagram is found at V,ii,2.

8.   Mill does not use the name 'hasty generalization'.

9.   Space restrictions do not allow me to discuss Mill's experimental methods. They are, however, the part of Mill's *Logic* that continues to be included in scientific-minded contemporary texts (e.g., M. Salmon, 93-104; Copi and Cohen, ch. 12), and that are therefore known to most logicians. For useful recent discussions see Mackie, 297-321, and Skorupski ch. 6. Mill's original discussion of the experimental methods is in III, viii-x.

10.   One contemporary text advises that hasty generalization 'arises from failing to meet the requirement of obtaining a large enough sample' (M. Salmon, 58), and another explains it as occurring 'when a person generalizes from a single anecdote or experience, or from a sample that is too small or too unrepresentative to support his conclusion' (Govier, 1988, 331).

11.   I am grateful to the Universities of Amsterdam and Lethbridge for supporting the research for this chapter, and to John Woods for invaluable discussion.

References

Allen, Derek (1990), 'Govier's Problems in Argument Analysis and Evaluation', *Informal Logic,* Vol. 12, pp. 43-62.

Aristotle (1928), 'On Sophistical Refutations', translated by W. A. Pickard-Cambridge, in Ross, W. D. (ed.), *The Works of Aristotle,* Vol. 1, Oxford University Press: Oxford.

Arnauld, Antoine, and Pierre Nicole [1662] (1964), *The Art of Thinking,* translated by James Dickoff and Patricia James, Bobbs-Merrill: Indianapolis.

Bacon, Francis [1620] (1937), *Novum Organum,* in Jones, R. F. (ed.), *Francis Bacon: Essays, Advancement of Learning, New Atlantis, and Other Pieces,* Odyssey: New York.

Copi, Irving, and Carl Cohen (1990), *Introduction to Logic,* 8th ed., Macmillan: New York.

De Morgan, Augustus (1847), *Formal Logic,* Taylor and Walton: London.

Eemeren, F. H. van, and R. Grootendorst, (1987), 'Fallacies in Pragma-Dialectical Perspective', *Argumentation,* Vol. 1, pp. 283-301.

Fogelin, R. J., and T. J. Duggan (1987), 'Fallacies', *Argumentation,* Vol. 1, pp. 255-62.

Freeman, James B. (1988), *Thinking Logically: Basic Concepts of Reasoning,* Prentice-Hall: Englewood Cliffs.

Govier, Trudy (1988), *A Practical Study of Argument,* 2nd ed., Wadsworth: Belmont.

Govier, Trudy (1989), 'Analogies and Missing Premises', *Informal Logic,* Vol. 11, pp. 141-52.

Hamblin, Charles (1970), *Fallacies,* Methuen: London.

Johnson, Ralph H., and J. Anthony Blair (1983), *Logical Self-Defense,* 2nd ed., McGraw-Hill Ryerson: Toronto.

Mackie, John L. (1974), *The Cement of the Universe: A Study of Causation,* Clarendon Press: Oxford.

Massey, Gerald J. (1981), 'The Fallacy Behind Fallacies', *Midwest Studies in Philosophy*, Vol. 6, pp. 489-500.

Mill, John Stuart [1873] (1961), *Autobiography*, in Lerner, Max (ed.), *Essential Works of John Stuart Mill*, Bantam Books: New York.

Mill, John Stuart [1843] (1973-74), *A System of Logic, Ratiocinative and Inductive; Being a Connected View of the Principles of Evidence and the Methods of Scientific Investigation*, in Robson, J. M. (ed.), *The Collected Works of John Stuart Mill*, Vol. 7-8, University of Toronto Press: Toronto.

Nagel, Ernest (ed.) (1974), *John Stuart Mill's Philosophy of Scientific Method*, Hafner Press: New York. Reprint of 1950 edition.

Quine, Willard van Orman (1961), *From a Logical Point of View*, 2nd ed., Harper and Row: New York.

Ryan, Alan (1970), *The Philosophy of John Stuart Mill*, Macmillan: London.

Salmon, Merrilee H. (1984), *Introduction to Logic and Critical Thinking*, Harcourt Brace Jovanovich: New York.

Salmon, Wesley C. (1984), *Logic*, 3rd ed., Prentice Hall: Englewood Cliffs, NJ.

Sextus Empiricus [2nd Century A.D.] (1933), *Outlines of Pyrrhonism*, translated by R. G. Bury, Harvard University Press: Cambridge.

Skorupski, John (1989), *John Stuart Mill*, Routledge: London.

Toulmin, Stephen (1958), *The Uses of Argument*, Cambridge University Press: Cambridge.

Walton, Douglas N. (1989), *Informal Logic: A Handbook for Critical Argumentation*, Cambridge University Press: Cambridge.

Whately, Richard (1826), *The Elements of Logic, Including 'Dissertation on the Province of Reasoning'*, Harper and Brothers: New York.

11 Kant and informal logic

Hud Hudson

Immanuel Kant is certainly not a philosopher who immediately comes to mind when one attempts to construct a list of the outstanding historical figures who have made significant contributions to those areas of philosophical investigation currently falling under the general heading 'Informal Logic'. The caricature of Kant is of a man obsessed with formality in all of its guises (in both his professional writings and in his private life), of a thinker who slavishly pursued his architectonic at the expense of truth (and even of plausibility), and of a philosopher who believed that the final word about logic had been said by Aristotle, after whom 'logic had not been able to advance even a single step'. As with most caricatures, this one contains some element of truth, but when we look more closely at Kant's writings, here, as elsewhere, he provides us with important insights in a number of areas, many of which are relevant to the study of informal logic.

In addition to the vast range of academic subjects taught by Kant during his series of appointments at the University of Königsberg, for over four decades he lectured in logic at least once a year. In accordance with university requirements, Kant's lectures were set against the backdrop of a then popular tradition of logic and metaphysics and were founded on textbooks authored by notable rationalists such as Christian Wolff and Alexander Baumgarten, and by the intellectual descendant of Wolff and Baumgarten, Georg Friedrich Meier. Meier's *Auszug aus der Vernunftlehre* [*Summary of the Doctrine of Reason*] of 1752 was Kant's particular text in logic, and despite its partial focus on methodological and psychological themes, it was heavily concentrated on topics which fall under the traditional scope of formal logic. Similar (but not entirely accurate) remarks have been made about Kant's own treatise on this subject, appropriately entitled *Logik*, which was compiled at Kant's request by Gottlob Benjamin Jäsche, and which (although published in 1800) was largely based on the lectures Kant had presented in 1782, the year immediately following the publication of the first edition of his masterpiece, *Kritik der reinen Vernunft* [*Critique of Pure Reason*]. Despite its own merits, much of the value of Kant's *Logik* is derived from its use as a tool for interpreting Kant's first *Critique* and, for that matter, from its intimate connection to and potential clarification of almost all of the writings which constitute the Kantian corpus; for instance, several of Kant's epistemological, metaphysical, moral, aesthetic, teleological, and religious doctrines are illuminated by the *Logik*. Of particular interest in our present investigation, however, it is also worth noting that his theories of concepts, judgments, inference, argumentation, fallacies, definition, and rhetoric are illuminated by those lectures, as well.[1]

As we will see, throughout his writings Kant works on and with a number of conceptions from older logical and rhetorical traditions which are of interest and relevance to contemporary informal logicians. It should be noted, however, that he does so in the context of *philosophical* argumentation, thereby providing something of a contrast to the approach employed by more recent argumentation theorists. Moreover, his treatment of these conceptions tends to be rather complex and obscure; he is a philosopher's philosopher. But despite the fact that Kant engages these topics at a different level, and despite the notorious difficulties associated with working through his contributions and criticisms, still, what he has to say is worth the effort it will require of contemporary informal logicians.

Taking his lectures as a starting point, then, but without unduly restricting our attention to the explicitly logical works, I propose to highlight some of the contributions Kant has made to issues in informal logic and thereby to make some effort to eradicate the caricature of Kant as the exclusive devotee of matters formal. In the first section, with respect to his contributions to a theory of argumentation, I will discuss Kant's widely-cited distinction between the analytic and the synthetic modes of investigation, and I will describe a particular type of argument structure which is championed by Kant, and which has been revived recently in moral theory, namely, the transcendental argument. In the second section, I will recount Kant's division of the types of logic, and I will investigate the features of Kant's distinctive theory of dialectic which emerges from that division, a theory which has had profound influence upon nineteenth- and twentieth-century conceptions of dialectic. In particular, I will focus on Kant's account of a unique type of fallacious reasoning which (on his view) both characterizes and undermines rationalistic metaphysics. And finally, in the third section, I will examine Kant's rather harsh criticisms of rhetoric and of oratory, and I will conclude my overview with some brief remarks concerning Kant's ethics and philosophy of history with emphasis on their significance for his views on rhetoric.

With respect to the special interests of informal logicians, the results of these investigations should reveal a clarification of Kant's views on analytic/synthetic distinctions, an unexpected connection between argumentation theory and normative ethics, the origins of one popular, current use of the term 'dialectic', the beginnings of a general theory of a kind of inevitable fallacy into which human beings are naturally drawn, and a new philosophical foundation for an old critique of the art of persuasion.

I. Kant's contributions to a theory of argument

The fact that Kant defended an analytic/synthetic distinction is widely known, but what is not so widely known is that there is nothing in Kant's writings answering to the phrase '*the* analytic/synthetic distinction', simply because there are several such distinctions drawn by Kant. Undoubtedly, the most famous analytic/synthetic distinction in Kant's work is the one between types of judgment, a distinction that gives rise to the subsequent investigation into *synthetic a priori judgments* upon which much of Kant's epistemology is founded. Very briefly, in the first *Critique* Kant describes analytic judgments as 'those in which the connection of the predicate with the subject is thought through identity', and he maintains that such judgments are merely explicative, adding nothing to our knowledge, but only making clear what was originally thought in the subject-concept. Kant describes synthetic judgments as 'those in which this connection [of the predicate with the subject] is thought without identity', and he maintains that they are ampliative, adding to our knowledge the relation of a predicate-concept to a subject-concept which is not already thought in that subject-concept. Not surprisingly, then, whereas the law of contradiction alone defines the former class of judgments, something more is required for the class of synthetic, ampliative judgments, since in such judgments the subject-concept does not already 'contain' its predicate-concept as one of its marks or constituent concepts [A6-A7/B10-B11].[2]

In addition to judgments, however, concepts, definitions, and methods also may be either analytic or synthetic. Kant's early account of the difference between the analytic and synthetic *method* arose from his characterization of the appropriate methodologies for mathematics, the natural sciences, and philosophy in his 1764 essay entitled *Untersuchung über die Deutlichkeit der Grundsätze der natürlichen Theologie und der Moral* [*Investigation of the Clarity of the Principles of Natural Theology and Morals*] (Ak. Ed. II, 273-301). Here Kant argues that the synthetic method is exhibited in mathematics, and that it consists of progressing from simple data in the form of definitions to complex conclusions derived from those data (e.g., consider Euclidean geometry). The analytic method, on the other hand, is exhibited in philosophy, and it consists of regressing from a given complex concept to its simple constituents.

It should be noted, however, that synthetic investigations may also begin with simple concepts (as opposed to simple definitions), and that analytic investigations may also begin with complex definitions (as opposed to complex concepts). Owing to Kant's dual conviction that mathematical investigations commence with definitions and that philosophical investigations terminate with definitions (thus providing a sharp contrast to one popular, contemporary school of analytic philosophy), he focuses on just one of the two possible starting points in each case when illustrating the two methods by way of these two particular disciplines. In fact, Kant's theory of definition in general is interwoven with his theory of analytic and synthetic methods, concepts and judgments. Whereas Kant carried on the tradition he had inherited of distinguishing between nominal and real definitions, he incorporated his own views on analysis and synthesis to produce a fourfold classification: analytic nominal definitions, synthetic nominal definitions, analytic real definitions, and synthetic real definitions. Kant's classification of types of definition becomes even more complicated, though, once we take into account his claim that analytic and synthetic definitions each admit of a further division into *a priori* and *a posteriori*. With respect to the analytic, then, we have two ways in which the concepts that figure in these definitions are *given*, and with respect to the synthetic, we have two ways in which the concepts that figure in these definitions are *constructed*. Setting aside the influence of Kant's theory of definition on his description of method, however, the distinction between the analytic and synthetic method can be clarified with section 117 of the *Logik*, where Kant distinctly and straightforwardly maintains that the analytic or regressive method moves from the composite to the simple, and that the synthetic or progressive method moves from the simple to the composite (Ak. Ed. IX, 149). By 1783, with the publication of his *Prolegomena zu einer jeden künftigen Metaphysik, die als Wissenschaft wird auftreten können* [*Prolegomena to Any Future Metaphysics*] (Ak. Ed. IV, 253-383), Kant had provided a sustained example of his distinction by offering two closely related philosophical treatments of the same topics which had been executed under these two different methods. In the *Prolegomena*, Kant takes, as given, a certain type of complex judgment (a synthetic *a priori* judgment), and then attempts to discover the only conditions under which what has been given is possible. With this regression from the complex to the simple, he employs the analytic method. Kant maintains, however, that in the first *Critique*, he carried out the same project in the synthetic style, first beginning with simple elements and then ascending to the complex whole. And again, in 1785, Kant describes his two-step approach in his *Grundlegung zur Metaphysik der Sitten* [*Foundations of the Metaphysics of Morals*] (Ak. Ed. IV, 385-463) with the distinction between the analytic and synthetic modes of investigation. In this book dealing with ethics, the first two sections of the work proceed analytically from the (complex) common knowledge of morals to the metaphysics of morals (which exposes the simple constituents of that complex knowledge), and the third section, in turn, proceeds synthetically from those simple constituents back to the complex and common knowledge (Ak. Ed. IV, 392).[3]

In addition to his emphasis on the various forms of analysis and synthesis, Kant is famous for his notion of a transcendental argument. Transcendental arguments are arguments designed to uncover necessary conditions which make possible certain types of judgments. The various structures, purposes, successes (or lack thereof), and even textual locations of Kant's own transcendental deductions are topics of intense philosophical discussion and disagreement. Kant exploited this argument form throughout his mature writings, attempting several transcendental deductions over the course of his career. In the first *Critique*, he offers a transcendental deduction of what he calls the categories of the Understanding in order to reveal the necessary conditions of the possibility of empirical knowledge, an argument which has been the subject of countless philosophical papers and books, references and reactions. Transcendental arguments also have a significant role to play in ethics. Some commentators have argued that in the *Foundations*, Kant offers a transcendental deduction of the moral law, and some commentators have argued that in his 1788 *Kritik der praktischen Vernunft* [*Critique of Practical Reason*] (Ak. Ed. V, 1-163), Kant abandons that project only to replace it with a transcendental deduction of the concept of freedom.[4]

Informal logicians may find that Kant's transcendental deductions have influenced current ethical theory and current argumentation theory in an especially interesting way. For instance, contemporary ethical theorists such as Jürgen Habermas have attempted to employ transcendental arguments to establish the unavoidability of accepting certain normative theses, if one is to participate in meaningful argumentation at all. Regardless of what verdict we pass on the philosophical significance of Kant's own transcendental deductions (or on the significance of their modern counterparts), the mere fact that he focused our attention on the character and various functions of transcendental argument has been openly acknowledged by his proponents and opponents alike as one of Kant's greatest philosophical contributions. In particular, informal logicians who are attempting

147

to identify just what the subject matter is that they are (or ought to be) studying may benefit from directing their attention to the project undertaken by Habermas and other contemporary, Kant-inspired, ethical theorists. The question to be answered is whether a theory of argumentation has anything substantial to tell us about normative moral principles, as Habermas has suggested with his transcendental argument. If the answer to that question turns out to be an affirmative one, then perhaps a certain portion of normative ethics is a candidate for being a subfield of study in informal logic, or at the very least, is more intimately connected to informal logic and to a theory of argumentation than the current literature might suggest.

Kant himself remained absolutely convinced of the fundamental importance of transcendental argument throughout his career, with his own efforts in this area most certainly ranking among his favorite philosophical achievements. In his work on aesthetics and teleology of 1790, *Kritik der Urtheilskraft* [*Critique of Judgment*] (Ak. Ed. V, 165-485), Kant offers a transcendental deduction of pure judgments of taste, and he offers a transcendental deduction of the principle of the formal purposiveness of nature. Moreover, he continued to work on a transcendental deduction of ether and (perhaps) on revisions of his deduction of the categories of the Understanding as well, until his death in 1804.[5]

II. Kant's conception of dialectic as a logic of illusion

In what has come to be called his 'precritical period' (i.e., everything before the publication of his first *Critique* in 1781), Kant was struggling (not always successfully) to retain what was valuable while rejecting what was unacceptable in the doctrines he had inherited from his rationalist predecessors, the very doctrines which dominated the intellectual scene in Germany in the first half of the eighteenth century. Many of Kant's works from this early period, especially those from the 1760s, are devoted to a critical appraisal of the general rationalist program and to arguments against the conception of reason advocated by the prominent figures of the German enlightenment.

Despite his uneasy relations with these champions of reason, Kant is frequently regarded as an unwavering disciple of traditional logic and is remembered for his claim that logic had been brought to completion by Aristotle, at least with respect to its certainty and content, if not in elegance of presentation (Ak, Ed. IX, 20). One work in particular, however, *Die falsche Spitzfindigkeit der vier syllogistischen Figuren* [*The False Subtlety of the Four Syllogistic Figures*] (Ak. Ed. II, 45-61), presents us with a sharp contrast to the picture of Kant as someone who was confined by his blind adherence to the tenets of traditional, scholastic logic. In this essay of 1762, Kant complains about the fashion of the day which restricted the approach he had to take to logic in his university lectures, and he straightforwardly rejects the standard division of the syllogism into four figures, on the grounds that it misrepresents the nature of inference. Kant here argues that there are only two types of inference, one for positive and one for negative judgments, and that both are adequately accounted for in the first syllogistic figure. He then offers an interpretation of the other figures which makes them out to be enthymemes, after which he not only denies that these other figures provide any genuine, independent forms of reasoning but also suggests that scarcely anything more useless has been the subject of such sustained, intelligent discussion. Finally, he completes his short piece by ridiculing scholastic logic with the image of a colossus who hides its head in the clouds of antiquity but who has feet of clay.[6]

In his later critical writings, when offering a classification of the various types and functions of logic, Kant makes clear the nature of his commitment to formal logic, as well as clarifying what he takes to be the limitations and proper scope of that discipline. He writes that general logic 'contains the absolutely necessary rules of thought without which there can be no employment whatsoever of the understanding', and special logic 'contains the rules of correct thinking as regards a certain kind of object' (A52/B76). Accordingly, general logic, or a logic of elements, abstracts from any differences of the objects of the understanding and treats the rules of thought apart from any application whatsoever, whereas special logic, or an organon, takes account of the similarity of certain objects of the understanding and regards the specialized rules of thought directed at a particular study (say, of Mathematics or of Biology). Moreover, general logic itself admits of a subdivision: Pure general logic is concerned 'only with principles *a priori*, and is a canon of understanding and of reason, but only in respect of what is formal in their employment', and applied general logic is concerned 'with the rules of the employment of the understanding under the subjective empirical conditions dealt with by psychology' (A53/B77; See also, Ak. Ed. IX, 18). According to Kant, since it alone has not become impoverished due to any association with empirical principles, *only* pure general logic is rich enough to constitute a science, and he is here, as elsewhere, quite harsh on logicians who have only disfigured (in their attempts to improve) this science by adding psychological, metaphysical, or anthropological chapters on the faculties and origin of knowledge, on certainty, and on prejudice (Cf. Bviii).

Incidentally, this remark would certainly appear to constitute a severe judgment on our own contemporary informal logicians who would attempt to give such an account of the rules of thought while remaining sensitive to the sources of error of doubt and of conviction, and to the feelings, inclinations, and passions which either enhance or restrict the application of the understanding in particular contexts (A54-A55/B78-B79). In fact, what certain informal logicians (i.e., those who endeavor to defend the so-called 'informal fallacies' from traditional criticism) often regard as among their primary virtues – namely, the recognition of the significance of the different contexts in which reasoning occurs and the recognition of the significance of the different passions and emotions which figure in argumentation – are here regarded by Kant as their ultimate weaknesses. Indeed, Kant argues that it is precisely because of its reliance upon such empirical principles that such an applied general logic can never aspire to be a science and that it will fail to be a canon or organon of anything.

Nevertheless, according to Kant, pure general logic is unable to furnish us with an adequate foundation upon which we can rest a theory of empirical knowledge. Accordingly, the search for an adequate foundation for empirical knowledge motivated Kant to propose another type of logic, a logic expressly concerned with a particular kind of content, and this, in turn, led Kant to formulate his views regarding the peculiar nature of the fallacies of rationalistic metaphysics. It is in the characterization of these fallacies that we will find our next item of interest for the history of informal logic.

Before turning to a discussion of these fallacies, however, we will require a *very* brief sketch of Kant's general epistemology and of Kant's views of the faculties and powers of the human mind in order to provide a background against which his intriguing theory of rationalistic fallacy may be understood. Kant's epistemology is driven, in part, by the recognition that our faculty of Sensibility is responsible for the contribution of certain *a priori* elements in cognition, namely, Space and Time, and that our faculty of Understanding is likewise responsible for the contribution of certain *a priori* elements in cognition, namely, a particular conceptual scheme upon which depends our ability to form judgments and subsequently to come to have empirical knowledge of ourselves and of nature. In his 'Transcendental Aesthetic' in the first *Critique*, he examines the former, and in his 'Transcendental Logic' from that same work, he examines the latter. The professed goal of the 'Transcendental Logic' is to show that there is a complete and unique list of non-derivative, *a priori* sources of knowledge (distinct from Space and Time), that they have their origin in the very nature of thought (and not in receptivity), and that they are necessarily applicable to all objects of possible experience. Unlike general logic, then, transcendental logic has a specified content, something Kant would call the pure manifold of the *a priori* intuitions (i.e., of Space and Time), and transcendental logic is thus concerned with the rules governing a particular type of thinking, the rules of synthetic *a priori* thought (A55-A57/B79-B82).

Kant's distinctive conception of dialectic emerges from this framework and from the further comparison of transcendental logic with general logic. Kant does admit that general logic furnishes a general criterion of truth with regard to form, but he notes that this is only a negative condition, a condition which no cognition can violate, but which is not sufficient to guarantee the truth of the content of those cognitions which are in accordance with it. This negative task of general logic is found in its Analytic, a logic of formal truth, and only when it is supplemented with information regarding content can we then generate knowledge of objects. However, when this use of general logic is mistakenly taken as providing more than a negative condition of truth, Kant maintains that we are engaged in Dialectic (A57-A61/B82-B86).[7]

Kant immediately compares his use of the term 'dialectic' with the use given to it by those ancients who regarded it as the title for a special type of science or art, ut then, revealing his unflattering opinion of their achievements, he writes that 'we can safely conclude from their actual employment of it that with them it was never anything else than the logic of illusion. It was a sophistical art of giving to ignorance, and indeed to intentional sophistries, the appearance of truth, by the device of imitating the methodological thoroughness which logic prescribes, and of using its 'topic' to conceal the emptiness of its pretensions' (A61/B85-B86). Whether or not Kant's historical charge is accurate will not be here disputed, but what is significant in this passage is the construal of dialectic as a *logic of illusion*, a characterization of dialectic which has profoundly influenced contemporary utilization and understanding of this concept. Rather than allowing such employment of dialectic to soil the dignity of philosophy, as Kant suggests it does when certain 'metaphysical jugglers' pretend that general logic is able to provide a positive, as well as a negative, criterion of truth, Kant proposes to reserve the term 'dialectic' for 'a critique of dialectical illusion' (A62/B86).[8]

150

Accordingly, when we investigate the corresponding division of an analytic and a dialectic in Kant's transcendental logic, the logic of content, we are conducting a two-fold inquiry: (i) we are formulating a negative condition of truth with respect to content (*i.e.*, we are specifying that unique conceptual scheme under which anything must be thought, if it is to be an object of knowledge for us), and (ii) we are conducting a critique of dialectical illusion with respect to content (i.e., we are offering a critique of the illegitimate attempt to extend the negative condition of truth with respect to content beyond those limits which are set by the special nature of the restricted subject matter of transcendental logic) (A62-A63/B87-B88). Consequently, whereas the error to be exposed by dialectic in general logic is the fallacious derivation of information about the content of any objects whatsoever from mere formal principles of that science, the error to be exposed by dialectic in transcendental logic is the fallacious derivation of information about non-sensible objects from the principles which constitute the conditions under which we must bring sensible objects in order to have knowledge of them. To that task of dialectic and to the nature of those fallacious inferences we may now turn.

Kant devotes the second division of his 'Transcendental Logic' to the study of 'Transcendental Dialectic', and it is this portion of the *Critique of Pure Reason* which contains Kant's critique of dogmatic metaphysics. A transcendental dialectic is concerned with a critique of transcendental illusions, i.e., of the sort of illusions which lead us into cognitive error, when, as Kant says, 'the subjective grounds of judgment enter into union with the objective grounds and make these latter deviate from their true function' (A294/B350-B351). Interestingly, he claims that this is neither a logical illusion of the sort which occurs when we commit a fallacy in reasoning due to neglect or inattention, nor is it an empirical (i.e., optical) illusion (A295-A297/B352-B353). Instead, Kant maintains, we here have a *natural* and *inevitable illusion* which arises when we mistake what is subjectively necessary in the connection of our concepts for an objective necessity in the determination of things in themselves.

Kantian terminology aside, what he seems to have in mind with this description is the dual thesis that there are basic rules which govern the employment of our faculty of Reason and that they occasion mistaken inferences about the nature of objects which fall outside the appropriate bounds of the uses of our Understanding. Significantly, Kant maintains that such transcendental illusions (and their corresponding fallacious inferences) do not simply vanish when critical attention has been brought to bear upon them and their invalidity has been thoroughly exposed, and in this respect, they differ from familiar logical illusions (and their corresponding fallacious inferences). However, we are not at the mercy of such illusions either. Although the astronomer cannot prevent the moon from appearing larger at its rising than when it is directly overhead, he can prevent his being deceived by this illusion, and consequently, he can avoid falling into fallacious inferences associated with that illusion. So too, then, the metaphysician cannot prevent the illusions which arise due to the very nature of his cognitive faculties, but he can prevent his being deceived by these illusions, and consequently, he can avoid the fallacious inferences underlying a rationalistic psychology, cosmology, and theology (A295-A298/B352-B355).

151

One interesting aspect of this account of dialectic is its explicit focus on 'natural illusions' and 'natural fallacies'. In other words, we are told that some fallacies have a special status; some fallacies are such that we fall into them precisely because we are the kinds of beings we are and because we possess the types of cognitive faculties we possess. More specifically, according to Kant, our Reason is the cognitive faculty at work in inference-drawing and system-building, and its function consists in constructing a completeness and universality in knowledge. In addition to the *a priori* intuitions of the Sensibility and the *a priori* concepts of the Understanding mentioned earlier, Kant argues that there are certain 'special *a priori* concepts, which we may call pure concepts of reason, or transcendental ideas' (A321/B378). Moreover, it is the purpose of these ideas to determine how we will utilize the faculty of Understanding in order to deal with experience in its totality. In Kant's terminology, this task involves the notion of an unconditioned ground for a whole of a synthesized series of conditions, and the task of these Ideas of Reason itself is the attempt to provide those unconditioned conditions for every object cognized by the Understanding (A326-A328/B383-B385). Unfortunately, this struggle for what he calls 'the unity of reason' and this search for unconditioned conditions will of necessity take us beyond the boundaries of experience, for nothing *in* experience could furnish this ground of all conditioned appearances. To go beyond the bounds of experience, however, is just to leave the proper confines of the special content of transcendental logic, and consequently, to sacrifice any hope of attaining *knowledge* of those unconditioned conditions.[9]

Kant's own account of the natural illusions and of the peculiar type of fallacious inferences which arise from the Ideas of Reason in their demand for unconditioned conditions falls into three divisions, each division corresponding to a doctrine of rationalistic metaphysics. In each of the following cases, then, we have a problem for pure reason. Very briefly: (1) The attempt to reveal the unconditioned unity of the thinking subject gives rise to the science of rational psychology, and to the fallacious inferences that characterize this transcendental doctrine of the soul, namely, arguments designed to show that the soul is a simple substance, which retains its identity over time. (2) The attempt to reveal the unconditioned unity of the series of appearances gives rise to the science of rational cosmology, and to the fallacious inferences that characterize this transcendental doctrine of the world, namely, arguments for the claims that the world has spatial and temporal limits, that all objects are composed of simple parts, that there is a causality of freedom, and that there is an absolutely necessary being. (3) The attempt to reveal the unconditioned unity of the condition of all objects of thought in general gives rise to the science of transcendental theology, and to the fallacious inferences that characterize this transcendental doctrine of God, namely, the traditional speculative arguments for the existence of God, i.e., ontological, cosmological, and physicotheological proofs. In his first *Critique*, Kant opposes these three rationalistic doctrines with his 'Paralogisms', 'Antinomies', and 'Ideal of Pure Reason', respectively.

Following this first sustained investigation into a critique of dialectical illusion, Kant returns to the topic of dialectic in his second *Critique* and in his third *Critique*, where he is once again concerned with the natural and inescapable illusions which arise from the interminable and insatiable demands of the faculty of Reason. Although the Kantian position I have here only sketched is rich with insights and with items of general philosophical interest, of special interest to informal logicians is the following: By locating the source of a particular kind of illusion and fallacious inference in the very nature of a certain type of thinking subject, Kant prepared the ground for a theory of fallacy which, although it may diverge considerably from his own, seeks to demonstrate the *natural* propensity of human beings in general towards a certain use (or misuse) of their reason.

III. Kant's critique of rhetoric and oratory

Kant's construal of dialectic as a logic of illusion also reflects his opinions of the value and functions of classical rhetoric and of oratory. When comparing the aesthetic value of the fine arts in section 53 of the *Critique of Judgment* he writes, 'Oratory [*Beredsamkeit*], insofar as this is taken to mean the art of persuasion (*ars oratoria*), i.e., of deceiving by means of a beautiful illusion, rather than mere excellence of speech (eloquence and style), is a dialectic [i.e., a logic of illusion] that borrows from poetry only as much as the speaker needs in order to win over people's minds for his own advantage before they judge for themselves, and so make their judgment unfree'.[10]

Admittedly, here as elsewhere, Kant's characterization of the components and functions of rhetoric is exceedingly narrow when judged from a classical point of view. But even with his one-sided emphasis on style, it would appear that Kant's opinions about rhetoric and oratory are mixed. Clearly, Kant thought of eloquence and style as redeeming features of rhetoric and as properly belonging to the fine arts. And, on occasion, he complimented (and perhaps even coveted) 'the grace of David Hume' and 'the elegance of Moses Mendelssohn' (Bxliii; Ak. Ed. IV, 262). Nevertheless, he did not regard the lack of such an excellence in his own writings as a *philosophical* failing. In the *Prolegomena*, for instance, when responding to those who had found the first *Critique* wanting in style, Kant wrote, 'I confess, however, I did not expect to hear from philosophers complaints of want of popularity, entertainment, and facility when the existence of highly prized and indispensable knowledge is at stake' (Ak. Ed. IV, 261, Beck translation). Kant, of course, recognized that eloquence and style can make a work more accessible and more popular, and he invited thinkers to reclothe his critical philosophy in just such an appropriate dress, but regardless of this admission, he hardly regarded rhetoric as an essential component of philosophy.

Despite his occasional approval of eloquence and style, however, Kant frequently offered very harsh criticisms of rhetoric. Interestingly, though, these attacks were not simply a parroting of standard eighteenth-century complaints; for Kant, the attack on rhetoric had a philosophical foundation grounded in his own epistemology, ethics, and political philosophy. When excellences in speech were enlisted in the service of the art of persuasion, Kant actively opposed the practice as a type of objectionable force which interferes with *freedom* and the ability to think for oneself, as 'an insidious art, an art that knows how, in important matters to move people like machines to a judgment that must lose all its weight with them when they meditate about it calmly'. Nor does it matter whether or not such force deceives in the best interests of those deceived: 'The art of using people's weaknesses for one's own aims (no matter how good these may be in intention or even in fact), is unworthy of any respect whatsoever' (Ak. Ed. V, 328n). According to Kant, it is not sufficient that someone performs an action which is right because persuaded to do so; he must perform it because it is right, and Kant, perhaps unlike Plato, regarded any person as equal to such a task, even those persons equipped with the rudest of understanding (A831/B859; Ak. Ed. IV, 404). The opposition, then, between Kant's notion of intellectual independence so crucial to his epistemology and ethics and his conception of oratory is severe. For Kant, noble lies preclude enlightenment, and the art of persuasion is little more than an art of fettering.

It is interesting to note, though, that the writings by Kant which are most helpful in clarifying his opposition to the type of rhetoric and oratory he here condemns (e.g., his essays on the themes of the enlightenment and his sometimes fanciful (but not frivolous) writings in the philosophy of history), come dangerously close to providing examples of the kind of appeal that Kant professes to find so distasteful in the third *Critique*. For example, in his 1784 *Beantwortung der Frage: Was ist Aufklärung?* [*What is Enlightenment?*] (Ak. Ed. VIII, 33-42) and in his 1786 *Was heisst: Sich im Denken orientiren?* [*What is Orientation in Thought?*] (Ak. Ed. VIII, 131-147), Kant spiritedly defends enlightenment themes by combining an (indirect) accusation of laziness and cowardice against his fellow citizens and professional colleagues with a plea for them to gather the courage to throw off the yoke of tutelage from their shoulders, and to make public use of their own reason at every opportunity.[11]

A leading idea in Kant's enlightenment essays and a primary source of his maligning of rhetoric and oratory can be found by examining his definition of 'tutelage' [*Unmündigkeit*] from the opening paragraph of *What is Enlightenment?* 'Tutelage is man's inability to make use of his understanding without direction from another' (Ak. Ed. VIII, 35). Kant argues that overcoming this tutelage, and acquiring through one's own efforts the ability to use one's own reason without direction from another is essential for a society to progress from the beginnings of an age of enlightenment to an enlightened age. The art of oratory, Kant seems to believe, is just one means of frustrating this progress by artfully persuading an audience before they judge for themselves, and so, by externally directing the reason of another through the use of a type of force. To the extent, then, that Kant saw the art of oratory as a type of coercion, as an obstacle to freedom, and hence, as nothing more than an impediment to being released from this tutelage, he also saw it as something deserving of no respect whatsoever.

Notes

1. For a discussion of the importance of Kant's *Logik* to the rest of his thought, see Collins, 1977 and Hartman and Schwarz, 1974, xv-cxv.

2. The identity of this third something which is required in synthetic judgments is a matter of long-standing disagreement among Kantian commentators. Incidentally, a rough and ready way of providing the present distinction (which may not be entirely accurate) is just to note that the negation of an

analytic proposition is a contradiction, whereas the negation of a synthetic proposition is not self-contradictory.

3. Those who would like to read Kant directly on these matters are encouraged to begin with either the *Foundations* or the *Prolegomena*. Both works are fairly brief, relatively accessible, and philosophical classics.

4. Other assorted interpretations of Kant's aims have their proponents as well, but determining Kant's stance on the transcendental deduction of the moral law and/or freedom is highly controversial. For a critical survey of the literature see part III of Allison, 1990. (Earlier in his book, Allison himself attempts a transcendental deduction for the Kantian claim that there is a universal propensity to evil in human nature.)

5. For a good introduction to transcendental deductions in general and to the particular debates surrounding Kant's own contributions to this type of argument see Förster, 1989.

6. Kant repeats portions of this objection in sections 56-80 of the *Logik*, Ak. Ed. IX, 120-131. For more on this and related matters see Beiser, 1992.

7. In short, no contradictory proposition is true, and thus we have at least a negative criterion of truth. Nevertheless, mere logical consistency does not also provide us with any substantial knowledge of objects.

8. Unfortunately, Kant sometimes deviates from his own proposed restriction on the meaning of this term, both in the first *Critique* and elsewhere.

9. In a stunning passage (given Kant's usual style) he describes the dogmatic battles which are fought outside the bounds of experience: 'Both parties beat the air, and wrestle with their own shadows, since they go beyond the limits of nature, where there is nothing that they can seize and hold with their dogmatic grasp. Fight as they may, the shadows which they cleave asunder grow together again forthwith, like the heroes in Valhalla, to disport themselves anew in the bloodless contests' (A756/B784).

10. Ak. Ed. V, 327, bracket additions, mine; all quotations from the *Critique of Judgment* are taken from the Pluhar translation (1987).

11. When exploring the tension Kant finds between the art of persuasion and enlightenment, between external force and self-directedness, it is instructive to compare Kant's enlightenment essays and his other efforts in the philosophy of history with his writings on education, *Pädagogik* [*Pedagogy*] (Ak. Ed. IX, 437-499). However, this source must be used with some

caution. For a general discussion of Kant's views on pedagogy and their relation to his views on the enlightenment, see Beck, 1978.

References

Allison, Henry E. (1990), *Kant's Theory of Freedom*, Cambridge University Press: Cambridge.

Beck, Lewis White (1956), 'Kant's Theory of Definition', *Philosophical Review*, Vol. 65, pp.179-191.

Beck, Lewis White (1978), 'Kant on Education', *Essays on Kant and Hume*, Yale University Press: New Haven, CT, pp.188-204.

Beck, Lewis White (ed.) (1985), *Kant on History*, Macmillan: New York.

Beiser, Frederick C. (1992), 'Kant's Intellectual Development: 1746-1781', *The Cambridge Companion to Kant*, Cambridge University Press: Cambridge, pp. 26-61. This collection also provides an excellent introduction to Kant's philosophy as a whole.

Blair, J. Anthony, and Ralph H. Johnson (eds.) (1980), *Informal Logic: The First International Symposium*, Edgepress: Point Reyes, CA.

Collins, James (1977), 'Kant's *Logik* as a Critical Aid', *Review of Metaphysics*, Vol. 30, pp. 440-461.

Dostal, Robert J. (1980), 'Kant and Rhetoric', *Philosophy and Rhetoric*, Vol. 13, pp. 223-244.

Förster, Eckart (ed.) (1989), *Kant's Transcendental Deductions*, Stanford University Press: Stanford, CA.

Habermas, Jürgen (1990), *Moral Consciousness and Communicative Action*, translated by Christian Lenhardt and Shierry Weber Nicholsen, MIT Press: Cambridge.

Hansen, Hans V. (1990), 'An Informal Logic Bibliography', *Informal Logic*, Vol. 12, pp. 155-184.

Hartman, Robert, and Wolfgang Schwarz (1974), 'Introduction to Kant's *Logik*, xv-cxv', translated by Hartman and Schwartz, Bobbs-Merrill: Indianapolis.

Johnson, Ralph H., and J. Anthony Blair (1985), 'Informal Logic: The Past Five Years 1978-1983', *American Philosophical Quarterly*, Vol. 22, pp. 181-193.

Kant, Immanuel (1900), *Logik*, in *Kants gesammelte schriften*, Vol. 9, Königlichen Preussischen Akademie der Wissenschaften (ed.), Walter de Gruyter: Berlin and Leipzig, pp. 1-150.

Kant, Immanuel (1929), *Critique of Pure Reason*, translated by Norman Kemp Smith, St. Martin's Press: New York.

Kant, Immanuel (1950), *Prolegomena to Any Future Metaphysics*, translated by Lewis White Beck, Bobbs-Merrill: Indianapolis.

Kant, Immanuel (1963), *False Subtlety*, translated by Thomas Abbott, Greenwood Press: Westport, CT.

Kant, Immanuel (1987), *Critique of Judgment*, translated by Werner S. Pluhar, Hackett: Indianapolis.

Körner, Stephen (1967), 'The Impossibility of Transcendental Deductions', *Monist*, Vol. 51, pp. 317-331.

Schaper, Eva (1974), 'Are Transcendental Deductions Impossible?', in Beck, L. W. (ed.), *Kant's Theory of Knowledge*, D. Reidel: Dordrecht, pp. 3-11.

12 Informal logic in the twentieth century

Ralph H. Johnson and J. Anthony Blair

I. Introduction

The purpose of this chapter is to discuss informal logic as it has existed in this century.

We begin, in section II, by listing seven ways 'informal logic' seems to be understood at present, including our favored sense. The term began to enter the philosophical vocabulary in the mid-1970s, referring to a new type of introductory logic course and, for some, to the associated developing theory.

Prior to the 1970s such material was taught, and philosophical work relevant to the background theoretical issues was carried on, but not under the label 'informal logic'. Our account of those 'predecessors', in Section III, must be sketchy in the extreme for reasons of space and time. We here also describe the monographs that had theoretical influence, the early influential texts, and the conference and journal activity that developed.

In section IV, we describe what in our view is the problematic of informal logic at the present time: the issues that are currently being addressed and the problems that need to be resolved.

Section V is a brief conclusion.

We must leave unexamined the many similar and roughly contemporaneous instructional and theoretical concerns being actively addressed elsewhere in the world besides the United States and Canada, for example in Australia and New Zealand, and in Europe.

Our main effort will be to characterize informal logic as it is conceived in the late twentieth century. The article is both descriptive and normative in approach. We will try report things as they were or are, to the best of our knowledge; and we will make clear where our own sympathies lie - how we think the enterprise is best conceived.

Historical fidelity requires mention of probable non-intellectual influences on the development of informal logic in the 1975-1985 period. We think political and social developments in the 1960s played a pivotal role. Student activism, kindled by the civil rights movement in the early 1960s and fanned by the anti-Vietnam war movement in the late 1960s and the related demand for 'relevance' in education associated with the

1960s, influenced students to expect their introductory courses to have a bearing on the reasoning and argumentation of current affairs and to demand such relevance when it was not apparent. Many instructors, often shaped by the same influences, were sympathetic. Hence the many simultaneous, independent attempts to replace the standard introduction to symbolic logic courses with a syllabus designed to teach how to assess critically the logic of natural language argumentation in public discourse. The new 'informal logic' course proved extremely popular. To attract enrollments at a time of increased competition for students within colleges and universities, philosophy departments introduced the 'new logic course'. A proliferation of textbooks solicited by market-conscious publishers contributed to more new courses. If these speculations are on target, then from the point of view of the history of ideas, the development of the informal logic movement in the late twentieth century merits study by not only historians of logic but also sociologists of knowledge.

II. What is informal logic?

Like 'pragmatism' or 'existentialism', the term 'informal logic' has many denotations: there is no established meaning. We here set out what we believe to be the principal ways the term is currently understood, including the one we prefer.

(1) *Ryle's distinction:* Ryle (1954) contrasts 'informal logic' with formal logic. For him, 'informal logic' consists of tracing the implications of 'full-blooded' concepts, whereas formal logic consists of the implications of topic-neutral logical constants. As he puts it, 'The Formal Logician . . . is working out the logic of *and, not, some*, etc., and the philosopher . . . is exploring the logic of the concepts of *pleasure, seeing, chance,* etc.' (119). What Ryle calls 'informal logic' is the enterprise of philosophy as he sees it: conceptual analysis of important philosophical concepts. As we use the term, informal logic is tied much more narrowly to the logical analysis and critique of arguments. (Pomeroy, 1982 argues for a connection between these two senses.)

(2) *'Formal' and 'informal' fallacies:* Fallacies have often been classified as formal or informal (see Carney and Scheer, 1964). In the minds of many, informal logic consists of the study of the so-called informal fallacies: the tasks of providing careful analyses of their characteristics and illuminating classifications of them. In our opinion, fallacies and fallacy theory have a central, but not defining, place in informal logic.

(3) *Baby Logic: logic without formal systems:* There is a widely-taught introductory logic course syllabus which includes some of the elementary ideas of deductive logic but no systematic treatment and little formal or symbolic apparatus, along with units on definition and language, on the informal fallacies, and on inductive reasoning, probability theory and scientific method (see Copi and Cohen, 1990). If logic is the study of formal deductive systems, such a course is only a 'baby', elementary, or introductory logic course, not a (formal) logic course proper. For many, 'informal logic' denotes the subject matter of such courses. However, that is not what we understand by the term (see (7) below).

(4) *Critical Thinking and Informal Logic:* In the minds of many who are familiar with these two terms, critical thinking and informal logic are different names for the same

thing. The labels are widely used interchangeably. There is a reasonable explanation for this identification, traceable to the purposes and the methods of the 'new' logic course textbooks of the 1970s that launched the informal logic movement. Most of these texts share three features: they (1) aim to foster critical thinking, by (2) teaching the analysis and critique of arguments, skills taught (3) using vehicles other than formal logic. (See Kahane, 1971; Thomas, 1973; Scriven, 1976; Johnson and Blair, 1977; Weddle, 1978; and Fogelin, 1978.) Informal logic connects centrally with the last two features. Since the educational end – to teach critical thinking – is conflated with the means – to teach the rudiments of informal logic, there is little wonder that informal logic and critical thinking are widely taken to be the same thing.

Govier (1987) argues that critical thinking and informal logic should be distinguished, because thinking can be critical without using or issuing in arguments. One can think critically about things other than arguments (e.g., art), and use other critical methods besides argument in doing so. In our view too, although there is a close connection, 'informal logic' and 'critical thinking' have different denotations.

(5) *Applied Epistemology:* Recently, some have argued that informal logic should be classified as applied epistemology, not logic. Battersby (1989) argues that it is epistemological norms, not rules of logic, that constitute the philosophical core of informal logic, and that there is a close theory-application parallel between informal logic and applied ethics; hence, informal logic should be called applied epistemology. Weinstein (1990) argues that a central task of informal logic is to develop an account of how acceptability is transmitted from premises to conclusions, and that 'the assessment of the strength of support premises afford conclusions can only be [made] when the domain within which the argument is presented is taken into account' (123) – which is nothing else than applied epistemology: 'the study of the epistemologies in use in the various domains of human understanding in order to ground the assessment of arguments as they occur within them' (123). (See also McPeck, 1981 and Goldman, 1986.) The focus of these arguments on the undeniable epistemological aspect of informal logic overlooks its pragmatic aspects, and in some cases relies controversially on the identification of logic with formal deductive logic.

(6) *The Null Set:* Another school of thought holds that there is nothing at all to informal logic: it does not reduce to something other than a branch of logic, such as epistemology; there is nothing to reduce. Hintikka (1989), who contends that informal logic is 'mythical' (20) and that the term is 'a solecism' (13), argues that all reasoning, inference and argument is deductive, logic is the theory of deduction, and theories of deduction are formalizable, and that therefore there can be no informal – i.e., non-formalizable – theory of reasoning, inference or argument: no informal logic. (See also Woods, 1980.) We are not persuaded that all the premises of Hintikka's argument are true, but we suspect the dispute here may be largely about definitions. In any case, as Woods and Walton put it, 'the expression has taken root and does some responsible semantic work' (1989, xxi).

(7) *Argument Evaluation:* We ourselves belong to a group of theorists who all take 'informal logic' to name a complex mix of practical and theoretical enterprises related to argument evaluation (see, among others, Johnson and Blair, 1977, 1980; Fogelin, 1978; Govier, 1985; Walton, 1989). At the practical level, they take informal logic to

160

embrace the knowledge and skills required for the tasks of identifying, analyzing and evaluating arguments. At the theoretical level, they include within informal logic, variously, the formulation or application of the theories, or components thereof, that underwrite those practical tasks. Thus, speech act theory and conversational implicature have been applied to the interpretation of texts as argumentative (Fogelin, 1978). The theories of argumentative exchange (such as various types of dialogue structure) (Walton, 1984) and of the structure of arguments pertain to the analysis of the arguments identified in texts. And fallacy theory on the one hand, and theories of what constitute cogent arguments on the other (see Part IV, below), are applied to argument evaluation. These theorists differ about where they put their emphases and disagree to some extent about theory, but the commonality of the overall approach constitutes the broadest consensus about the nature of informal logic that exists at the present time.

To give an example, and to provide a reference for the rest of this article, here is how we have characterized informal logic:

> By informal logic we mean to designate a branch of logic which is concerned to develop non-formal standards, criteria, procedures for the analysis, interpretation, evaluation, critique and construction of argumentation in everyday discourse. (Johnson and Blair, 1987, 147)

We distinguish informal logic from formal logic, not only by methodology by also by its focal point: the social, communicative practice of argumentation can and should be distinguished from both deductive inference and deductive implication, which in our view are the proper subjects of formal logic. Our concern is with the logic of *argumentation*: the cogency of the support that reasons provide for the conclusions they are supposed to back up.

A note about terminology: Aside from Ryle's use, the first occurrence of 'informal logic' we know of in something like the usage we take as canonic is in Carney and Scheer (1964), where it appears without explanation as the title of a section and seems to denote logical matters not taken up by formal logic. The term next appears, still without explanation, in the subtitles of Munson (1976) and Fogelin (1978). We first used informal logic' in the title of the First International Symposium on Informal Logic in 1978.

Obviously, the term 'informal' will be as wide-ranging as its counterpart: 'formal'. Here we follow the lead of Barth and Krabbe (1982, 14ff.) who helpfully distinguish three senses of 'formal'. 'Formal$_1$' is the sense deriving from the Platonic idea of form and taken to be the ultimate metaphysical unit. 'Formal$_2$' is the form of sentences and statements as these are seen in modern logic. Thus, the syntax of the language to which sentence S belongs might be precisely formulated as 'formalized$_2$'; or the validity concept for S is defined in terms of the logical form$_2$ of the sentences which make up the argument. In this sense, most modern and contemporary logic is formal$_2$. 'Formal$_3$' refers to 'procedures which are somehow regulated or regimented, which take place according to some set of rules'.

In terms of this distinction, informal logic takes its meaning from a contrast with formal$_2$. However, there is nothing in the informal logic enterprise that is opposed to form$_3$, the idea that argumentative discourse should be regimented, i.e., subject to rules, criteria, standards or procedures (though not to algorithms). Nor does the project of informal logic deny that for *theoretical* purposes formalizations$_2$ within the statement of the theory might be useful and desirable. What is denied is that the criteria are to be found by reflection on the logical form$_2$ of the involved statements, and that its translation into logical form$_2$ is necessary or illuminating for the analysis and evaluation of argumentation in natural languages.[1]

'Informal' also has the connotation of lack of rigor, but what formalizing$_2$ does is make rigor *economical* (amenable to succinct formulation); it is not a condition of the theoretical possibility of rigor. In line with Aristotle's wise admonition, informal logic seeks precisely the degree of rigor that is appropriate in the context of interpretation, criticism, or theorizing about argumentation.

III. Twentieth century developments

1. 1900-1970

We can be brief here, because there is little to say about informal logic in this period. The reason is instructive. This period is the hey-day of mathematical logic. Under the influence first of Frege, then of Russell and Whitehead and later of Carnap and others, logic became mathematicized. Formal methods and approaches to logic became, accordingly, the approach of choice. The concern was to show that at its outer limits logic was virtually indistinguishable from mathematics. Logic was formal science par excellence. It did not take long for this approach to filter down into the logic tuition of the twentieth century.

There was little or no concern for *logica utens*, for what logic could do for life. Moreover the focus on proof or deductive demonstration meant such logic had virtually no application as a tool for the analysis and evaluation of actual argumentation - a restriction objected to in the critiques of Toulmin (1958), and Perelman and Olbrechts-Tyteca (1958).

There are no doubt many who might be mentioned as writing in the spirit of what later came to be called informal logic. Among those who published before the Second World War, we think of John Dewey for his *How We Think* (1933) and *Logic, The Theory of Inquiry* (1938), Robert Thouless for his *Straight and Crooked Thinking* (1930), L. Susan Stebbing for her *Thinking to Some Purpose* (1939).

After the war, Max Black (1946) and Monroe Beardsley (1950) wrote textbooks that in many respects anticipated the informal logic texts that appeared a quarter century later. For example, Beardsley says his book will be especially concerned with arguments, and its main theme is whether the reasons given when someone tries to convince us of something ought to convince us (11). In a section on 'the anatomy of argument' Beardsley introduces the tree-diagram method later adapted by Thomas (1973) and it or some modification of it is now used widely in textbooks. During the same period, the early exemplars of what we have called the 'global' introductory logic textbook began

162

to appear (Johnson and Blair 1980), Copi's (1953) perhaps being the most widely used. This is the text used in the 'baby logic' course mentioned above.

Thomas's use of Beardsley's tree-diagraming convention is the exception; for the most part, later informal logic texts did not turn to the earlier books for inspiration or ideas. Many writers, the authors of this article among them, felt themselves to be swimming against the current, and doing so in indifferent if not hostile waters. This feeling was not paranoia.[2] Furthermore, their own logical training as graduate students was in formal logic, and the preoccupation of logicians with symbolic logic and logistic systems had shaped their sense of what was legitimate and proper in logic education. They were quite aware, in developing the syllabi for the new courses they were teaching, and which evolved in due course into new textbooks for such courses, that they were bucking conventional wisdom and also developing their own theory as they went. There was a felt need both for legitimation and theoretical nurture. The figures we list next are philosophers to whom many of the 1970s writers turned for both sorts of sustenance.

2. Main theorists

a. Stephen Toulmin, *The Uses of Argument* (1958): Toulmin sees himself as challenging what might be called the mathematicization of logic, attempting to free logic from the geometric model and arguing that logic would do better to model itself after jurisprudence. To this end, he develops his own approach to understanding the layout of arguments. His elements are not the traditional premise, conclusion and assumption. Instead, Toulmin suggests arguments are more perspicuously interpreted as consisting of *claims* supported by grounds (*data*), with the inference relying on a *warrant* ruling that data of that sort support such claims. Warrants themselves may be supported by *backing*. The support for the claim is usually *qualified*, and certain conditions of *rebuttal* may be acknowledged.

Toulmin's contribution was an innovation in the theory of argument. Though its immediate effect on logic was nil, Toulmin's model has had wide influence in other areas: speech communication theory, rhetoric and more recently informal logic.

The following reservations may be entered. First, not all argumentation can be assimilated to the jurisprudential model without distortion, since it has certain assumptions that do not apply universally, such as the adversarial character of much legal argumentation. Second, Toulmin's model does not capture the dialectical character even of legal argumentation. In spite of his intentions, Toulmin's model is more fitted for monological than dialogical argument. Third, if one were to use jurisprudential argumentation as an inspiration, the likelihood is that it would generate several different models, not just one, since there is not one type of legal argumentation, but many (e.g., criminal and civil litigation differ, and both differ from negotiation argumentation). These criticisms, it should be added, are entirely in the spirit of Toulmin's approach to argumentation – sensitivity to context: be empirical rather than a prioristic, and expect differences in different domains. These matters of philosophical approach have had more influence on informal logic than the model itself, though Toulmin's example has helped validate resistance to the hegemony of formal logic.

b. Chaim Perelman and Lucy Olbrechts-Tyteca, *The New Rhetoric* (English translation in 1968, first published in French in 1958): This work's influence on informal logic is more by way of its legitimizing function and certain of its general features than by way of the impact of its details. The first chapter in particular, 'the framework of argumentation', with its relegation of the domain of formal logic to demonstration *in contrast to* argumentation, its emphasis on the importance in argumentation of the speaker and the audience, the distinction of truth-oriented discussion from victory-oriented debate, the idea that individual deliberative reflection can be argumentative in character – these and other general ideas have found their way into informal logic theory. In contrast, the lists of patterns and types of argument and their classification, which form the vast bulk of this big book's contents, have received little attention. However, due to influences from Dutch argumentation scholars (van Eemeren & Kruiger, 1986; Schellens, 1986), and working somewhat parallel to the Austrian argumentation scholar, Kienpointner (1992), Walton's theorizing has begun to find a central role for a conception of argument schemes (see his *Argument Schemes for Presumptive Reasoning*, 1996) whose lineage traces in part back to Perelman and Olbrechts-Tyteca.

c. Charles I. Hamblin, *Fallacies* (1970): Hamblin's book provided two sources of theoretical inspiration. First, his historical surveys of fallacy theory and of individual fallacies demonstrated the antiquity of the subject; and his trenchant critique of the accounts of individual fallacies demonstrated the need for improvement. Second, his argument that a revised fallacy theory requires a revision in the theory of argument along dialectical lines, and his accompanying contribution to what he calls formal dialectic, have led philosophers to approach these large tasks, trying to improve on his accounts. Hamblin inspired in particular Woods and Walton (see 1989) to launch their extensive studies and analyses of the fallacies, and through them, many others. Paradoxically, this influential work, famous for its characterization and condemnation of 'the standard treatment' of the fallacies, has been used by critics of informal logic as 'the standard treatment' of current fallacy theory, and as a substitute for careful attention to the detailed analyses of fallacies inspired by the very book they appeal to. Today, Hamblin's complaint, 'The truth is that nobody . . . is particularly satisfied with this corner of logic' (11) is no longer justified without considerable qualification.

d. Nicholas Rescher, *Plausible Reasoning* (1976) and *Dialectics* (1977): Some informal logicians have turned to one or both of these works by Rescher with a view to applying their theory to informal logic. Woods and Walton (1982) used Rescher's method of plausibility screening in handling conflicting advice from authorities in their treatment of *ad verecundiam*. In *Dialectics*, Rescher dips back into the scholastic tradition to borrow and revitalize the disputation model of argumentation. The effect of this move is to counteract the Cartesian model, which is solipsistic, with an approach that emphasizes 'the communal and controversy oriented aspects of rational argumentation and inquiry' (Rescher xiii). Rescher's modelling of dialectical argumentative exchanges has been influential, as has his associated account of burden of proof (see Blair and Johnson 1987).

e. John Woods and Douglas Walton: A single bibliographical reference here is impossible. Most of Woods and Walton's joint work on fallacies is collected in *Fallacies*

(1989). Their other main joint work is their textbook, *Argument: The Logic of the Fallacies* (1982). The fallacies treated include *ad verecundiam, petitio principii, ad baculum, ad hominem*, composition and division, post hoc, *ergo propter hoc, ad ignorantiam*, equivocation, *ad populum*, and many questions. Each has written on informal logic individually, Woods in several articles and Walton in articles and in several books (see Hansen's bibliography, 1990, and Woods and Walton's, 1989). Woods and Walton, collectively and individually, have been eclectic theorizers, borrowing from whatever branch of logic or other theory that might have application to produce as precise, rigorous and complete an account of whatever topic they are tackling at the moment. It has been their view that not just one or two, but several kinds of reasoning and dialogical interaction are instantiated in argumentation and require theoretical accounting for. Where possible, theorists would do well to try to make use of established logical theory to model the reasoning of this or that kind of argument. Always the objective is a theoretically mature analysis, but 'the . . . urgent work for now is to clear away the pretheoretical rubbish which obscures fundamental insights and impede[s] coherent theoretical effort' (1989, xiv).

3. Developments in post-1970s textbooks

a. Howard Kahane, *Logic and Contemporary Rhetoric: The Use of Reason in Everyday Life* (1971: 6th ed., 1992): To understand the emergence of informal logic, one must understand how this textbook came to be. Kahane's own words are helpful. In the introduction to the first edition, he writes:

> Today's students demand a marriage of theory and practice. That is why so many of them judge introductory courses on logic, fallacy and even rhetoric not relevant to their interests.
>
> In class a few years back, while I was going over the (to me) fascinating intricacies of the predicate logic quantifier rules, a student asked in disgust how anything he'd learned all semester long had any bearing whatever on President Johnson's decision to escalate again in Vietnam. I mumbled something about bad logic on Johnson's part, and then stated that *Introduction to Logic* was not that kind of course. His reply was to ask what courses did take up such matters, and I had to admit that so far as I knew none did.
>
> He wanted what most students today want, a course relevant to everyday reasoning, a course relevant to the arguments they hear and read about race, pollution, poverty, sex, atomic warfare, the population explosion, and all the other problems faced by the human race in the second half of the twentieth century. (vii)

Kahane wants logic to be useful, to be *relevant*. Why? Here the cultural context we discussed in the Introduction comes to the fore. Kahane's text can be seen as one type of pedagogical response to the demand for relevance in logic instruction.

Kahane takes what had until then been but one section of the traditional logic course – the part on fallacies – and makes that the core of his approach. In so doing, he is going back to the *De Sophisticis Elenchis* rather than the *Prior Analytics*, to the tradition in logic that becomes known as the informal fallacies. Although Fearnside and Holther (1959) have already done as much, Kahane does more, for he attempts to breath new life into the fallacy tradition. He expunges the old examples such as amphiboly and the artificial or invented examples of most texts, he restricts his treatment to fallacies with some currency in contemporary political rhetoric, introducing catchy new nomenclature, and he fills his text with examples of actual, lively arguments, taken from the politics and social issues of the day. In addition, he adds new fallacies to the traditional list, among them *provincialism, red herring* and *suppressed evidence*. Finally, Kahane replaces the traditional chapters on scientific method and probability with chapters on advertising and on the news media, and a supplement on evaluating textbooks.

Kahane's text was an important breakthrough, and it paved the way for the informal logic movement. But it was not the only progenitor to challenge the conventional assumptions about logic tuition as found in logic texts.

b. Stephen Thomas, *Practical Reasoning in Natural Language* (1973; 3rd ed., 1984): Albeit with some indebtedness to Beardsley's *Practical Logic* (1950), Thomas's book represents a quite different approach to the teaching of logical criticism. He places heavy emphasis on the task of laying out clearly the logical structure of the argument (129 pages altogether in the first edition in chapters 1 and 5) - far more than any other text. In all this material, *Thomas makes no reference at all to the traditional schemata of formal deductive logic.* He combines classical validity with inductive strength in his criterion for adequacy of premise support for the conclusion. By showing how logical analysis and critique can be carried out without employing the standard notion of logical form, Thomas makes a signal contribution to informal logic. In addition, Thomas has the first discussion in an informal logic text of the principle of charity (see Rescher, 1964 for an earlier appearance). And like Kahane, he too has an eye firmly on the sorts of issues that are likely to come up in today's world outside the classroom.

c. Michael Scriven, *Reasoning* (1976): Scriven's text is important for several reasons. For one, since Scriven was the most prominent philosopher of the early authors, his writing an informal logic text helped to legitimize the new approach. Like the others, he avoids the apparatus of formal logic, which he sees as having little transfer, as relying on questionable translation possibilities, and as in any case having costs outweighing any possible benefits. Instead, he presents a seven-step method of argument analysis, one that involves clarification of meanings, identification of premises and conclusions, portrayal of the argument's structure, formulation of assumptions, criticism of the premises and inferences, consideration of other relevant arguments, and overall evaluation. Scriven extends Thomas's method of tree diagrams; he is the first to discuss at length the ethics of argument analysis, including a new formulation of the principle of charity; he discusses the differences between strong and weak criticism; and his text contains the first real discussion of the principle of discrimination (proportion the critique to the gravity of the offense).

In our opinion the textbooks by Kahane, Thomas and Scriven are the first generation of informal logic texts. Each breaks new ground. Together, they prefigure the remarkable divergence of approach of later texts. In fact, their only main points of agreement are that (1) all target real life arguments, and (2) all eschew the recourse to formal apparatus found in formal logic texts, or even of standard introductory logic texts.

4. Other developments

A field of inquiry requires communication between inquirers. By the late 1970s informal logic had developed to the extent that in 1978 about 80 people attended the First International Symposium on Informal Logic at the University of Windsor. Following the conference and prompted by the participants, Blair and Johnson began in early 1979 the *Informal Logic Newsletter*, publishing news about informal logic, articles and teaching material thrice yearly. The proceedings of the first symposium were published in 1980 by Edgepress. In 1983 there was a Second International Symposium at Windsor. Participants at the symposium formed the Association for Informal Logic and Critical Thinking, which has since sponsored numerous sessions on informal logic in conjunction with the American Philosophical Association and Canadian Philosophical Association annual meetings. Many papers of the symposium were published in the journal, *Informal Logic*, which Blair and Johnson established as the successor to the *Newsletter* in 1983, publishing three issues annually. In 1989 a Third International Symposium on Informal Logic was held at Windsor. Some of its papers have been published in *Informal Logic*, others appear in *New Essays in Informal Logic*(1995). Many informal logic papers also appear in the long-established journal, *Philosophy and Rhetoric*, as well as being scattered throughout other journals (see Hansen, 1990).

Since 1981, an annual critical thinking conference at Sonoma State University has been an hospitable environment for informal logicians to present their ideas to interested North American colleagues.

In 1986 many informal logicians from North America participated in the first Conference on Argumentation held at the University of Amsterdam, which brought together from around the world scholars working on argumentation from a variety of points of view besides logic. This conference was followed by the founding of a new quarterly journal, *Argumentation*, which publishes a broad variety of articles on all aspects of argumentation. A second Amsterdam Conference on Argumentation was held in 1990 and a third in 1994. Besides the Amsterdam conferences, another source of interdisciplinary stimulation for some informal logicians have been contacts with members of the argumentation group of the speech communication community in the United States, through its journal, *Argumentation and Advocacy* (formerly, *Journal of the American Forensic Association*), and the biennial Speech Communication Association-American Forensic Association sponsored conference at Alta, Utah.

So much for a quick sketch of the history of informal logic in this century. (See Johnson and Blair, 1980 and 1985 for our earlier accounts.)

IV. The problematic: issues in informal logic

In this section we present what are currently the main issues in informal logic. The first is the question of fallacies, which has two components: (a) fallacy theory as whole, and (b) the individual fallacies. The second issue concerns the interpretation of argumentative texts in general and of particular arguments in such texts, including how exactly to comprehend and to display the structure of the argument, and other problems involved in the task of reconstruction. A third issue concerns the normative question: by what standards and according to what theory should one evaluate the argument once reconstructed?

1. Fallacies and fallacy theory

a. *The viability of fallacy theory:* There has been an enduring interest in the question: are there fallacies? Do the fallacies represent a viable approach to argument evaluation? For the most part, the playing field divides into two parts: those who question the viability of fallacy theory; and those who defend it. Defenders of fallacy theory subdivide into those who believe a unified theory of the fallacies is necessary, and those who do not.

Hamblin first raised the question of the viability of fallacy theory in general by showing that the treatment of fallacies found in the textbooks were often conflicting, often confused, and on the whole completely inadequate. Some ten years later two influential articles, building on Hamblin, also challenged the viability of fallacy theory. In the first, Finocchiaro (1981) criticizes the accounts of fallacies found in textbooks (in the spirit of Hamblin but looking at a different selection) and also suggests that the very charge of fallacy is not infrequently a creation of the critic. The fallacy approach stresses negative instead of positive evaluation, and thereby illustrates an important but unfortunate bias in the theory of evaluation. In the second, Massey (1981) also criticizes textbook accounts of fallacy and argues that there cannot be a logic of fallacies. His argument is based on the definition of fallacy stemming from Hamblin: an argument that appears to be valid but is not. Massey argues that since there cannot be a theory of invalidity, it follows that there cannot be a theory of fallacy. A somewhat different challenge is that of Hintikka (1989), who argues that instead of seeing fallacies against the background of critical discussion, we should view them against the background of the highly-structured form of discourse practiced in the Lyceum.

In defense of fallacy theory, Govier (1982) argues that the challenges raised by both Finocchiaro and Massey make important but undefended assumptions regarding a theory of argument. Johnson (1987) argues against some of the traditional points raised against fallacy theory, such as that the ways of going wrong are infinite and hence that there cannot be any theory of fallacy, nor any reliable classification. Johnson (1989) contends that Massey's position rests on a questionable conception of fallacy. Moreover it makes assumptions about what an adequate theory must look like that are biased against informal logic. Woods (1992) offers a defense of fallacy theory that connects the interest in fallacy with rationality theory and takes a dim view of the prospects for a possible unifying theory.

At this point in the debate, the objections directed at fallacy theory, however serious, have not been sufficiently persuasive either to cause the abandonment of fallacies or to dissuade theorists from the attempt to give better accounts of fallacy theory in general and of the individual fallacies in particular.

Among those sympathetic to fallacy theory the main bone of contention, apart from vigorous disputes over the best analyses of individual fallacies, is between those who argue for a unified theory of fallacy, one that is not tied exclusively to logic, and those who believe that a unified theory might be impossible, and that proof theoretic treatment is a powerfully illuminating tool worth trying for. Van Eemeren and Grootendorst maintain that 'ideally, one unified theory that is capable of dealing with all the different phenomena, is to be preferred' and 'it is important not to exaggerate the role of logic' (1992a, 103). Woods and Walton have been content to analyze fallacies one at a time, trying to use a variety of logics to 'provide solid generalizations' (1989, xix), and Woods has insisted that any integrated theory of the fallacies should preserve their often striking differences (1992, 43). Recently, Walton (1995) has developed a pragmatic theory of fallacy according to which a fallacy 'is an argumentation technique, based on an argumentation scheme, misused to block the goals of dialogue in which two parties are reasoning together' (xi). Although on Walton's view there are many argumentation schemes, and several different types of dialogue, his theory is unifying in its general conception of fallacy.

b. *Studies of the individual fallacies:* Hamblin's criticisms struck a nerve (though recently there has come a call for a re-evaluation of Hamblin's critique, see Johnson, 1990a and 1990b). As we have noted, they inspired a large body of work by Woods and Walton. So where do matters stand now as regards our accounts of the individual fallacies? Are there now definitive analyses of the traditional fallacies? Are there new fallacies worthy of inclusion in the repertoire? There can be little question that the current analyses of most fallacies are more clear and precise than hitherto in the history of the subject.

Tighter and more finely focused book length studies of fallacy have been more prominent in the last decade. Most of them have viewed fallacy in the context of argumentation and have shown the benefits of the rhetorical concern for context and audience (see Walton, 1992). There have also been many more article-length studies of the individual fallacies, (e.g., Brinton, 1985 and Wreen, 1987). For a record of recent work on fallacy and particular fallacies, the reader should consult H. V. Hansen, 'An Informal Logic Bibliography' (1990), which lists, since Hamblin's book appeared, some twenty-two articles on *ad hominem* and *tu quoque*, ten on *ad verecundiam*, thirteen on other '*ad*' fallacies, and thirty-one on all other fallacies. However, the best source of recent work on fallacies and fallacy theory is Hansen and Pinto (1995), which includes historical selections from the principal theorists, papers on contemporary fallacy theory, criticism and teaching, several papers analyzing individual fallacies, and an up-to-date bibliography of recent work on fallacies.

In spite of challenges and criticisms, the topic of fallacy has remained a significant focus for research.

2. Argument analysis

The informal logic turn to actual arguments forced theorists to face up to the ill-organized, incompletely stated, wandering-off-topic arguments found normally in written and spoken texts. With the exception of Fogelin (1978), informal logicians have tended not to address the complex theoretical issues arising from the attempt to explain how we manage to interpret such discourse, leaving this task to linguists, speech communication theorists, and philosophers of language. The doctrine in textbooks has been *ad hoc* rather than theoretically motivated. Where informal logicians have focused their attention is the issue of how to lay out the statements playing argumentative roles in such discourse in a perspicuous way from the point of view of evaluating the argument.

As we have noted, Toulmin's model has had little impact on informal logic and much more on argumentation theory in speech communication. Beardsley's diagrams, mentioned above, with their distinction between convergent, divergent and serial arguments, were more influential. Thomas adds the concept of a linked argument. Beardsley's and Thomas's diagrams contain each premise written out in full. Scriven adds the wrinkle of numbering the sentences playing an argumentative role and then making a diagram of the supporting relationships using just the circled numbers and lines joining them. He also introduces the convention of using a minus sign to symbolize negative support, so the he can diagram 'balance of considerations' arguments. Scriven's third innovation is to use letters to represent reconstructed 'missing' premises and putting them in the diagram at the appropriate place to 'reconstruct' the argument to show their role in joining with stated premises to strengthen the inference. Johnson and Blair (1977) adapt Scriven's diagramming method to longer arguments. Later texts have modified and amplified these basic approaches to the task of representing the structure of arguments.

Recently, the conceptions of argument structure underlying such diagramming have come under critical scrutiny. For example, there is an unresolved ambiguity as to whether each unit in the diagram is a distinct premise or an argument as such (that is, a set of premises. The so-called linked structure seems to capture sets of premises working jointly, whereas the so-called convergent structure seems to capture different lines of argument. Snoeck Henkemans (1992), applying the Amsterdam pragma-dialectic argumentation theory of van Eemeren and Grootendorst (1983), argues that conceiving arguments as dialogical discussions aimed at dispute resolution permits the removal of these and other confusions. Recent articles by Yanal (1991) and Conway (1991) also discuss the 'linked-convergent' distinction.

Attention to the structure of actual examples of arguments has invariably been accompanied by the attempt to account for 'assumptions' - 'missing', 'hidden', 'unexpressed', 'tacit' or 'unstated' premises. If an arguer clearly intends one statement to support another, but it doesn't, there is a presumption that the arguer expected the listener or reader to understood as read some additional proposition(s) that, when added to the initial statement, enable the entire set to be relevant, or to provide stronger support. Aristotle's enthymemes are an instance. But how shall the missing premise be formulated? Which argument should be reconstructed - the speaker's, the strongest possible (given what's stated), some other? Should the argument be reconstructed so the premises logically imply the conclusion (so that the logical form of the resulting argument is deductively valid), or so that they provide strong support, or merely so that they are relevant, or something else? Should the missing premises supplied be (likely to be) believed by the arguer, known to the arguer, what the arguer (likely) expected the listener to believe, or something else? There has been considerable discussion in the informal logic literature of such questions surrounding the problem of missing premises, but no resolution of them (see Hansen's 1990 index entry for a list of articles).

A crucial question for informal logic is what theory of evaluation or criticism to use. Suppose we have laid out the structure of the argument, giving as plausible a reconstruction as we can in accordance with the principle of charity, and without recourse to logical form. Now we face the question: How good is this argument? Qua informal logician we must be able to answer this question without recourse to 'soundness' (true premises, deductively valid inference). How do we answer?

a. *Fallacy as a theory of criticism*: Immediately, of course, fallacy theory suggests itself for this role: a good argument will be free of fallacy, and the presence of a fallacy is at best a prima facie weakness and at worst a fatal flaw in the argument. The problem with this intuition is that there is as little consensus within the realm of fallacy theory about how to shape the theory and use it for critical purposes as there is about whether the theory is viable. That said, we will discuss one framework that has been quite widely adopted. According to it, an argument must satisfy the criteria of relevance, sufficiency and acceptability, and a fallacious argument violates one or more of these criteria. This account is first appears in Johnson and Blair (1977) and later in Govier (1985), Damer (1987), Freeman (1988), Little, Groarke and Tindale (1989), and Seech (1993). Herewith a few comments on the status of each of these criteria.

Relevance: First, there is no widely accepted account of probative relevance – the relevance of premises for conclusions. This is unsurprising, since relevance has received little attention from informal logicians until recently. Grice (1975) makes relevance one of the governing criteria for conversational implicature, but his account does not provide any theoretical enlightenment. Sperber and Wilson (1986) have the most definitive account to date, but it does not settle the question of the nature of probative relevance. A conference on relevance in 1991 at McMaster University was noteworthy for the variety of approaches, of ways of understanding the question of relevance, and of solutions that found expression there (see van Eemeren and Grootendorst, 1992b for most of the papers).

Second, it has been objected that sufficiency presupposes relevance: if premises satisfy the sufficiency requirement, they must be relevant. This is true, but relevance is a separate requirement because some problems with arguments are specifically relevance failures; for example, *straw person* and *red herring*.

Sufficiency: Of the three criteria, this one has so far attracted the least amount of sustained discussion. It goes without saying that no one seriously believes that anything like an algorithm for sufficiency will ever be available. The question whether the premises provide sufficient evidence for the conclusion has three dimensions. First, are the appropriate types of evidence presented? Second, within each type, is enough evidence of that kind provided? Third (what might be termed dialectical sufficiency), does the arguer deal with the appropriate kinds of objection?

Acceptability: The criterion of acceptability is the informal logician's counterpart to the truth requirement in the traditional doctrine of soundness. Influential in this respect was Hamblin who argued that truth was an inappropriate criterion for arguments with a given audience, context, and occasion, being both too strong (who can be sure of the truth?) and too weak (it would have to be *known* truth). His complaint was not unlike that of the deconstructionists: the idea of truth presupposes an impossible God's eye position from which to view matters. Many informal logicians have adopted acceptability as a requirement, but Johnson (1990) raises questions about it. He argues that on any construal acceptability is problematic, and in any case it may be too weak a criterion.

b. *The natural-language approach*: Scriven opposes using the fallacies approach for the purpose of argument criticism, arguing that doing so requires building into the identification process all the skills needed for analysis without the taxonomy, and that turns fallacy criticism into a formal approach with a tricky diagnostic step (1976, xvi). He thinks there already exists in natural language a rich critical vocabulary that is sufficient and suitable for critical purposes, for example: reason, evidence, conclusion, thesis, relevant, sufficient, inconsistent, implication, presupposition, objection, assumption, ambiguous, vague, and so on. Scriven's method of evaluation is to raise the questions embedded in his seven-step method cited above.

In criticizing the inferences, Scriven asks the critic to inquire whether, given the truth of the premise(s), the conclusion is true or likely to be true. He thus has broadened the conception of validity beyond syntactic and semantic entailment in ways not unlike Thomas. The test of a reliable inference is whether it withstands counterexamples. He requires the arguer to look for other arguments that bear on the issue, those pointing to a different conclusion and other arguments favoring the stated conclusion. Thus one must go outside the frame of the argument in order to evaluate it. And the critic must in the end make an overall judgement. (See Hitchcock, 1984 for an application of Scriven.)

c. *Toulmin-type theories*: Toulmin and others take the view that standards of good argument are specific to each field or discipline (see Toulmin, Rieke and Janik 1979). We have seen that McPeck (1981) and Weinstein (1990) think the important standards for an argument are furnished by the epistemology of its field. The middle ground position between the 'all standards are field dependent' view and the 'important standards are field invariant' view (the latter includes some fallacy theorists) is occupied by Siegel (1988) who argues that there are significant field invariant and field dependent standards.

In summary, at this point, it seems clear that there continue to be divisions among theorists about the kind of normative theory which should be used in the approach to argumentation.

d. *Probative logic/presumptive reasoning*: Scriven (1986) argued for the need to develop what he called 'probative logic' as the central logic of argumentation, and to relegate to subsidiary roles the logics of deduction and probability. Probative logic is the logic of the reasoning of practical arguments. Scriven has since discussed its role in the reasoning of evaluation (1995). This is the logic of inferences which are neither entailments nor inductions, yet can be 'good enough to bet the farm on' (1995, 67).

Without reference to Scriven, but acknowledging the influence of Rescher's notion of 'plausible reasoning' (Rescher, 1976) Walton has been developing a theory of 'presumptive reasoning' (1995) which has the same objective as Scriven's probative logic – namely to account for non-monotonic reasoning, that is, reasoning which is neither inductive nor deductive, and is inherently subject to correction or qualification. Walton treats argumentation schemes as the inference warrants of such reasoning.

In our view, this is one of the most significant recent developments in informal logic, since it addresses the central question of the distinctiveness of the 'logic' of this field.

V. Concluding remarks

This paper has of necessity been but a brief scan of the informal logic movement of the past twenty-five years or so, of its antecedents and its preoccupations. Clearly. informal logic has established itself as a legitimate field of inquiry – as a branch of logic, in our view, not incompatible with formal logic, but covering a large body of reasoning and argumentation not well-modeled by monotonic logic. Informal logic has begun to contribute to and learn from cognate fields. Walton and Krabbe, a formal dialogue theorist, have collaborated on a book (1995). Scholars working in informal logic and in speech communication in North America have collaborated with Dutch argumentation theorists on a handbook of historical backgrounds and contemporary developments in these overlapping fields (van Eemeren, Grootendorst and Snoeck Henkemans, 1996; see also Hansen and Pinto, 1995). And scholars from all three communities are currently collaborating with researchers in artificial intelligence on a multi-volume Handbook of Practical Reasoning (see Gabbay and Ohlbach, 1996 for the proceedings of a recent conference which brought these groups together). With Walton's most recent books (1995, 1996), we have for the first time a more or less unified and mature theory of informal logic for examination and further dialectical development. In short, the field appears to be flourishing.

Notes

1.   For additional discussions of the term 'form' and its variant meanings and how these affect the understanding of informal logic, see Johnson and Blair (1991, 131-150) and Govier (1988, ch. 10).

2.   Scriven, an established and respected philosopher of science, could not get his publisher, McGraw-Hill, to take on the manuscript of *Reasoning* until his own privately published and promoted edition proved to be commercially viable. The authors' *Logical Self-Defence* (3rd edition, 1993) was panned by the first set of publisher's readers, formal logicians, at least one of whom, incidentally, did not even bother to read the manuscript through before recommending rejection

References

Austin, J. L. (1962), *How to Do Things with Words*, Oxford University Press: Oxford.
Austin, J. L. (1970), *Philosophical Papers*, 2nd ed., edited by J. O. Urmson, Clarendon Press: Oxford.

Barth, E. M., and Erik C. W. Krabbe (1982), *From Axiom to Dialogue: A Philosophic Study of Logics and Argumentation*, de Gruyter: Berlin.

Battersby, Mark E. (1989), 'Critical Thinking as Applied to Epistemology', *Informal Logic*, Vol. 11, pp. 91-99.

Beardsley, Monroe C. (1950), *Practical Logic*, Prentice-Hall: Engelwood Cliffs, NJ.

Black, Max (1955), *Critical Thinking*, 2nd ed., Prentice-Hall: Englewood Cliffs, NJ.

Blair, J. Anthony, and Ralph H. Johnson (eds.) (1980), *Informal Logic: The First International Symposium*, Edgepress: Point Reyes, CA.

Blair, J. Anthony, and Ralph H. Johnson (1987), 'Argumentation as Dialectical', *Argumentation*, Vol. 1, pp. 41-56.

Brinton, Alan (1985), 'A Rhetorical View of the *ad Hominem*', *Australasian Journal of Philosophy*, Vol. 63, pp. 50-63.

Carney, James D., and Richard K. Scheer (1964), *Fundamentals of Logic*, Macmillan: New York.

Conway, David A. (1991), 'On the Distinction Between Convergent and Linked Arguments', *Informal Logic*, Vol. 13, pp.145-158.

Copi, Irving (1953), *Introduction to Logic*, Macmillan: New York.

Copi, Irving and Carl Cohen (1990), *Introduction to Logic*, 8th ed., Macmillan: New York.

Damer, T. Edward (1980), *Attacking Faulty Reasoning*, Wadsworth: Belmont, CA.

Dewey, John (1938), *Logic, The Theory of Inquiry*, Irvington: New York.

Dewey, John (1933), *How We Think*, Heath: Boston.

Eemeren, Frans H. van, and Rob Grootendorst (1983), *Speech Acts in Argumentative Discussions*, Foris: Dordrecht.

Eemeren, Frans H. van, and Rob Grootendorst (1992a), *Argumentation, Communication, and Fallacies: A Pragma-dialectic Perspective*, Lawrence Erlbaum Associates: Hillsdale, NJ.

Eemeren, Frans H. van, and Rob Grootendorst (eds.) (1992b), *Argumentation*, Vol. 6.

Eemeren, Frans H. van and Tjark Kruiger (1987), 'Identifying Argumentation Schemes', in Eemeren, F. H. van, R. Grootendorst, J. A. Blair, and C. A. Willard (eds.), *Argumentation:Perspectives and Appraoches*, Proceedings of the 1986 Amsterdam Conference on Argumentation, Foris: Dordrecht, pp. 70-81.

Eemeren, Frans H. van, Rob Grootendorst, J. Anthony Blair, and Charles A. Willard (eds.) (1992), *Argumentation Illuminated*, Sic Sat: Amsterdam.

Eemeren, Frans H. van, Rob Grootendorst, and Francisca Snoeck Henkemans (eds.) (1996), *Fundamentals of Argumentation Theory: A Handbook of Historical Backgrounds and Contemporary Developments*, Lawrence Erlbaum Associates: Mahwah, NJ.

Fearnside, W. Ward, and William B. Holther (1959), *Fallacy, The Counterfeit of Argument*, Prentice-Hall: Engelwood Cliffs, NJ.

Finocchiaro, Maurice A. (1981), 'Fallacies and the Evaluation of Reasoning', *American Philosophical Quarterly*, Vol. 18, pp. 13-22.

Fogelin, Robert (1978), *Understanding Arguments: An Introduction to Informal Logic*, Harcourt, Brace, Jovanovich: New York.

Freeman, James B. (1988), *Thinking logically: Basic Concepts for Reasoning*, Prentice-Hall: Englewood Cliffs, NJ.

Goldman, Alvin (1986), *Epistemology and Cognition*, Harvard University Press: Cambridge.

Govier, Trudy (1982), 'Who Says There Are No Fallacies?', *Informal Logic Newsletter*, Vol. 5, pp. 2-10.

Govier, Trudy (1985), *A Practical Study of Argument*, Wadsworth: Belmont, CA.

Govier, Trudy (1987), *Problems in Argument Analysis and Evaluation*, Foris: Dordrect.

Grice, Paul (1975), 'Logic and Conversation', in Cole, P. and J. Morgan (eds.), *Syntax and Semantics*, Vol. 3, Academic Press: New York.

Hansen, H. V. (1990), 'An Informal Logic Bibliography', *Informal Logic*, Vol. 12, pp.155-184.

Hansen, H. V., and Robert C. Pinto (eds.) (1995), *Fallacies: Classical and Contemporary Readings*, The Pennsylvania State University Press: University Park.

Hintikka, Jaakko (1989), 'The Role of Logic in Argumentation', *The Monist*, Vol. 72, pp. 3-24.

Hitchcock, David (1983), *Critical Thinking: A Guide to Evaluating Information*, Methuen: Toronto.

Johnson, Ralph H. (1987), 'The Blaze of Her Splendours: Suggestions About Revitalizing Fallacy Theory', *Argumentation*, Vol. 1, pp. 239-253.

Johnson, Ralph H. (1989), 'Massey on Fallacy and Informal Logic: A Reply', *Synthese*, Vol. 80, pp. 407-26.

Johnson, Ralph H. (1990a), 'Hamblin on the Standard Treatment', *Philosophy and Rhetoric*, Vol. 23, pp. 153-67.

Johnson, Ralph H. (1990b), 'Acceptance Is Not Enough: A Critique of Hamblin', *Philosophy and Rhetoric*, Vol. 23 pp. 271-287.

Johnson, Ralph H., and J. Anthony Blair (1993), *Logical Self-Defense*, 3rd ed., McGraw-Hill Ryerson: Toronto.

Johnson, Ralph H., and J. Anthony Blair (1980), 'The Recent Development of Informal Logic', in Blair and Johnson (1980).

Johnson, Ralph H., and J. Anthony Blair (1985), 'Informal Logic: The Past Five Years, 1978-83', *American Philosophical Quarterly*, Vol. 22, pp. 181-196.

Johnson, Ralph H., and J. Anthony Blair (1987), 'The Current State of Informal Logic and Critical Thinking', *Informal Logic*, Vol. 9, pp. 147-51.

Johnson, Ralph H., and J. Anthony Blair (1991), 'Contexts of Informal Reasoning: Commentary', in Voss, James F., David N. Perkins and Judith N. Segal (eds.), *Informal Reasoning and Education*, Lawrence Erlbaum Associates: Hillsdale, NJ, pp. 131-50

Kahane, Howard (1992), *Logic and Contemporary Rhetoric, The Use of Reasoning in Everyday Life*, 6th ed., Wadsworth: Belmont, CA.

Kienpointner, Manfred (1992), *Alltagslogic: Struktur und funktion von argumentationsmustern*, Frommann-Holzboog: Stuttgart-Bad Cannstatt.

Little, J. Frederick, Leo A. Groarke, and Christopher W. Tindale (1989), *Good Reasoning Matters*, McLelland and Stewart: Toronto.

Massey, Gerald (1981), 'The Fallacy Behind Fallacies', *Midwest Journal of Philosophy*, Vol. 6, pp. 489-500.

McPeck, John (1981), *Critical Thinking and Education*, Martin Robertson: Oxford.

Munson, Ronald (1976), *The Way of Words: An Informal Logic*, Houghton Mifflin: New York.

Nisbett, Richard E., and Lee Ross (1980), *Human Inference: Strategies and Shortcomings of Social Judgement*, Prentice-Hall: Englewood Cliffs, NJ.

Norris, Stephen, and Robert Ennis (1989), *Evaluating Critical Thinking*, Midwest Publications: Pacific Grove, CA.

Perelman, Chaim, and Lucy Olbrechts-Tyteca (1958), *La nouvelle rhetorique: Traite de l'argumentation*, Presses Universitaires de France: Paris.

Perelman, Chaim, and Lucy Olbrechts-Tyteca (1969), *The New Rhetoric*, translated by John Wilkinson and Purcell Weaver, University of Notre Dame Press: Notre Dame, IN.

Pomeroy, Ralph (1982), 'Ryle on (and for) Informal Logic', *Informal Logic Newsletter*, Vol. 5, pp. 23-25.

Rescher, Nicholas (1964), *Introduction to Logic*, St. Martin's Press: New York.

Rescher, Nicholas (1976), *Plausible Reasoning: An Introduction to the Theory and Practice of Plausible Inference*, Van Gorcum: Assen.

Rescher, Nicholas (1977), *Dialectics: A Controversy-Oriented Approach to the Theory of Knowledge*, State University of New York Press: Albany.

Ryle, Gilbert (1954), *Dilemmas*, Cambridge University Press: Cambridge.

Schellens, Peter Jan (1987), 'Types of Argument and the Critical Reader', in Eemeren, F. H. van, R. Grootendorst, J. A. Blair, and C. A. Willards (eds.), *Argumentation: Analyses and Practices*, Proceedings of the 1986 Amsterdam Conference on Argumentation, Foris: Dordrecht, pp. 734-41.

Scriven, Michael (1976), *Reasoning*, McGraw-Hill: New York.

Scriven, Michael (1987), 'Probative Logic', in Eemeren, F. H. van, R. Grootendorst, J. A. Blair, and C. A. Willards (eds.), *Argumentation: Across the Lines of Discipline*, Proceedings of the 1986 Amsterdam Conference on Argumentation, Foris: Dordrecht, pp. 7-32.

Scriven, Michael (1995), 'The Logic of Evaluation in Practice', in Fournier, Deborah M. (ed.), *Reasoning in Evaluation: Inferential Links and Leaps*, Jossey-Bass: San Francisco, *New Directions for Evaluation*, No. 68, pp. 49-70.

Seech, Zachary (1993), *Open Minds and Everyday Reasoning*, Wadsworth: Belmont, CA.

Siegel, Harvey (1988), *Educating Reason: Rationality, Critical Thinking and Education*, Routledge: New York.

Snoeck Henkemans, A. F. (1992), *Analyzing Complex Argumentation*, Sic Sat: Amsterdam.

Sperber, Dan, and Deirdre Wilson (1988), *Relevance: Communication and Cognition*, Harvard University Press: Cambridge.

Stebbing, Susan L. (1939), *Thinking to Some Purpose*, Whitefriars Press: London.

Thomas, Stephen N. (1984), *Practical Reasoning in Natural Language*, 3rd ed., Prentice-Hall: Englewood Cliffs, NJ.

Thouless, Robert (1930), *Straight and Crooked Thinking*, Hodder and Stoughton: London.

Toulmin, Stephen (1958), *The Uses of Argument*, Cambridge University Press: Cambridge.

Toulmin, Stephen, Richard Rieke, and Allan Janik (1984), 2nd ed., *An Introduction to Reasoning*, Macmillan: New York.

Walton, Douglas N. (1984), *Logical Dialogue Games and Fallacies*, University Press of America: Lanham, MD.

Walton, Douglas N. (1985), *Arguer's Position: A Pragmatic Study of 'Ad Hominem' Attack, Criticism, Refutation and Fallacy*, Greenwood Press: Westport, CT.

Walton, Douglas N. (1989), *Informal Logic, A Handbook for Critical Argumentation*, Cambridge University Press: Cambridge.

Walton, Douglas N. (1991), *Begging the Question*, Greenwood Press, New York.

Walton, Douglas N. (1992), *The Place of Emotion in Argument*, The Pennsylvania State University Press: University Park.

Walton, Douglas N. (1995), *A Pragmatic Theory of Fallacy*, The University of Alabama Press: Tuscaloosa and London.

Walton, Douglas N. (1996), *Argument Schemes for Presumptive Reasoning*, Lawrence Erlbaum Associates: Mahwah, NJ.

Walton, Douglas N., and Eric C. W. Krabbe (1995), *Commitment in Dialogue: Basic Concepts in Interpersonal Reasoning*, State University of New York Press: Albany.

Weddle, Perry (1978), *Argument, A Guide to Critical Thinking*, McGraw-Hill: New York.

Weinstein, Mark (1990), 'Towards a Research Agenda for Informal Logic and Critical Thinking', *Informal Logic*, Vol. 2, pp. 121-143.

Willard, Charles Arthur, and J. Robert Cox (eds.) (1982), *Advances in Argumentation Theory and Research*, Southern Illinois University Press: Carbondale and Edwardsville.

Woods, John (1980), 'What is Informal Logic?', in Blair and Johnson (1980), pp. 57-68.

Woods, John (1992) 'Who Cares About the Fallacies?', in van Eemeren, *et al.* (1992), pp. 23-48.

Woods, John, and Douglas Walton (1982), *Argument: The Logic of the Fallacies*, McGraw-Hill Ryerson: Toronto.

Woods, John, and Douglas Walton (1989), *Fallacies: Selected Papers 1972-1982*, Foris: Dordrecht.

Wreen, Michael J. (1987), 'Yes, Virginia, There is a Santa Claus', *Informal Logic*, Vol. 9, pp. 31-39.

Yanal, Robert J. (1991), 'Dependent and Independent Reasons', *Informal Logic*, Vol. 13, pp.137-144.

Index of names

Holther, William B. 97n, 103, 166
Howell, Wilbur Samuel 8, 84, 97n, 101
Huby, Pamela 5
Hudson, Hud 7
Hugh of St. Victor 51
Hume, David 71-72, 75, 78, 97n, 114, 153

Jean Buridan 55, 60
John Scotus Eriugena 56
John of Salisbury 51-52
Johnson, Ralph H. 1, 7, 135, 160-61, 163-64, 167-171, 173n
Johnstone, Henry W. 109
Jongsma, Calvin 101

Kahane, Howard 160, 165-66
Kant, Immanuel 5, 7, 71-72, 75, 78, 82, 127, 144-57
Kirwan, Richard 101
Kneale, Martha 2, 3-4, 13, 52
Kneale, William 2, 3-4, 13, 52
Krabbe, Erik C. W. 123n, 161, 173

Lindsay, Thomas 101
Little, J. Frederick 171
Locke, John 6, 7, 67, 85, 87, 101, 109

Massey, Gerald J. 141n, 168
McKerrow, Raymie E. 6, 101
McPeck, John 160, 172
Mill, John Stuart 7, 46, 68-69, 71, 81n, 101-2, 115, 125-43
Moses Maimonides 58
Murphy, James J. 53

Olbrechts-Tyteca, Lucy 9, 119, 123n, 162, 164

Paul of Venice 58, 61
Perelman, Chaim 9, 119, 123n, 162, 164
Perreiah, Alan R. 5, 62

Peter Abelard 52, 58
Peter of Spain 51-52, 55
Pinto, Robert C. 169, 173
Plato 2-4, 7, 12-16, 19, 22, 25-38, 40, 42-43, 45-46, 57, 103, 154
Pomeroy, Ralph 159
Poulakos, John 4

Quine, Willard van Orman 140

Ramus, Peter 8, 69
Rescher, Nicholas 164, 166, 172
Robert Kilwardby 51
Robinson, Paul 27, 29
Russell, Bertrand 6, 75, 125, 162
Ryle, Gilbert D. 27, 28, 37, 159, 161

Salmon, Merrilee H. 142n
Scheer, Richard K. 103, 159, 161
Schmidt, Michael F. 102, 111
Schopenhauer, Artur 8
Scriven, Michael 160, 173n, 166, 170, 172
Secor, Marie J. 119, 120
Sextus Empiricus 8, 68
Sidgwick, Alfred 8
Siegel, Harvey 12
Snoeck Henkemans, A. F. 170, 173
Spinoza, Benedict de 63
Stebbing, Susan L. 97n, 162

Thomas Aquinas 60-61
Thomas, Stephen N. 160, 162-63, 166, 170, 172
Thouless, Robert 97, 162
Tindale, Christopher W. 171
Toulmin, Stephen 129-30, 162-63, 170-72

Wahl, Russell 6
Walton, Douglas 5, 27, 44, 109-10, 112, 122n, 137, 160-61, 164-65, 169, 172-73
Watts, Isaac 6, 7, 84-98, 101
Weddle, Perry 160

179